Environmental Politics

The second edition of *Environmental Politics: Stakeholders, Interests, and Policymaking* shows students that environmental politics is fundamentally a clash of competing stakeholders' interests, and environmental policy the result of their reconciliation. But developments in environmental policymaking over the past several years have been little short of earthshaking. The text not only marks changes in the formal lawmaking process itself, but covers recent elements reshaping environmental politics, such as:

- the dramatic shift of policymaking influence from the federal to state and local levels;
- the participation of new actors on the environmental policy stage, most notably the faith community;
- the changing roles of business, science, and labor groups in environmental policymaking;
- the consolidation of the varying missions of environmental advocacy groups to fight global warming;
- the increasing role of both the media and the judiciary.

Written by an expert with more than 25 years of "smoke-filled room" experience in environmental policymaking, *Environmental Politics: Stakeholders, Interests, and Policymaking* gives students an insider's view of how policies are forged.

Norman Miller has served on the faculties of Rutgers University, Rollins and Meredith Colleges, and North Carolina State University. He is currently a member of the Global Warming and Energy Subcommittee of the national Sierra Club, and the Executive Committee of the Sierra Club's North Carolina Chapter. Previously he worked in both the legislative and executive branches of New Jersey state government in a variety of environmental policy capacities. He is also an academic member of the Society of Environmental Journalism.

Environmental Politics

Stakeholders, Interests, and Policymaking

Second Edition

Norman Miller

Routledge
Taylor & Francis Group

NEW YORK AND LONDON

First edition published 2002 by CRC Press
This edition published 2009
by Routledge
270 Madison Ave, New York, NY 10016

Simultaneously published in the UK
by Routledge
2 Park Square, Milton Park, Abingdon, Oxon OX14 4RN

*Routledge is an imprint of the Taylor & Francis Group,
an informa business*

Typeset in Garamond by RefineCatch Limited, Bungay, Suffolk
Printed and bound in the United States of America on acid-free
paper by Edwards Brothers, Inc.

Library of Congress Cataloging-in-Publication Data
Miller, Norman
Environmental politics : stakeholders, interests, and policymaking /
Norman Miller.—2nd ed.
p. cm.
Includes bibliographical references and index.
1. Environmental policy. I. Title.
GE170.M54 2008
363.7′056—dc22   2008015013

ISBN10: 0–415–96105–X (hbk)
ISBN10: 0–415–96106–8 (pbk)
ISBN10: 0–203–89008–6 (ebk)

ISBN13: 978–0–415–96105–9 (hbk)
ISBN13: 978–0–415–96106–6 (pbk)
ISBN13: 978–0–203–89008–0 (ebk)

To Andrea, who didn't volunteer for a second tour of duty, but served admirably; and to Jonah and Daniel, ultimate beneficiaries of sound environmental policy

I have never regarded politics as the arena of morals. It is the arena of interests.

Aneurin Bevan, British Labour Politician

Contents

Preface

Every book is, at its roots, a personal narrative, an attempt to rationalize the experience of its author. This book is no exception. It was conceived long before I sat down at my computer to try to draw some overarching conclusions about what in my experience as a foot soldier in the environmental wars might be interesting and instructive to others. But it did not come together until several years after I had left the field of battle and had the opportunity to undertake some mental reconnaissance flights over the theater of war. Over time, I came to understand the relation between the battles and the war, to determine which strategies succeeded and which failed, to sort out the victors and the vanquished, and to try to anticipate to the extent possible what battles lay ahead and what weapons may be needed to fight them effectively.

In the 1970s, I was assigned to the Environment Section of the New Jersey Legislature's research staff. I did not know then, nor could I have known, that environmentalism was destined to become the most significant socio-political movement of the last half of the 20th century, that it would generate an unprecedented body of law, and that it would be responsible for the continuing expenditure of vast sums of public and private revenues as well as change our culture and our view of the world. I was innocent as well of just how public policy was formulated. I brought to my work the only kind of understanding that people who have not been intimately involved in policymaking can have, a civics-textbook notion that laws are the product of the informed deliberation of elected, albeit partisan, officials and technically proficient administrative personnel, and that these laws are implemented effectively by governments at all levels for the public good.

My experience was an assault on these preconceptions. I was shocked when, at a committee meeting I staffed on the Clean Air Act, the first three rows of seats were commandeered by members of classic and antique car clubs, there to oppose the stricter regulations justifiably imposed on older, more polluting automobiles. I was distressed when television reporters were reluctant to cover what we regarded as a potentially catastrophic circumstance—the contamination of almost 50% of the state's potable water supply by leaking underground storage tanks—because the story could not have a dramatic visual vehicle. Underground tanks are, after all, impossible to film.

Over the years, I looked on as education officials participated actively in the consideration of legislation reducing real estate taxes adjacent to riparian land because these monies were dedicated to securing school bond funds; as licensed well-drillers welcomed regulations that would cause them only minor inconvenience and cost, but that would drive out competition from incompetent practitioners and moonlighters; as farmers failed to support farmland preservation programs because they wanted to preserve their options as land speculators; and as animal rights activists split with their environmental colleagues over the testing of health hazards of suspect chemicals because such tests would be conducted on animals. As staff, we had to struggle to bring the expertise of the state's scientific community to the committee room because it was a community that needed to preserve its economic opportunities as advisors to industry, advisory groups, and governments, not the general public.

Returning to the military imagery with which I began, for it is consistent with three basic truths that I discovered during the course of my work in environmental politics. The first is that policies are more often the product of combat than deliberation. The second is that the combatants are multiple and varied, do not always wear uniforms that identify their missions, and change sides when it suits their purposes to do so. The third truth is that winning strategies in the political world depend as much on activities off the designated battlefield as on it. My book was an effort to explain the environmental policy consequences of these truths.

The first two of these truths were stressed throughout the text because they constituted what I saw as the guiding principle in environmental policymaking; interests are a major driving force. The third, though, is more subtle in its manifestation. A central idea of the first edition was that the previous several decades witnessed an evolution in environmentalism from a high-minded conservation movement to a populist, grassroots social force, with a corresponding shift in the locus of advocacy from the corridors of government to the broad social and physical environment we all inhabit daily. The public became more anxious about their own personal environments, and the full range of interests involved in making public policy had to address that concern—in newspaper ads, in op-ed pieces, on websites tacked on to television spots, even in the promotion of "green packaging." Public opinion became more influential than ever, and appeals to it—explicit as well as subliminal—were all around us. Environmentalism had insinuated itself into the fabric of our culture and lifestyle.

In beginning work on this second edition, I fully expected to simply update the earlier work. I naively assumed that the trends I had written about would continue in a straight line of development, but my expectations were again unrealized. Over the past dozen years or so, a whole new era of environmentalism has dawned, necessitating a corresponding transformation in environmental policymaking. The sources of these changes are, principally, two. First, there developed an almost universal recognition and acceptance of the reality and stark potential consequences of global climate change. Interests across the spectrum, from environmental advocacy groups to business concerns, had to review and recast their missions and practices to come to terms with this growing phenomenon. Climate change, and its attendant energy and air quality implications, has veritably dwarfed other environmental concerns.

The second factor was the drastic change in the federal government's posture with regard to climate change. Historically, major environmental problems and challenges—air and water pollution, endangered species, oil spills, toxic and hazardous waste management—were addressed legislatively by the federal government, with local levels of government serving principally in administrative capacities. Furthermore, the George W. Bush administration has been, for a variety of reasons, dismissive of the threat of global climate change. No substantive federal policy on climate change has been developed or advanced, or even discussed. This policy vacuum created by the federal government had to be, and was, filled by others.

While this second edition, like its predecessor, is organized around the crucial role of interest group competition in policymaking, it has had to be significantly recast to reflect this evolution in environmentalism. Those interests are now in a very different political place. State and local governments, formerly the handmaidens of Washington, are now at the forefront of a nationwide campaign to control carbon emissions not only by adopting their own strict regulatory standards, but also by developing, funding, and promoting energy conservation and alternate sources that do not rely on fossil fuels. Environmental advocacy groups that pursued distinct, if synergistic, missions have closed ranks around a common cause; climate change, after all, challenges both conservationist and ecological and environmental quality goals. Many in the business community have come to recognize that climate change represents a threat to its profitability, and has thus altered many of its practices even as some of its corporate giants uncharacteristically lobby the federal government to regulate greenhouse gas emissions. Organized labor has flipped from an ally of management to an environmental collaborator, while the faith community, only tepidly involved in politics for most of the past century, has emerged, remarkably, as an activist force, awakening the members of its churches, as well as the federal government, to the new threat to God's creation. And the media who, until recently, found global climate change insufficiently newsworthy for regular coverage now fill our newspapers and TV and computer screens almost daily with its effects. Even the courts have established new ground, stepping out more aggressively than ever to enforce statutory and regulatory measures that address global warming.

In this new edition I have sought to describe and document the dramatic eruptions in environmental policymaking and their ultimate effect on our response to the most significant ecological threat in our history—global climate change.

In *Cases on Environmental Politics*, the companion to this text, I allow the interests to speak for themselves, in their own voices. Their positions and viewpoints illustrate and exemplify the new politics that constitutes environmental policymaking, or, more colloquially, "put meat on the bones" of current environmental discourse. The casebook complements the text by adding depth and specificity to possible class discussions on policies taken up in that text while providing materials to stimulate lively class debate. I have added as well an extensive bibliography of books and articles that have proven instructive and useful to me not only in putting this book together, but also in pursuing a wide variety of classroom strategies. It will, as well, enable students to conduct their own more extensive research on aspects of environmental politics of particular interest to them.

Acknowledgements

First, I want to thank my wife, Andrea, who allowed marital dedication to triumph over good sense in agreeing to join me once again on the journey. As before, she served as patient sounding board for ideas and critical reader of every chapter. This text is much the better for her indispensable contributions to it.

My appreciation goes as well to the two editors at Routledge with whom it was my privilege to work. In a number of long conversations, Michael Kerns generously shared with me his expertise in political science and his long experience as editor, and thus helped inform—and ground —my thoughts and perceptions. I shall miss our policy discussions. Development Editor Elizabeth Renner performed both macro and micro functions admirably, keeping me on task and the project on track. Her keen editorial eye improved the style of the manuscript and kept it focused on its intended audience. Eliana Perrin, in the course of guiding me through the vagaries of the electronic editing program, thankfully took the opportunity to make constructive substantive and stylistic improvements to the text. Andrew Perrin read several chapters and, as always, made perceptive comments and asked thorny questions.

Chapter I

The Evolving Landscape of Environmental Politics

> Politics: A strife of interests masquerading as a contest of principles. The conduct of public affairs for private advantage.
>
> (Ambrose Bierce)

In this definition from *The Devil's Dictionary*, Ambrose Bierce, one of America's most celebrated cynics, was obviously mocking the hypocrisy of our political life, but Americans have come to accept his characterization with equanimity. Today, few citizens are under any illusions that those with axes to grind or causes to pursue organize themselves and plead their special cases to lawmakers. Indeed, they regard such activities as a fundamental right of democracy. It is only when certain of these "special pleaders" gain disproportionate power and influence, especially by contributing vast sums of money to election campaigns, that the public bristles. Americans, to be sure, like a level playing field, but they generally have no problem with the game itself.

Despite their acceptance of the role of lobbyists or "lobbiers," as the representatives of special interests have been known for almost two hundred years, Americans have generally regarded one or another of the major parties as the guardian of their interests. Today, most people see politics exclusively as a battle between two camps—Republicans and Democrats—representing ideologies that are correspondingly dual and opposing—Right and Left, Conservative and Liberal. Such a view provides those citizens who have only a passing interest in politics—which is to say, regrettably, most of our citizens—a formulation that does not often, if ever, encourage revision or refinement, and it allows the media to cover elections and disputes over major issues as sporting events, with all the drama and conflict inherent in such contests.

Moreover, the popular conception is that the political battlefields are almost invariably the national and state capitols, and, on the local level, city halls. Such a situation, citizens believe, puts most of them on the sidelines and leaves participation, even close observation, to the political professionals and those with the luxury of much spare time. But today's environmental politics are playing out all around us, every day, wherever we may reside or work, and all of us are, consciously or unconsciously, participating. It is the goal of this book to sharpen the reader's awareness of the components and forces operating in environmental politics not only to understand why and how we as a society address the problems we do, but also to empower that reader to actively take part in making those politics serve not only personal but socially desirable ends.

Ideology, Partisanship, and Interests

It is important to recognize that viewing environmental politics exclusively as partisan or ideological combat can be misleading; the forces at war are numerous and the battlefield itself complex. To be sure, the two political parties over the years have staked out broad policy orientations, manifest in their election campaigns and carefully cultivated to secure the support of their traditional social and economic constituencies. If the Democratic Party, judging from voting records and priorities, has by and large garnered the support of the environmental community, it is because environmental issues are broadly based and invested with a wide spectrum of social and civic concerns. Democratic orientation is more grassroots. Addressing environmental problems almost invariably requires federal government action and the appropriation and application of substantial levels of public funding. Democrats have more confidence in the role of the public sector. Republican orthodoxy, on the other hand, preaches small government and reliance on the free market to incentivize appropriate environmental behavior.

But the many who subscribe to the widely shared perception that the Democratic Party has co-opted the environmental agenda must account for the fact that the formative National Environmental Policy Act and the establishment of the Environmental Protection Agency were formal accomplishments of the administration of Richard Nixon, though supported by bipartisan majorities. They must also recognize that several landmark environmental laws, like the Endangered Species Act of 1973, the Toxic Substances Control Act and the Resource Conservation and Recovery Act of 1976, and the Clean Air Act of 1990 Amendments of 1990, were all signed into law by Republican presidents, though, again, with substantial Democratic support. Thus, party affiliations and ideologies are, by themselves, insufficient to predict policy outcomes. Any of a wide variety of events and circumstances often has more influence on policymaking than more traditional factors.

Consider the following:

- In 1982, Representative John Dingell, a Democrat from Michigan and

Chairman of the House Committee on Energy and Commerce, joined forces with the Reagan administration in attempting, though unsuccessfully, to scale down many of the core provisions of the Clean Air Act of 1990. Obviously, his alliance with the major interest group in his state, the automobile manufacturers, was more compelling than his loyalty to party. Until 2007, under pressure during deliberations on the omnibus energy bill, Representative Dingell opposed legislative initiatives to require auto manufacturers to increase fleet averages for fuel efficiency, known as CAFÉ standards. In taking this uncompromising stand, he differs from most of his Democratic colleagues. Similarly, Senator Robert Byrd has continually opposed any legislation that would regulate the practice of mountaintop removal in the service of his state's coal mining industry, a practice at odds with the disposition of most Democrats. On the other side of the coin, Republican Senator Chuck Grassley of Iowa has joined his Democratic colleague Senator Tom Harkin in ardently supporting federal subsidies for biofuel development that would represent an economic boon for their state's corn growers. The Senators are state representatives first and party loyalists second.

- In 1987, Alfonse D'Amato, a conservative Republican Senator from New York, enthusiastically assumed a leadership role in support of EPA's newly proposed regulations toughening air quality standards. At the same time, Chicago Mayor Richard M. Daley, a lifelong organization Democrat and strong ally of the Clinton administration, opposed those same standards. Senator D'Amato was more concerned with the ability of the State of New York to meet federal ambient air quality standards, which would be facilitated by imposing stringent new requirements on Midwest power plants whose emissions were wafting to the Northeast, than with the niceties of political philosophy. For his part, Mayor Daley was worried that the new regulations would disproportionately punish large metropolitan areas such as his by crippling industrial development, encouraging suburban sprawl, and promoting more auto traffic. The population concentrations in urban areas would make compliance with the regulations more difficult. Party politics often stops at the state's or city's boundary.

- The Chemical Industry Council of New Jersey actively supported proposed legislation granting the state intrusive and comprehensive powers not only to inspect their clients' facilities, but also to prescribe a whole range of procedures they must follow in the handling of certain chemicals and the management of their businesses. The Toxic Catastrophe Prevention Act of 1993 was introduced in the wake of the explosion at a chemical plant in Bhopal, India, the most serious industrial accident in world history. Because New Jersey has the second largest concentration of chemical plants in the U.S., opposing any measure that proposed prevention of such an accident in the state would have seriously tarnished the industry's image.[1]

- A coalition of 52 business leaders in the West tried to block a U.S. Forest Service plan to triple commercial logging in the Sierra Nevada Mountain area north of Lake Tahoe. Business' departure from its historical alliance with the timber industry was in response to a shift in this area away from extractive industry and toward recreation and tourism. As one of the coalition businessmen put it: "We're a tourism economy now, and people come up here to see trees standing, not on the ground."[2]

- Similarly, a civil war raged among Alaskans over whether to include the Tongass National Forest in the ban on new road building throughout the national forest system. Some Alaskans support retaining the exception in the interests of continued timber harvesting, but others who make their living guiding tourists and sport fishermen through the rich natural areas want the increased protection that extending the ban to the Tongass would bring.[3] In an analogous situation, 54 business groups have lobbied to stop oil and gas drilling near Yellowstone Park in Wyoming; as in Alaska, tourism was deemed more important than mineral extraction.[4]

- The Alliance for Safe and Responsible Lead Abatement, an industry group whose job is to protect drinking water from the health hazards of lead, opposed an EPA proposal to *relax* building containment requirements in favor of landfill disposal of contaminated materials. The EPA proposal would have given much of the work now conducted by the constituents in the Alliance to general contractors. Further, the Alliance advocated stronger rather than weaker standards through grass roots appeals for public support, in the best tradition of environmental activism.[5] Similarly, manufacturers and suppliers of environmental technologies whose products would enjoy the wider market that strict environmental standards would generate have formed the Environmental Industry Coalition of the United States, Inc. to promote strong waste minimization and pollution prevention requirements before Congress and state and local governments. In both cases, the economic interests of the constituent members guided their political activities.

- Two business groups have undertaken opposing campaigns in connection with the Kyoto Global Warming Treaty. One—The Business Roundtable, representing 200 large companies—viewed the treaty as a significant economic threat, while a separate segment of that group, representing 13 blue-chip corporations, foresaw potential economic benefits. How the treaty negotiations play out would determine how individual interests are affected.[6] Differing interests divided two segments of the textile industry over the Central American Free Trade Agreement (CAFTA). The National Textile Association foresaw their fortunes threatened by increased competition from Central America, but the National Council of Textile Organizations saw growth in the textile industry spurred by growth in demand for yarn and other fabric components.[7]

- Contrary to usual practice, a Native American tribe, the Skull Valley Band of the Goshute, is fighting the State of Utah to have their reservation designated and licensed as the site of a storage facility for half of the nation's civilian nuclear waste, and thus enjoy the jobs and other economic benefits that would flow from such designation. The dispute is emblematic of that in several other venues, where economically disadvantaged populations—to the chagrin of government officials and environmental justice groups—are willing to bear the risks of exposure to toxic and radioactive materials or emissions in exchange for the economic benefits that would come with them.[8]

In Wyoming, owners of land on which livestock and wildlife thrive and which preserves sources of clean water are battling owners of the mineral rights beneath them, where rich methane gas deposits await extraction. The water resources are desperately needed, of course, but the revenues that the methane would generate might rescue a state with a low tax base and shrinking population from potential financial ruin.[9]

If, as these cases demonstrate, positions on environmental issues are often unrelated to partisan or ideological considerations, the collaborations that self-interest promotes are often between groups that have historically been at odds, and give renewed meaning to the old saw that "politics makes strange bedfellows." The uneasy relationship between business and labor has nevertheless inspired at least two joint efforts. The signing of the Global Warming Treaty in Kyoto, Japan in 1997 brought together two old adversaries—the United Mine Workers and the Bituminous Coal Operators Association. The potential for job loss and higher energy prices that they see in the treaty has caused the two sides to temporarily put aside their differences to fight a common enemy.[10] More recently, another collaboration between traditional enemies, the Alliance for Sustainable Jobs and the Environment, finds its member environmental groups and labor unions overlooking their historic differences to fight off their common threat, the World Trade Organization.[11]

Finally, longtime antagonists—cattlemen and environmentalists—joined in support of land trusts as a way to protect western open spaces from development by providing a mechanism to allow cattle to graze them. Long opposed to the grazing of land, environmentalists saw "cows" as preferable to "condos."[12] A comparable situation has inspired an unlikely alliance of environmentalists and developers, both of whom opposed a proposed mining project in Colorado. The area around Mt. Emmons, the tentative site of the project, has seen a conversion over the last 30 years from mining and ranching to recreational activities like hiking, camping, and skiing, on which the local economy now depends.[13] This is the New West. The Old West seeks to restore mining to the area.

In other unlikely alliances: the Utah Outdoor Industry Association joined environmentalists in opposing the Administration's opening of pristine backcountry to off-road vehicles, economic development, and natural resource exploitation, undermining what the Association regards as the state's biggest economic driver;[14] and environmentalists and the National Rifle Association (NRA) both worked to add conservation provisions to the 2002 Farm Bill.[15] In other circumstances, unlikely clashes occurred between ranchers within the same scenic Montana area over a proposal to build a rail link to transport coal;[16] and a dispute between the neighboring states of Montana and Wyoming over the draft of water from coal-bed methane.[17]

Finally, now gaining attention is the battle between Republican policy and the Republican base. "[R]anchers, cowboys, small property owners and local government leaders—the core of the Republican base in the Rocky Mountain West—are chafing at the pace and scope of the Bush administration's push for energy development."[18]

Environmental policy positions, then, are less often a function of ideology, of belief in certain core values that collectively constitute a commitment to social needs and aspirations, than to self-interest, principally, though not invariably, economic interest. Such an assertion may seem blasphemous, especially since the environment has achieved almost religious status among some segments of the population, and "environmentalist" is a label that virtually everyone wears with pride. Yet the self-interest involved in the formulation of environmental policy simply mirrors its role in our nation's political economy as a whole. It was, after all, Adam Smith, the apostle of free-market capitalism, who argued that the greater social good is best served by each person's pursuit of his or her own interests, and that it is the role of our particular political system to nourish the conditions for a competition that reconciles individual and collective ends.

It is, therefore, well grounded political theory that public policy derives from the healthy combat among competing interests, a war won usually by those who control the political process, or who have the financial resources to access it and bend it to their own purposes. Environmental policy is no exception. What makes the politics of environmental policymaking especially complex and contentious is that environmental issues as they have evolved by the early years of the 21st century embrace an incredibly broad and diverse universe of phenomena, circumstances, and conditions. They reach into virtually every aspect of our lives. It is interesting and relevant to observe, however, that that evolution has taken place generally in three distinct phases, with distinctly different interests and stakeholders.

Its initial conservationist phase was inspired by the interests of a generally well-educated, upper-middle class constituency that had the luxury of much leisure and opportunity for outdoor recreation. The next phase can be characterized as the "domestication" of environmentalism; public health and safety concerns over drinking water and air quality in homes and toxic chemicals in workplaces began to overshadow the natural resource focus of its earlier years, and brought almost everyone in the society into the impacted and involved population. The politics of this phase was tracked as an almost daily subject in the media.

But the latter years of the 20th century and the first decade of the 21st have witnessed the emergence of the third phase. A single, dominant environmental issue—global climate change—has veritably dwarfed all other environmental issues. If the second phase can be seen as contracting the environmental focus, global climate change and its related elements—energy policy and air pollution control—have turned environmentalism on its head and given it a planetary dimension.

Conservationist Origins

For most of our country's history, at least until the middle of the 20th century, the origins of what was later to become known as environmentalism resided in the conservation of natural resources—the country's oceans, rivers, lakes, and coastal zones; its parks and forests and wilderness areas; its agricultural lands; and, of course, the wildlife, flora, and fauna for which those resources provide habitat. The term that was applied to their protection and management was "preservation" or "conservation," depending upon whether you were an adherent of John Muir or Gifford Pinchot, early 20th century representatives of different schools of conservation. Their epochal struggle over the proposed construction of the dam and reservoir at Hetch Hetchy in Yosemite National Park to meet the suddenly emergent water supply needs of San Francisco in the wake of the 1906 earthquake—the first major battle in the war of environment politics—was over man's relationship to nature, specifically the extent to which this natural resource should be utilized to meet man's needs. The central issue in this debate had far-reaching philosophical and ethical implications, but it had little practical significance. Except for the residents of San Francisco, whose potable water supply needs would eventually be met by Hetch Hetchy, the dispute barely touched the everyday lives of most Americans.[19]

For the better part of the next several decades, land use issues continued as the principal objects of environmental attention. The interests involved were, accordingly, those of sportsmen and outdoorsmen—hunters, trappers, fishermen, hikers, bikers, and campers—as well as those of loggers, miners, and ranchers, who would profit financially from a Pinchot-supported multiple use policy reconciling preservation of the land's aesthetic and ecological values with carefully managed and controlled exploitation of its resources. Though bitterly fought, the politics of conservation were clearly delineated, with the sides sharply drawn and the issues relatively circumscribed.

But shortly after mid-century, things changed dramatically. The evolution from conservation to what we now commonly call "environmentalism" brought with it a new mix of issues and concerns, and a corresponding proliferation of advocacy groups. While the initial water and air pollution statutes in the 1950s represented the earliest federal efforts to gain a measure of control over those environmental threats, the evolution was accelerated by one woman and one book.

The "New" Environmentalism

Rachel Carson's *Silent Spring* played an important role in the development of environmentalism, bringing public health issues to its core conservation and natural resource concerns. *Silent Spring* documented the potentially lethal effects of chemical pesticides, particularly DDT, not only on their intended targets, but on all life, contaminating everything with which they come in contact and reaching humans by infiltrating the food chain as well as air and water supplies. Eventually, she warned, they threaten "the very nature of the world—the very nature of its life." By implication and extension, she attacked the abuse of science and the worship of technology, as well as the burgeoning post-World War II industrialism that was imposing increasing burdens not just on natural resources but on public health. The substance of her claims, and the dramatic terms in which she cast them, captured the public's attention. But the book went beyond description; it called for a new public consciousness of the dangers around us, and for a more activist government to control them. In essence, it called for a new politics of environment.[20]

As we now know, over the next several decades the public consciousness that Carson awakened did develop, not only of the chemical pesticides that were her immediate target, but of an ever broadening list of domestic toxic threats. Industrial activities created ever-mounting and often uncontrolled repositories of solid and hazardous wastes; nuclear power plants generated radioactive waste stockpiles that society has yet to devise the means to sequester from humans; and oil spills fouled previously pristine areas of our coastlines. People became concerned not only about the deterioration of their parks and forests, but also about their more immediate surroundings. Henceforth they would be anxious not only about the purity of the water in oceans, lakes and streams, but the safety of the water from their faucets. The quality of the ambient air—worsening under the onslaught of increased automobile traffic—remained an issue, but it was joined by worry over indoor air pollution—"sick building syndrome" as it is called—as well as by radon infiltration of homes in some geographical regions. Microwave ovens and cellphones, sports utility vehicles and diesel trucks, decaffeinated coffee and food dyes, fertilizers and herbicides, lead paints and asbestos coatings, automobile batteries and used motor oil, antibacterial household detergents and antibiotic medications, plastic food wraps and dry cleaning chemicals, and, ironically, alternatives to the very pesticides that were responsible for the movement in the first place—food irradiation and genetic modification—all these and countless others were alleged to threaten public health and the environment, and, accordingly, became the subject of political wrangling and, in many cases, of legislation and regulation.

The identification of this growing matrix of potential risks raised a whole host of legal, ethical, and social questions, as well as potential liabilities and costs. Manufacturers, retailers, and governments clashed over the question of who was responsible for the safe management of these risks, and whether appropriate warnings and notices were sufficient to discharge that responsibility. Many disclaimed responsibility entirely and invoked the "buyer beware" principle. Employers clashed with workers over the safety of their workplaces, especially those that are the sites of industrial activities necessarily involving hazardous materials.

There were new land use questions, and these, too, took on a more local cast. The conservation of natural areas for their aesthetic qualities, as habitat and as recreational resource is, as we have noted, historical. But recently, more thorny issues came to the fore. Builders and developers steadfastly resisted legal requirements to incorporate in their plans the impact of their construction on flood-prone areas, on wetlands, on habitats of endangered or threatened species, and on fragile waterfront areas. All these challenge the extent to which government regulation can go without treading on the constitutional right to private property. People became more sensitive, too, to the siting in their neighborhoods, for example, of unwanted solid waste, hazardous waste, and sewage treatment facilities, that at worst exposed them to potentially higher levels of pollution, or at least reduced the value of their homes and property. The "not in my backyard" (NIMBY) syndrome became a familiar chant of these people. Many were opposed even to any new development at all that increased traffic and air pollution, and gave rise to the politically charged phenomenon of suburban sprawl.

Finally, civil rights and questions of ethics became inextricably entangled with environmental activities and conditions. *Where* to site facilities that may expose surrounding populations is an environmental matter to be sure, but it has also become a civil rights matter, as such sitings have tended to follow the path of least political resistance, i.e. in economically disadvantaged and minority communities. Furthermore, national environmental issues have spread abroad, with the increasing exploitation by transnational corporations of impoverished third world labor and by producing the low cost goods that reflect, in part, the environmental compromises made in the interests of economic competitiveness. More significant has been the bitter disputes over the commodification of third world rainforests and other irreplaceable natural resources essential to maintaining biodiversity in response to the desperate basic needs of indigenous populations. Even animals became an interest group. The production of cosmetics and fur coats, which involve what many consider the unethical treatment of animals, became hot-button issues, and garnered their own constituencies and created their own demands.

The transformation from conservation to environmentalism unleashed at mid-century caused a sea change in environmental politics. In marrying public health with conservation, the new environmentalism extended its reach to the whole population, and made each and every citizen a stakeholder in the environment's well-being. In bringing the concerns in from the outdoors, it became a factor in our daily lives—what we eat and how we grow it, where we live, what we buy, where we work, and even where we play. Witness, for example, the attention that environmental stresses associated with golf course maintenance and leisure cruise ship operations are now commanding.

This fundamental change in the environmental agenda generated an explosion of new issues and new interests. No longer could one view the environmental wars as simply bilateral—government versus the private sector, environmentalists versus business, developers versus preservationists. The interests that have been created are, rather, much more numerous and complex, and occupy many more narrow and focused niches. As the enumeration of policy positions on a range of issues recited earlier in the chapter suggests, they are also frequently unexpected and unorthodox. Now we have, as a particular issue may dictate, builders and developers of residential property on opposite sides of the political table from industrial and commercial builders and developers; producers of high sulfur coal are fighting off their low sulfur coal counterparts (a battle that translates into a regional war) with respect to clean air regulatory regimes; and the national giants in any number of industries often separate themselves from the "mom and pop" operations in that same industry. Even wilderness hikers and rock climbers are doing battle, most recently over the prohibition imposed by the National Forest Service on fixed anchors on rocks, which climbers argue are fundamentally indistinguishable from fixed markers on hiking trails.[21] Finally, it must be recognized that state and local governments have interests different not only from the federal government but from each other as well.

If the combinations and permutations of interests are almost endless, so too are the organizations, associations, alliances, interest groups, coalitions and lobbies—permanent, temporary, and ad hoc—that have been created and entered into in order to influence public opinion, and represent these interests in the formal policymaking process. Because the impact of legislative and regulatory policies can be subtle yet significant, and because counter interests are all around (even where one may not expect them), each group feels it needs its own representation, and its own public relations effort.

The changing role of environmental organizations will be discussed later but it might be appropriate here to hint at one of those changes with political ramifications. There are those interests with less financial support and fewer members than their national counterparts. Their survival often depends upon their linking up with other sometimes only tangentially related interests to maximize their political power and funding. Co-op America, for example, is a program to consolidate and direct the buying power of American consumers toward environmentally benign products, but it associates itself as well with those who are working more broadly for social justice—opposing sweatshops, promoting work for the disabled, and, in general, improving the life, skills, self-esteem, and dignity of men and women in low income areas. It is generally acknowledged that U.S. environmental policy is the result of the combat and ultimate reconciliation of competing interests. But it is the central premise of this book that the number, nature, and impact of those interests have changed so dramatically over the past few decades that they constitute a new politics of the environment, and that viewing environmental politics through the interest-group lens is key to understanding how we got where we are today with respect to environmental policy and, perhaps more importantly, where we are going and what forces will shape that destiny.

To be sure, the lawmaking process and the major combatants in the environmental wars in some measure remain in place, and thus continue to merit our examination. But both have had to accommodate themselves to the changing environmental landscape. New legislative strategies have been devised and old ones revived to meet the new political scene, and the rulemaking protocol has undergone a virtual metamorphosis. Both the legislative and regulatory processes, at least in practice, now upset many of our elementary school civics class notions of how they operate. The nature and impact of these changes on environmental policy are the subjects of Chapters 2 and 3 respectively. The role of state and local governments has undergone the most significant expansion of any "interest group" in response to the federal government's failure to sufficiently address the dramatic manifestation of global warming, and the energy policies needed to address it. Why this has happened, and its effect on the historic responsibility of state and local governments to implement environmental law, are taken up in Chapter 4.

In the mind of most people, the real environmental war is between big business, whose industrial and commercial activities have imposed the most strain on the environment, and the environmental establishment, which has served as agenda setter and self-appointed watchdog of government's regulation of the private sector. Seen in the broadest terms, that, of course, continues to be true. But the environmental establishment and the business community have themselves undergone significant reinvention in response to the growing influence of the new complex of environmental concerns, again in response to broad recognition of the threat of global warming. Each has been criticized by the purists under its tent, but the reality is that they have come much closer to each other, have even worked together on specific programs, for practical, if not ideological, reasons. Further, each has sprouted new "branches" that operate independently, but serve many of their same ends. Environmental justice groups and the more controversial eco-terrorists supplement, but by no means mirror, the efforts of more mainstream environmental organizations. Similarly, corporate-funded conservative and libertarian think tanks and a consortium of interests constituting the Wise Use movement try to emasculate the government's environmental work and keep environmental organizations in tow. They strengthen the anti-environmental forces in the halls of government and in the popular media, but allow the business establishment to pursue the same goals in more politically conventional ways. The environmental and business camps, and their respective evolutions and allies, are examined in Chapters 5 and 6 respectively.

Chapter 7 discusses the newly energized relationship between labor and environmentalists. Organized labor has played a dual, somewhat paradoxical role, siding with business interests when jobs are at stake and siding with environmentalists when business practices jeopardize their health and safety. In this century, however, the two have most often found common cause.

Probably the fastest growing new alliance is that between religion and the environment. As we shall see, environmentalists and spiritual leaders are increasingly joining in efforts to redirect the environmental agenda by reawakening society's spiritual values and rethinking man's fundamental responsibility to nature.

Chapter 8 takes up another newly enlisted participant in the environmental wars—the scientific community. Another legacy of the movement inspired by Rachel Carson is the inclusion of public health concerns under the environmental umbrella, a legacy that puts the grounding of much environmental policy beyond the reach of laymen and thereby creates a substantial role for scientific experts. Despite the reticence of scientists to provide the superficial answers to complicated problems that policymakers seek, interest groups of all stripes have eagerly sought them out and capitalized on the credibility with the public they can bring to their positions. The resulting politicization of science is examined in detail in this chapter.

These changes in the policymaking process and in the composition and strategies of the major participants in that process would represent significant political change by themselves. But the changes go beyond refurbished theaters and old actors in new roles. New participants with deep influence have emerged from the redefined environmentalism. The most significant of these are the media, discussed in Chapter 9. What I call the "domestication" of the environmental agenda has made the media important players in environmental politics today. It is not a role that the media either sought or willingly accepted. As environmental issues and concerns centered increasingly on our homes and workplaces and food and lifestyles, newspapers and television found much more in environmentalism that directly engaged their audiences, though, in the minds of many environmentalists, that has not been an unmixed blessing. Those issues that have been given the most prominent treatment are by no means the most significant or threatening. Nevertheless, by some "invisible hand" (to borrow Adam Smith's famous phrase), public concerns are communicated to official policymakers. For that reason, interest groups from across the spectrum routinely enlist the media in their efforts to set the agenda and bring visibility to their causes.

A look at the judiciary, a branch of government that is taking on an increasingly significant policy role, especially as the friction between the other two branches of government increases is the subject of Chapter 10.

However the aforementioned processes, protocols, and stakeholders debating a wide variety of issues have shaped environmental policies for most of the past century, one issue—global climate change—will determine the future direction of environmental policy. While our responses to it are still being formulated, climate change has already been the catalyst for significant changes in environmental policymaking. The shadow of climate change hangs over every element of the political process discussed in this book. Two omnibus energy bills Congress considered in the early years of this century have had the dual goal of reducing the nation's dependence on foreign oil and the control of CO_2 emissions that accelerate climate change. One or another of the several bills that will ultimately be merged has accordingly given new life to a declining nuclear industry, because its plants emit no greenhouse gases. On the other hand some include provisions to support technologies like sequestration that minimize the unacceptable levels of CO_2 emitted into the atmosphere by conventional coal plants. Provisions to stimulate the development of renewable energy and alternate sources are similarly aimed at controlling the emissions that most threaten the climate.

Subsidies for biofuel production, intended to partially supplant fossil fuels to power cars, planes, and buses, are included for national security reasons, but the varying levels of greenhouse gases that different biofuels emit has also been a factor in the deliberations. In addition to promoting more environmentally benign fuels, legislation has taken up the fuel efficiency of automobiles, food production, and new building construction.

The wide variety of legislative proposals to address global climate change have stimulated more intense and expanded activity by the many lobbyists whose role it is to make any enactments as profitable for their clients as possible. Stakeholders across the spectrum from automobile manufacturers to corn growers have new interests to preserve or promote. The result has been a potpourri of initiatives all over the partisan map.

But those legislative efforts have been too few and too tentative, in part because the competing interests have fought to a veritable standoff. The failure of the federal government to carve out a strong, clear set of policies that address climate change and its attendant energy implications has required state and local governments, individually and collaboratively, to fill the void left by the federal government.

Climate change's potential effects on a whole range of insults to the ecosystem have given environmental advocacy groups a banner behind which to marshal their forces.[22] Further, the business community has come to recognize that not only society's interests, but also its own bottom line, are threatened by climate change. Climate change has as well given both the labor movement and the faith community new reasons to review and renew their larger missions.

Finally, the potential manifestations of climate change are, inevitably, tracked principally, though not exclusively, by the projection of trends, simulation by models, and the extrapolation of data from a wide variety of sources and disciplines. Unlike most subjects that undergo scientific scrutiny, climate change cannot be readily tested in the laboratory or on human subjects. As such, climate change represents the quintessential challenge for the application of science in policymaking. While scientists identified the phenomenon decades ago, and have become increasing confident of their earlier predictions of its catastrophic effects and their causes, the inherent uncertainty in these determinations have allowed skeptics just enough leeway to cloud public opinion and forestall a fully-fledged, coordinated national effort.

The broad and systemic evolution of environmentalism has made it the most significant social and cultural movement since the second half of the 20th century. It also has been the most profound—and interesting— political movement. But in recent years, due to geophysical changes caused partly by man's own actions, global climate change has taken environmentalism to a whole new plane. Environmentalism began as a broad national effort to preserve and protect natural resources. It evolved into a multifaceted social movement that brought local public health and safety together with its core mission. It has now gone global!

Central Ideas

Environmental politics is driven by interests as well as ideology and partisan considerations. Over the past several decades the number and nature of interests has changed dramatically, transforming environmental politics from contests waged by powerful interests over conservation to wars over public health. But in recent years, the advent of global climate change has totally dominated environmental politics, causing the various interests and stakeholders to re-evaluate their missions and practices.

Chapter 2

Legislation: Leveling the Playing Field and Leveraging the Process

> If you like laws and sausages, you should never watch either being made.
>
> (Otto von Bismarck)

> Discovering a workable definition of environmental law is a little bit like the search for truth: the closer you get, the more elusive it becomes.
>
> (William H. Rogers)

The formal procedure by which laws are enacted at the federal level and by the states was designed to reflect the most cherished values of democratic society—openness, equity, inclusiveness, and stability. It is a process intended to be deliberative, structured, and predictable. It is an expression of the founding father's core beliefs in the principles of the separation of powers and checks and balances, and provides our citizens with the comfort—justified or not—that power is shared, and that everyone participates, either directly or through representatives. Americans assert with pride that they are "a nation of laws, not men."

At the same time, and paradoxically, Americans knowingly smile at Chancellor von Bismarck's famously cynical characterization of the making of laws cited above. For the realities of the legislative process are more complex than might be expected from a superficial analysis of the bare-bones procedure itself. Simple common sense would inevitably lead us to the fundamental truth that those in positions of authority and wealth, and those with the greatest stake in its results, exercise disproportionate power. And so the statutes, clear and compelling as they may appear, belie the extraordinary mix of influences that go into their formulation.

Because environmental issues affect us in such profound ways and involve such a multiplicity of interests, they subject the legislative process to its greatest strains. As noted earlier, over the course of the last half century or so the body of laws enacted in the environmental area have influenced almost every aspect of our daily lives, and mandated the appropriation of more public and private monies than the body of law in any other area. Perhaps more significantly, environmentalism and politics are inextricably linked because substantive values, to say nothing of behavior, are at stake. Every major policy supports some interested party's view of the world and adversely affects someone else's. That is why the collective process for solving problems related to the environment is inherently adversarial. As suggested above, the legislative process tries to minimize or at least manage these divisions. It also tries to provide the circumstance for the reconciliation of conflicts, and allows problems to be thoughtfully and rationally resolved. By and large it does, but at virtually every step in that process are entry points for interested parties—public and private—to promote their causes, or opportunities to stifle threats to those causes, and that is why politics finds its way into lawmaking.

A Brief History

In order to appreciate environmental politics as it is currently practiced, it might be useful to have a brief perspective on its history. Until roughly the middle of the last century, environmental threats to private property and public health were generally handled by the courts in accordance with common law principles, and, in certain limited areas, by state and local governments. Under common law, the burden was on those who called for action to demonstrate how a specific party engaged in acts or created a circumstance that specifically and unreasonably caused environmental harm to them. A plaintiff had to suffer personal damages in order to bring an action against a polluter or developer. The concept of "public injuries" was a foreign notion, and economic interests were given deference over social needs in controversies over land use.[1]

All that dramatically changed in the latter half of the 20th century. The post-World War II economic boom, in the absence of any significant governmental restraints or oversight, imposed an increasing burden on the nation's resources. Pollutants created by industrial activities were routinely discharged into the air and water bodies; solid wastes were dumped into public landfills, along with any number of toxic wastes; and pesticides developed from a wide range of untested chemicals were often indiscriminately applied in agricultural and horticultural production. The nation's reserves of wood, oil, and minerals were extracted with little restraint, and wetlands and habitats of endangered species were claimed by rampant development. By mid-century, some of the signs of these profligate activities had begun to manifest themselves.

But the modest initial efforts of the federal government to address these problems did not, at first, generate private sector resistance. Two measures—the Federal Water Pollution Control Act of 1970 and the Air

Pollution Control Act of 1977—were broad, general approaches to their respective problems, and the robust economy fueled by this economic boom subsumed most of the regulatory costs imposed by these measures.[2] Further, few interests at this time had sufficient expertise and research capacity to get deeply involved in the lawmaking process. It was not until later, when it became apparent that the goals of these statutes were not being achieved, that their more rigorous reauthorized versions began to command more attention.

The Shift

In 1962, Rachel Carson's *Silent Spring* set in motion an early, and bitter, war of environmental politics. Its allegations against the chemical industry aroused deep public concern over the health effects of broad pesticide applications and stimulated sharp debate over the proper role of government in addressing this threat. In doing so, it foreshadowed subsequent battles over endangered species, toxic and solid waste reduction and disposal, "Superfund" site cleanup, marine protection, nuclear power generation, and a host of other issues. From that point on, environmental policy would be in the public consciousness, and the media and any number of new local environmental watchdogs would join the newly vigilant national organizations in advancing an aggressive agenda, and begin to shape federal action to address public concerns.

After the broad, comprehensive framework to address the nation's overarching environmental problems was set in place, more narrowly focused measures to address specific pollutants followed. Particular attention was paid to air or water supplies, special classes of toxins, threatened or endangered species, ecologically fragile areas like wetlands and coastal areas, and a host of other newly emerging potential health threats like lead, electromagnetic fields, and food additives. As the focus of the problems narrowed over the last half of the 20th century, environmental issues crept closer to home. Concern over ocean and lake quality was shared with fears over the quality of water flowing from residential faucets. The quality of ambient air competed for attention with anxiety over indoor air quality, particularly radon. Additionally, the environmental safety of our workplaces, schools, and food supplies commanded increasing legislative attention. The first years of the 21st century, however, have represented a pendulum swing back to issues of broader—even global—concern, as we shall see later.

This "domestication" of the environmental agenda in the latter years of the 20th century was accompanied by two other factors that gave rise to a more activist political climate. As the next chapter details, the EPA exercised its growing authority by tightening regulatory standards across the board as our capacity to detect and remove increasingly microscopic concentrations of pollutants improved. These regulations increased the cost of compliance for the business community, which satirically dubbed the effort as "hitting the vanishing zero." But the private sector was, at least until the late 1980s, on the defensive due to a series of highly publicized, galvanizing events that aroused the public: the oil spill off the Santa Barbara coast; the Love Canal and Times Beach episodes; the nuclear accidents at Chernobyl and Three-Mile Island; the Bhopal disaster at an American chemical plant in India; and the Valdez oil spill off the coast of Alaska. These environmental disasters—or near disasters—energized the environmental movement, generated increased membership and funding, and virtually earned it the proxy of the American public. Those feeling the pinch of an activist legislative agenda had to turn, again as noted in the next chapter, to the less visible regulatory arena for relief.

Environmental statutes, then, have historically taken on the cast of public problem solvers and the protectors of the public welfare. Their goals—set out in introductory "Declarations of Goals and Policy" sections—establish laudable objectives to be achieved by their operative provisions. They either promote the public welfare or, even more compelling, prevent potentially catastrophic threats to public health and safety, or the ecosystem. As such, they are hard to impeach and they seldom are. Rather, those who, for example, emit pollutants into the air or contaminants in the water are often forced to adopt strategies that minimize the effect of the statutes on their operations, or somehow escape their purview altogether by advocating thresholds of applicability that exclude them. These strategies can be best understood in light of the legislative process itself, to which we now turn.

The Skeletal Legislative Process

It might be best to describe this process as it is set out in our public school civics textbooks before going into what has complicated and, in the view of some, corrupted that process. The bare-bones lawmaking procedure, which prevails today principally at the state level, starts formally with the introduction of a legislative "bill," which is simply a proposal for a new law or for amendment of an existing one. Such bills are formally sponsored by a member of Congress, either a Representative or a Senator, and entered into the agenda and given a number. Once a bill is introduced, or "put in the hopper," it is referred to a committee or committees in the body of the House of its sponsor. The full Congress cannot collectively consider each introduced bill; it would be far too cumbersome, confusing, and time-consuming to do that. The complexity of issues would make such collective consideration counterproductive. Nor do any substantial percentage merit, or receive, serious examination.[3] To facilitate the process, Congress organizes "standing reference committees," each with a particular subject matter, on which its members presumably have some expertise and whose jurisdictions are significantly affected by that subject matter. Reference committees are, correspondingly, supported by subcommittees that represent a further division of labor. Subcommittees are far more numerous and influential at the federal level than at the state level; indeed, with respect to major legislation, subcommittees do the bulk of the work. Even at the state level, it is not uncommon for more than one committee to consider a bill, and virtually mandatory that the appropriations committee be one of those committees when the referred bill involves substantial public expenditures. After a bill is considered, discussed, and amended as deemed appropriate by the members of the committee, it is "reported" by a majority vote of the members. Once an agreed upon version of the bill clears all relevant subcommittees and committees, it is put on an agenda awaiting full House vote. A majority vote passes the bill, except in the special circumstances noted later.

Upon a favorable vote by the full House, the bill moves to the other body, where it follows essentially the same path. If identical bills are introduced in the two Houses, the bills can move sequentially or concurrently. In both cases, identical versions of the bills must pass both Houses. In state legislatures, bills usually continue to bounce back and forth until the same version can be mutually agreed upon. At the federal level, "conferences"—meetings between representatives of the House and Senate—reconcile differences between the two versions and prepare a "conference report."[4] Minor differences between the House and Senate versions of bills are usually worked out by compromise.

When agreement on a bill has been reached, and the reference committees and the full Houses have voted on it favorably, it is sent to the President for final approval and passage into law. The President can veto it, conditionally veto it with recommended changes, or sign it. A Presidential or gubernatorial veto can be overridden by a larger majority of the full House, generally two-thirds, but conditional vetoes are usually either accepted with the recommended changes or negotiated with the administration. This, in skeletal form, is the trip that a bill takes into law.

In the latter decades of the 20th century a significant new form of legislation, omnibus legislation, became the choice vehicle for consideration of major issues at the federal level. Omnibus bills, which are several measures packaged as a single bill, are a response, in part, to the growing number and complexity of issues. The nature of omnibus bills is such that they represent an important and widely supported core proposal. Because these bills are more likely to be enacted, lawmakers try to quietly incorporate more controversial related proposals. They are subject to less committee scrutiny; in fact, omnibus bills are often accorded expeditious consideration, which gives the ancillary proposals they carry along a correspondingly better chance of becoming law.[5] But their growing popularity is attributable to more than just their role as expeditious managers of an increasing workload. They bestow considerable political advantages, as discussed below.

Political Opportunities

It should be obvious that, despite the superficial objectivity of the process, many political and policy implications are submerged in it. At virtually every stage, interested parties can penetrate the procedure, and move, stall, or amend a bill's provisions to suit their purposes. The points and stages at which this interference can occur merit closer attention because they are highly political and partisan.

Since the process is initiated by the introduction of a bill, this is where to start. Where do bills come from? The short answer: "From a variety of sources." It must be noted that the legislation banning DDT spurred by Rachel Carson's *Silent Spring* is not typical. It is rare that a book achieves such public notice that it drives public policy, but in the social and political milieu of the 1960s, it happened. It was not until 30 years later that another book, *Our Stolen Future*, captured comparable attention and, again, served as the catalyst for a major law, the Food Quality Protection Act of 1996.[6] *Our Stolen Future* alleged that a class of chemicals, known as endocrine disrupters, were potentially responsible for a number of adverse health consequences, including reduced sperm counts (hence its title). In both thesis and reception, in some ways, it echoes its influential predecessor.

Still, books are rarely catalysts for legislation. Somewhat more common, though not typical, are major environmental incidents such as those cited above that stimulate legislative action. Though these events do pull together all the forces needed to move legislative responses decisively, they fortunately do not occur with sufficient frequency to shape policy, and environmental advocates cannot very well hope, even privately, for new environmental calamities to renew their mandate. When an environmental circumstance has the potential to drive policy, such as a drought or flood, the media can often turn it into a political issue. Somewhat more commonly, less spectacular issues are raised by interest groups of all kinds, including an investigative report they may have commissioned, or by their being aggrieved by the implementation of an existing law, though that is generally reserved for the regulatory or judicial processes, since appropriate implementation is in the jurisdiction of administrative agencies or the judiciary. On occasion, a court decision will identify a problem that only a new law, or a change in existing law, can resolve.

Interest groups with sufficient influence with legislators sometimes go beyond the active promotion of a measure to literally produce a draft bill for introduction, a practice that is no doubt rather more common than generally acknowledged. Two examples of improper interest group involvement in the very earliest stage of the legislative process can be found in the preparation of legislative bills that gained notoriety from press exposure in the mid-1990s and earlier in 2000. In 1995, a prominent wood products company drafted key provisions of a bill that would have insulated alleged violators of a law from being prosecuted by the EPA in certain circumstances (among which was theirs).[7] Then, in June 2000, a pesticide lobbyist openly admitted to crafting a bill for a Congressman that would have effectively blocked implementation of the same Food Quality Protection Act of 1996 that derived from *Our Stolen Future*.[8] Only slightly less proactive and aggressive are the number of firms who call the Capitol to offer legislative strategy and advocacy services. Such firms usually carry out quite traditional lobbying responsibilities, but in providing advertised services such as preparing bills for lawmakers and developing their legislative strategies, they can penetrate and skew the legislative process by contacting key legislators before the bill is formally considered by Congress. It hardly needs to be pointed out that the ability of well-financed, politically connected interests to get a measure on the agenda is infinitely greater than that of a lesser group, particularly at the national level. Congressional support agencies are in a unique position to define issues that need to be addressed. Finally, members of Congress themselves, especially Chairs of influential committees, can and do bring ideas and needs to their representatives, who, in turn, have them prepared for introduction.

Though at the top of the Executive Branch, the President serves key legislative functions. Not only does the President formally sign bills passed by Congress into law at the end of the legislative process, but he or she initiates legislation and plays the dominant role in setting the Congressional agenda, at least for the first months of the administration or session of Congress. Presidents almost invariably come into office with several priorities, many of which they prominently promoted during their campaigns for office or advocated in their annual messages to Congress.[9] It is a mere formality for them to have a member of Congress formally draft these ideas into formal legislation and introduce them.

Legislative Leadership and Committees

Another major element of politics in the process resides in the officers themselves. The Houses have leaders—the Speaker in the House of Representatives and the Majority Leader in the Senate. (The President of the Senate is the Vice-President of the United States, with the sole legislative responsibility of breaking tie votes.) They have many sources of influence through the selection of committee chairs, the control over the agenda they maintain by committee references, and the allocation of monies in political action committee funds (PACs) to which lobbyists contribute. Either by themselves or through the committee chairs they appoint, they can kill bills, or accelerate their progress through the successive stages. Committee chairs also have a substantial degree of control. They are under no obligation to consider any particular bill referred to their committee. In truth, there are more bills introduced than can possibly be considered, and so only a small percentage appears on a committee agenda, much less gets voted on. Bills can, of course, be heard and tabled, in effect killing them. So either by tabling them or failing to take them up at all, committee chairs can bury bills they don't like, or that their more influential constituents don't support. When one speaks of the influence and access of politically and economically powerful interests, then, it can refer not only to public votes, but to the almost invisible control of the legislative agenda through its presiding officers and chairs.[10]

Further, committee members themselves sometimes use the bill review process to advance the specific interests of their constituents even on measures unrelated to the one at hand. Technically, of course, lawmakers are United States Senators and United States Representatives, and formally committed to protect and promote the welfare of the nation, but because they are elected by the voters in their respective states, they are expected to represent their more local interests as well. The principal constituent concerns of a Senator from, say, New York are in most cases radically different from those of a Senator from Iowa or Montana. Thus it may well, and often does, serve the interests of all concerned to "trade" votes on proposals before them. By supporting a measure important to a fellow committee member, or House member for that matter, in exchange for their vote on an issue important to his or her constituents, a legislator can secure something significant to his electorate while giving up little in return. This common practice is called "logrolling." Thus are majorities among diverse political and economic interests achieved.

Omnibus Legislation

As briefly discussed above, omnibus legislation scrambles—and further politicizes—the traditional legislative process in important ways. First, omnibus legislation implicitly grants increased power and authority to party leaders, who are in the position both of determining what other bills will be permitted to be attached to the major proposal, and the capacity to coordinate the package. Because the aggregate of bills in the omnibus package have different—and sometimes competing—goals, member accountability is blurred. Constituents cannot readily discern which or which combination of proposals their representatives support.[11] Furthermore, omnibus packages are carefully crafted first as a means to get minority interests accommodated and thus increase their likelihood of enactment. At the same time, by widening the scope of the package, the number of secondary bills increases as do their chances of passage on the shoulders of the omnibus package itself. Not only do omnibus bills help build coalitions among members of different parties, but they can also coerce the support of a President who is interested primarily in the over-arching proposal.[12] In the environment sphere, the Energy Policy Act of 2005 and the reconsideration of many of the same issues in counterpart House and Senate Bills (2007), are classic examples of omnibus legislation. These examples embrace some combination of bills to provide federal funding for:

- oil interests to encourage drilling;
- incentives to facilitate ethanol production;
- requirements for utilities to generate percentages of electricity from alternate or renewable sources;
- requirements for inreased energy efficiency for lighting and appliances;
- money for expansion of biofuels research;
- improved fuel economy standards for vehicles;
- climate research and for carbon capture and storage emitted from coal plants.

Similarly, the farm bill of 2007, currently under negotiation, comprises bills on:

- subsidies;
- conservation;
- ethanol;
- other biofuel promotion;
- organic product certification, and more.

In both cases, the multiple goals are facilitated by the fact that omnibus legislation packages them and makes it possible for them to traverse the labyrinthine course of committee and subcommittee referrals. It is thus not difficult to understand why omnibus legislation has dramatically increased in popularity in recent years, and especially in a political climate of divided government.

The Bill Review Process

As noted earlier, introduced bills are referred to appropriate standing refer-ence committees and then usually sent to subcommittees, or, in the case of bills that cross jurisdictions, to multiple subcommittees. It is at the subcommittee stage that proposals receive the most scrutiny. The Cabinet officers and other administrative agencies participate in legislative hearings as well. The first committee action taken on a bill is usually a request for comment by the government agency or agencies with regulatory jurisdiction over the subject matter. Most obviously, they represent the Administration, since their officers are Presidential appointees. Less generally recognized is that they have their own interests as well. Environmental regulatory agencies like the EPA, the Department of Energy, and the Department of the Interior have institutional interests in what policies emerge and the shape they take, since their authority and budgets are potentially at stake. Quite aside from the considerable policymaking influence administrative agencies exert in adopting regulations, they have an interest in the laws themselves, which give or deny them the authority and funding to carry out the provisions of the statute. It would be naïve to assume that these agencies would actively pursue the general public interest without thinking at all of their own concerns. "Bureaucrats" are often accused of "careerism" when they promote policy initiatives. Although it is their alleged regulatory excesses that are at the source of these critiques, their very real influence on legislation is often overlooked.

The process by which committees review legislation offers a host of opportunities for the input of the subcommittee members as well as the interest groups that have the time, expertise, and money to stay abreast of the congressional calendar. Because, as noted earlier, the titles and missions of major bills promise to be all things to all people, changes to the introduced draft are offered during these meetings, which are much more sparsely attended, and, by and large, out of the public eye. Still, requests for changes advanced by interest groups are most often technical in nature so as not to appear to oppose the lofty objectives of the proposal. As generally well informed as committee members are, they can seldom challenge the data or rationale provided by experienced lobbyists steeped in the particular subject matter. Legislative staffers are the principal guides for committee members on detailed matters, but, again, they cannot pretend to possess the expertise of the private sector's legislative agents. Often, by the time a bill wends it way through the committees and subcommittees in each House, it is most often different from the introduced draft in significant ways. Partisan, geographic, and interest group considerations have been forced upon it at every stage, and while the reported bill may have the same title and public purpose, it often shows the scars of the legislative wars. The procedure by which various differences among subcommittee members are reconciled into a new or amended version is called a "markup." The goal is to secure maximum agreement on the bill's provisions, and to keep the "scars" as invisible as possible.

It should be apparent, however, that the virtues of this step-by-step, open and deliberative process are, at the same time, its limitations. They make the legislative process dispositive toward certain kinds of policy outcomes and resistant to others—except, of course, when dealing with a highly charged emergency. Because the public prefers incremental to dramatic change, only some of the potential alternatives for dealing with a problem are considered, generally the most practical and readily implemented. Limitations on the amount of information available to policymakers and on their time together with the need for consensus preclude comprehensive change. The process is open also to legislative mischief. Subcommittee members opposed to a measure, who, as an alternative to voting against it, may choose to add seemingly supportive amendments that would actually diminish the likelihood of its passage.

If its members reach consensus on a bill, the committee "reports" it favorably, together with a written report that summarizes the bill, notes any committee revisions and digressions from existing law, and presents the views of executive branch agencies. Any committee member may append to the report any dissenting view he or she may have. Cost estimates and estimated regulatory impacts are included.[13]

Finally, as floor challenges to bills are becoming increasingly common, committee chairs are called upon to get the bill on the calendar for vote by the full House, market it to potential opponents, and anticipate any procedural obstacles to its enactment. Thus, for all kinds of practical and political reasons, bills proceed to enactment, if at all, by easy, though halting, stages, and not by the clear and direct route the step-wise process may suggest.

If the progress of a legislative proposal on its journey into law is, finally, muddied and unpredictable, so apparently is its placement on an agenda. As can be inferred from the barebones process the consideration of a proposal begins at its introduction, after which it is carried along a pre-scribed path. But recent research has disclosed that its viability as a high agenda issue at the front end of the process is dependent on a more complicated set of circumstances.[14] Specifically, its status as a priority is the result of a confluence of circumstances and factors. It must be recognized as the potential solution of a present problem that requires action. Further, the political climate must be favorable to developing a consensus for its consideration. Finally, it must engage the support of elected officials and their appointees, who, ultimately, have a greater influence on the agenda than political participants outside of government. But these factors are not sequential; rather they may well manifest themselves randomly, and "windows" of opportunity may open up at unpredictable times. Those who would advance proposals should be mindful of these factors and, to the extent possible, capitalize on them.

Along with the disposition to modest, incremental change is a short-term policy bias. The two- and six-year terms of office to which legislators are elected, and the fact that most budgets are required to be submitted annually, inevitably dispose lawmakers to those policies that show immediate results, and reduce immediate costs. This disposition is especially harsh on environmental problems, which do not generally submit themselves to quick fixes. Gross environmental and ecological conditions take time to address effectively, and initial investments often cannot demonstrate a return for long periods of time. Again, spills or accidents that constitute crises can be responded to in the short term through initiatives and quick infusions of money, but most environmental problems swim against the legislative current. Perhaps that is why crises, or the appearance of them, are so often exploited by environmental groups, and why the dramatic presentation of them in the media has been such a potent driver of legislative action.

The decentralization of power in the legislative process that protects the public from autocratic rule also works against prompt constructive action. It is an axiom in the halls of government that it is much easier to keep something from happening than it is to make something happen. If those many and varied interests playing into the process offset each other, or get caught up in partisan wrangling, legislative gridlock is the result. When these circumstances obtain—as they often do during the final months of an administration—ways to get around the plodding, multi-step legislative process are sought. It was not hard to find them during the Clinton administration, especially during his second term.

The systematic and deliberative procedure by which legislation is formally enacted notwithstanding, especially contentious issues—and especially contentious times—often call for extraordinary strategic maneuvers. The 1990s were such times, and, accordingly, Congress and the President revived and expanded tactics that enabled them to circumvent or co-opt the other in order to pursue goals that they almost surely could not achieve through the conventional process. These tactics were the use of "riders" and executive proclamations respectively. Let it be stressed clearly at the outset that both of these tactics are perfectly legal, and each has been utilized throughout our nation's legislative history. But recourse to these tactics in the area of the environment increased dramatically in the 1990s, during which the Executive and Legislative branches were for the most part controlled by different parties and were as bitterly at odds as they have been for years. Let's take a closer look at them, for they became strong forces in shaping environmental policy.

Legislative Riders

The "rider" is a legislative maneuver that attaches a measure that wouldn't be passed on its own to a bill likely to pass at the last stage just before full House vote and after committee consideration. These stealth provisions, though not related to the main purposes of the bills they hijack, have been responsible for countless initiatives that have become part of our established law. Unlike the Constitutional authority vested in all but a half dozen or so state legislatures, the Federal Constitution permits provisions on issues unrelated to the purpose of the original bill to be voted on together with the original bill by the lawmaking body. Thus, special interests may prevail upon lawmakers to attach a controversial provision it desires onto a popular bill, which "carries" it to passage (thus the nickname). In this way, riders escape the scrutiny built into the legislative process—at committee hearings and during floor debate.

The most common vehicles for riders have historically been appropriations and spending bills for a variety of reasons: appropriation bills inherently have a diversity of purposes and often have substantive urgency about them, particularly those dedicated to relieving some grievous situation. Too, major department appropriations bills must often be enacted to keep agencies of government running. Finally, budget legislation is shielded from filibusters in the Senate, thus minimizing debate and opposition. A classic example was the Kosovo Emergency Funding Bill in 1999. The bill was to "provide needed aid for those suffering from the ravages of natural disaster and war," but the conference committee sought to capitalize on the crisis by loading it up with anti-environment riders in the final version of the bill.[15] In the end, though, most of these riders were negotiated out of the enacted law.

During the 1990s, riders continued to play an active role in environmental policymaking. The reason can be traced back to the election of the 104th Congress, and Speaker Newt Gingrich. Despite the best efforts of previous administrations, and the rising influence of anti-regulatory forces since 1980, virtually all polls confirmed that the public remained strongly committed to environmental protection, whatever the cost. Environmental activism did not comport well with the platform of Congressional Republicans and many conservative Democrats. The unveiling of an old tactic, the rider, and the advent of omnibus legislation, seemed like an ideal way to advance the environmental agenda, especially as the anti-environmental initiatives embedded in the Contract With America failed to secure Senate passage and largely fell by the wayside.[16]

President Clinton first encountered this tactic when he made an active effort to resolve the issue concerning logging in the Pacific Northwest by trying to find a meaningful compromise between those who wanted to protect the resource and the economic interests promoting the continuation of logging. The environmental forces appeared to have won with the Fiscal 1995 Rescissions Bill proposing more than $17 billion in spending cancellations for budget accounts approved by the preceding Congress. But Representative Charles Taylor attached a rider to it to increase logging on U.S. Forest Service and Bureau of Land Management lands. The rider provided for the suspension of all federal environmental laws to log the ancient forests of the Pacific Northwest and "salvage" log at least 6.2

billion board feet of trees affected by wildfire or insect infestation. While the President did veto this particular bill, he signed a similar one 90 days later. The game was on.

Expectedly, President Clinton was faced with a series of fiscal 1996 appropriations bills laden with anti-environmental riders. These measures were by no means purely budgetary; they contained significant policy implications. Among them were measures to eliminate EPA's role in protecting: wetlands; to restrict energy conservation and efficiency programs; to impose a moratorium on listing for protecting any additional threatened and endangered species; to establish a timber plan permitting considerable logging of the Tongass National Forest in Alaska; and to reduce the scope of the California Desert Protection Act by relieving the National Park Service of the responsibility to manage the Mohave National Preserve. In addition, an omnibus bill in the House of Representatives consolidating the proposals would have cut funding for environmental programs and reduced EPA's budget by 10%. President Clinton's threat to veto the entire measure ultimately saved most of the programs and the EPA budget, but provisions to halt endangered species designations and expediting the logging of ancient forests were signed into law as part of emergency spending legislation. It was only the first of what was to become a continuing assault on environmental protection through this essentially clandestine legislative strategy.[17]

In an unsuccessful attempt to forestall this stealth strategy, Representative Henry Waxman introduced The Defense of the Environment Act, a bill that would require open floor debate and a separate vote on all proposals that would have the effect of weakening environmental protection. Meanwhile, the practice continued. The Alaska delegation, which holds influential seats on appropriations and resource committees, advanced a number of riders to spending bills designed to facilitate exploitation of Alaska's natural resources. Further, riders to the Veterans Administration, Housing and Urban Development Appropriations bill that would have interfered with EPA efforts to clean the air in national parks, and delayed cleanup of toxic mercury and PCBs and federal action to protect children from harmful pesticides were also introduced.

In 1998 more than 40 anti-environmental riders were attached to bills funding the budgets of the Departments of Commerce, State, Interior, Defense, and Agriculture, and the EPA.[18] The issues were more than fiscal, covering a range of topics from climate changes, mining waste, wildlife protection, and royalties for extracting oil from public lands, to grazing on public property. In another defensive strategy, Representative Norm Dicks successfully advocated a directive to House negotiators on a measure funding the Department of Interior to reject Senate riders. Though of little substantive influence, it was one of a number of elements that collectively led to the ultimate negotiation of a bill without the riders.

To demonstrate that Republicans were not the sole practitioners of legislation by rider and that interests prevail over partisanship, Senator Robert Byrd of West Virginia, the senior Democrat on the Appropriations Committee, sponsored a rider that would have exempted mountaintop coal mining practices in his state, a measure opposed by House Democratic leaders as well as a group of House Republicans. If enacted, the provision would have effectively overturned a Federal court decision finding that West Virginia's mining companies were in violation of clean water and surface mining laws.[19]

The result of rider-wrangling in the 105th Congress was, by and large, won by environmental interests. Only a rider preventing the Department of Transportation from raising fuel economy standards for cars and light trucks was subsequently enacted. But riders proliferated in Fiscal 2000 appropriations bills, and continued efforts to obstruct compliance with U.S. commitments under the Kyoto climate change treaty, to forestall fuel efficiency standards known as "corporate average fuel economy" or CAFÉ standards. Riders to promote "logging" of forests and to minimize or eliminate reviews by regulatory agencies were also embedded in them. In fact, the Natural Resources Defense Council, from a link on its website, identified 70 Fiscal 2000 budget riders that were modified and defeated. But even when riders fail to be enacted, their goals are frequently embodied even less visibly in the "report language" through which Congressional committees express their "legislative intent." Such language, though technically not "the law," must be taken seriously by regulatory agencies.

So pervasive and potentially threatening have anti-environmental riders become that environmental organizations have established separate website links for the sole purpose of tracking and scorecarding these riders.[20] That most such riders have failed to be enacted is attributable, at least in large part, to the increased exposure that the rider strategy has been subject to in the last several Congresses. At a minimum, anti-environmental riders have strained the resources of the environmental activists, gotten measures onto the legislative agendas that could not make it on their own, and not infrequently forced compromises that would otherwise not have been made.

If Congress has sought to advance issues and interests through recourse to riders and proposals appended to priority bills and omnibus legislation when those issues and interests could not survive the open legislative process, the Executive Branch has engaged in its own extra-legislative tactics to accomplish purposes it probably could not have gotten Congress to agree to. In fact, on the day after the nation celebrated its 274th birthday on July 5, 2000, the *New York Times* devoted facing pages to two related executive branch exercises of singular power. The first described the battle raging over the proposal of the White House to preclude, by regulation, road building on 43 million acres of national forest land and thereby impede further development on as much as one-quarter of the nation's entire forest system. The National Forest Service was, of course, holding extensive hearings on the proposal, but the ultimate power remains in the Executive Branch.

The other story more generally described the quite deliberate efforts of the President to rule by "decree" whenever he felt that he could not accomplish his goals by process. It publicized the various tools available to him—executive orders, memoranda, proclamations, and regulations—that he has used, and will continue to use until he leaves office, to move initiatives that would otherwise stand little chance of passage by Congress. This is no mere sideshow. The Office of Management and Budget estimates that President Clinton averaged one executive order a week during his terms in office. Policymaking by the executive alone has a long and hallowed history, but President Clinton perhaps exploited it more fully than any of his predecessors.

While more stringent air pollution standards have secured wide publicity and engendered much nationwide controversy, the most actively exploited and controversial initiative that the Executive Branch undertook at the turn of the century is the protection of special natural and wild areas from commercial exploitation and development via another tack. Sensing the relentless efforts of Congress through challenges both legislative and judicial to land use regulations based on Constitutional "takings" principles, President Clinton exploited the authority in the Antiquities Act of 1906, a law that allows the President to act unilaterally. The law states: "The President of the United States is authorized, in his discretion, to declare by public proclamation historic landmarks, historic and prehistoric structures, and other objects of scientific interest that are situated upon the lands owned or controlled by the Government of the United States."[21]

There are, as a close reading of the law will reveal, subtle but real differences between what can be designated a "monument" and what can be preserved as simply "wilderness" or natural lands. Those treasures that can be protected by Presidential proclamation are special, particular resources rather than whole ecosystems. Nevertheless, President Clinton saw in the authority vested in him by the Antiquities Act of 1906 a chance to build a preservation legacy—and endear himself to a significant component of the environmental community—by setting aside vast areas of Federal lands without, and even in the face of, an angry Congress.

President Clinton's first significant act under this authority was the designation of 1.7 million acres of red rock cliffs in southern Utah as the Grand Staircase-Escalante National Monument in September of 1996. He sought to enhance the significance of the designation, and its symbolism, by signing the proclamation virtually at the site where President Theodore Roosevelt proclaimed the Grand Canyon a monument in 1908, and thus immunized it from commercial exploitation.[22]

While the President's act was, of course, lauded by preservationist groups like the Sierra Club and the Southern Utah Wilderness Alliance, as well as the region's celebrity environmentalist Robert Redford, it was bitterly denounced by the entire Utah Congressional delegation as well as the lone Democrat in the Utah State Legislature. They lamented the adverse effect of the designation on what is regarded as the largest known coal reserves in the U.S. The Utah Association of Local Governments was also outraged, principally because mining royalties are dedicated to funding public schools, further exacerbating the political fallout of the declaration. And joining the chorus of angry cries were those of the Western States Coalition, county government agencies, and citizen groups. All pledged to fight the designations with every weapon in their power, but most admitted that they were not optimistic about their chances.

Officials opposed to the designation denounced the manner in which it was made as much as the action itself. Senator Orrin Hatch, while conceding that the Antiquities Act of 1906 gives the President very broad powers, nevertheless asserted that blocking it would be extremely difficult. Other legislators called it an undemocratic abuse of power.

Clearly, President Clinton's act excluded a wide range of interests—mining, tourism, and education to name but a few—from the public debate. And the vehemence of the reaction signaled the difficulty the President would have had in pursuing his objective through the open legislative process. That was the rationale for invoking the Antiquities Act of 1906. His action did provoke more than a verbal response just as the proliferation of riders spawned "defensive" legislative measures, however fruitless. Included among those responses were a lawsuit brought by the Western States Coalition grounded in a claim of overreach; a Joint Resolution passed in the Alaska Legislature that would require Congressional consent before withdrawals under the Antiquities Act could be made; and a bill that would weaken presidential authority, specifically providing for public participation in the declaration of national monuments. Additionally, Congressman Hansen introduced a measure to require Congressional as well as gubernatorial and state legislative approval of designations in excess of 5,000 acres. In sum, opponents of Clinton's act at once claimed that he exceeded his authority and that the act should be changed to require broader participation in such decisions. None of these challenges had much of a chance of passage, but they did direct anger and frustration into formal channels of opposition.

These various formal initiatives did not discourage President Clinton from continuing the practice. In early January, 2000, utilizing the same authority, he designated three additional monuments and expanded a fourth. These additions, which were considered monuments, brought the total acreage newly set aside by Clinton to 2.7 million acres, with his expressed intention to subsequently add another 6 million. As they had before, opponents sought legislative remedies in vain.

It is generally agreed that any succeeding president, or a veto-proof majority of Congress, can overturn the declaration of a monument, just as a veto-proof majority of Congress can enact riders over presidential objection. No declaration of a monument has, however, ever been overturned by Congress nor rescinded by a succeeding president, no doubt because doing so would be a very public anti-environmental action, whereas riders more often than not are "unhorsed" before crossing the finish line. The respective histories of these two strategies may well reaffirm the power of the executive, but, more significantly, they betoken the frustration policymakers often experience with the traditional legislative process and their persistent desire to achieve their goals, if necessary, by going around rather than through it. In President Clinton's case, there was the additional factor of his being in the final year of a second term. Republicans were not favorably disposed to his building an environmental legacy by this backdoor tactic, but as the President's term wound down, they seemed helpless to prevent it.

As relations between the two branches becomes more strained, or as their workload gets increasingly overwhelming and the issues more complicated, Congress takes increasing recourse to unorthodox strategies. However serviceable the hallowed legislative process may be to formulate and carry out our nation's policymaking during ordinary times, the very elements intentionally built into it to slow the enactment of proposed measures are those that get short-circuited as new protocols are introduced.

The past half dozen years or so have witnessed a reversion to the centralization of power and authority in the Office of the President, and the Republican majority in both houses, at least until the 2006 midterm election, by and large supported him. For example, the omnibus Energy Policy Act of 2005 represented a legislative triumph for the Administration. It appropriated billions of dollars in subsidies to the fossil fuel and nuclear industries, strong supporters of the Republican Party, while allocating a small percentage of that amount to conservation and alternate energy sources.[23] On the other hand, the broad parameters of the energy policy package introduced in 2007, after the Democratic Party secured modest majorities in both Houses in the 2006 mid-term election, generally reversed these priorities. Early deliberations, however, found Democratic Senators Obama and Byrd advancing the interests of their constituents by promoting coal, industries important to Illinois and West Virginia respectively, and Democratic Senator Levin and Democratic Representative Dingell, both of Michigan, supporting the automobile manufacturers by stifling new requirements for fuel efficiency standards. The diverse and competing components of this package were ultimately sorted out in

Conference, and the President's threatened veto if the bill's final version failed to increase support for oil exploration didn't happen. The Energy Independence and Security Act of 2007 did provide support for oil exploration, and, accordingly, the President signed it into law in December.

Thus the deliberation and transparency that have historically characterized our policymaking process are giving way to increasingly complex issues and the corresponding balkanized interests of Congress and the President. Overarching issues such as energy and farm policies scramble the usual partisan alignments, and replace them with practices that allow members of Congress to advance the needs of their constituents, often without regard for party ideology. Finally, interests often trump process and partisanship.

Central Ideas

The legislative process is designed to be fair and open to all, so that the policies it enacts reflect broad public consensus. But as it has come to be practiced, it is dispositive toward certain interests and policy outcomes. A variety of circumstances have generated substantial changes to the legislative process, concentrating power and reducing transparency. Newly emergent legislative strategies seek to deal with increasingly complex issues.

Chapter 3

Environmental Regulation and the Evolution and Capture of the EPA

Administrative agencies of the regulatory kind are established to carry out the terms of the treaties that the legislators have negotiated and ratified. They are like armies of occupation left in the field to police the rule won by the victorious coalition.

(Earl Latham)

I'll let you write the substance on a statute and you let me write the procedures, and I'll screw you every time

(U.S. Representative John Dingell)

This chapter takes up the broad and complex issue of environmental regulation, the aspect of the process that has the most impact on environmental policymaking and is, therefore, the most politically contentious. First we will look at the formal procedures by which regulations are adopted, since these procedures are dispositive toward certain kinds of policy outcomes. We will then take up the regulatory arena itself—the turbulent history of the Environmental Protection Agency (EPA) and its evolving operational protocols. As the principal institutional embodiment of environmental protection, EPA has historically been the focal point of the myriad social, political, and economic forces that are exerted whenever any substantive environmental issue has been up for public consideration. With the advent of the modern environmental movement, it fell to the EPA to be the workhorse in developing and enforcing rules to carry out new environmental laws. But several factors, including a backbreaking workload, increasingly complex technological challenges, a political climate favoring federalism, and persistent pressures from the business community required gradual modifications of its operational principles. More recently, however, its necessary independence has been eroded by an aggressive and unabashedly business-friendly Chief Executive, President George W. Bush, and its very integrity has correspondingly suffered.

The Politics of the Regulatory Process

In the popular mind, and even in the minds of many actively involved in environmental policymaking, "rules and regulations" are synonymous with "laws"; the terms are routinely used interchangeably to refer to any environmental requirement. Yet rules and regulations, while they have the force and effect of law, are very different from laws (formally referred to as "statutes") and those differences are significant. Understanding what they are, who develops them, and the process by which they are adopted is crucial to understanding environmental politics, and to effective participation in the policy arena.

What are the differences between regulations and laws, and why is it important to distinguish between them? The differences between regulations and laws are significant because many, if not most, of the major battles on environmental issues have been fought over regulations, not laws. As noted in the previous chapter, many of the major environmental laws are dedicated to achieving broad policy objectives: the air ought to be free of contaminants that threaten human health; the waters of the nation ought to be "fishable and swimmable"; and those who spill toxic chemicals on lands or into waters ought to be responsible for cleaning them up, with their money, not the public's. Because these are lofty and laudable objectives, they were not, by and large, controversial. Who, after all, would quarrel with any of these—at least publicly? This is why even the most broad-based and ambitious of such laws—The Clean Air Act of 1990, "Superfund," and the Farm Bill of 2002, to take three notable examples—were passed with healthy, bipartisan majorities.

This is not to say that the enactment of environmental laws is a friction-free, amicable process. As we have seen in Chapter 2, it is not. There is often much debate over whether the solution to one or another problem is the responsibility of government at all, or whether the marketplace should be allowed to resolve problems in its own way. Even when the appropriateness of government action is conceded, there is often disagreement over whether the objectives in question ought to be pursued at the national or state level. There is also disagreement, especially with respect to land use issues, over whether government involvement tramples on higher, sometimes constitutional, rights, e.g. the right of landowners to use their property as they please. Finally, even when all these issues are resolved, special interest groups vie for control of the agenda, clash over how a problem should generally be addressed, and work to get themselves excluded from the purview of whatever is being proposed. Overarching all these issues are battles of the respective political parties to protect their turf, and their respective constituencies. But except when statutes themselves have "reauthorization" provisions, provisions that require Congress to revisit the law at regular intervals, evaluate their record of effectiveness, and amend them as appropriate (e.g. the Clean Air Act of 1990), or when a program's funding source expires (e.g. "Superfund"), or when a significant problem with the programs' implementation develops (e.g. the Endangered Species Act of 1973), laws seldom get revisited, and the battle moves to the regulatory arena. The Reagan administration, widely regarded as the most anti-environmental presidency until that of George W. Bush, announced at the outset its goal to rein in environmentalism. But it sought to do so by making it more difficult to adopt strict regulatory standards and by relaxing enforcement of laws already on the books, rather than by amending the laws themselves or vetoing new bills. It also reduced EPA's funding, hampering its ability to fulfill the responsibilities given to it by law. Indeed, the Republican National Party Platform of 1980 acknowledged that "virtually all major environmental legislation reflected a bipartisan concern over the need to maintain a clean and healthful environment," even as it "declared war on government overregulation." Thus, the Reagan administration's efforts to change laws were few, modest and tentative. But its assault on regulations was direct and comprehensive.

What Are Regulations and Who Develops Them?

Broadly defined, regulations are the specifically prescribed ways of carrying out the policy objectives of the laws. Legislators cannot, after all, be expected to know exactly what must be done to realize these policy objectives. They want to keep landfills from leaching but do not have the expertise to prescribe how they should be engineered to isolate the wastes from human contact. They want to assure that nuclear power plants do not release radioactivity, such as at Chernobyl, but they obviously do not know what risk elimination systems are necessary or what training programs for employees are appropriate. The federal Clean Air Act goal of air relatively free of toxic pollutants has no opponents, but the control of contaminants discharged continuously into the air from hundreds of thousands of industrial and commercial activities and millions of cars involves thousands of scientific and technical determinations. Standards for each statutorily identified contaminant, a protocol for automobile inspection and maintenance programs, a formula for reformulated gasoline, as well the identification of specific technologies to minimize pollution at its source, and balancing costs and practicality against efficiency and effectiveness are all largely beyond the expertise of those who make the laws.

Much the same is true in the area of land use. The values of wetlands and the need to preserve them have also been embodied in law. In creating this law, politicians were confronted with the questions of how to define wetlands, and what criteria to adopt for their designation. Obviously, this must necessarily be the business of experts. If the overarching question with regard to air is "how clean is clean," the question with respect to wetlands may well be "how wet is wet." Do lands have to be veritable swamps to qualify, or do they simply have to support hydrophytic vegetation? And how wide do buffer areas around them need to be to protect the resource? For that matter, how extensive an area is required to preserve the habitats of threatened or endangered species?

Therefore, in order to realize their policy objectives, legislators must turn to engineers, scientists, land use planners, lawyers, economists, and specialists in a variety of other disciplines to set the protocols, standards, methodologies, equipment specifications, tolerances, dosages, and time frames necessary to make sure that what they want to happen, happens. These are the "regulators," the personnel staffing the administrative agencies who field the questions enumerated above. The answers they provide are loaded with implications for a whole range of interests. But before getting into that, we must look at who they are and the process by which the regulations themselves are developed.

We have seen that federal laws are enacted by legislators, officials elected every two or six years and therefore directly accountable to those they represent at regular intervals. They thus have to be ever mindful of their constituents' interests and concerns. Regulations, on the other hand, are developed principally by administrative personnel who usually hold permanent full-time positions, often, though not invariably, protected by "civil service," the government counterpart to tenure in academia. To that extent the line staff is personally insulated from external pressure. These staffers are, appropriately, selected for their technical expertise in a given area, and are publicly invisible and anonymous. They develop their regulations collectively, in settings that are almost never covered by the press, and do not attach their names to their products. Unlike laws, regulations have no "sponsors."

It should be noted, however, that these regulatory personnel do work under the immediate supervision of agency heads, who have to sign off on draft regulations before they go to public comment. These supervising administrators are most often political appointees, and it is their job to reconcile individual regulations with the broad goals and policies of the agency and the President as well as with the demands of the external world. It is their role to maintain a larger perspective, if for no other reason than to insure the viability and credibility of the agency's decisions. The tensions between core staff and administrators, as might be expected, are not infrequently strained. A dramatic and potentially far-reaching example of this is the EPA's denial, in December of 2007, of California's request for a waiver of federal preemption of its greenhouse gas mitigation program. California and 16 other states sought to implement a program that would establish standards for CO_2 emissions stricter than those of the federal government, but needed EPA approval. EPA Administrator Stephen L. Johnson denied the waiver over the strenuous objections of his staff and of former EPA Administrator William Reilly. In justifying his decision, Johnson argued that California's measure was obviated by the recently revised fuel efficiency standards and that the climate threats posed by greenhouse gas emissions were not limited to California and therefore required a broader approach. But in doing so, he was obviously following the direction of the White House and sympathizing with the automobile industry that did not relish observing different standards in different states. This denial has now been appealed in the courts.

Further, regulators are in an organizationally anomalous position. While they are administratively located in the executive branch of government and work under the supervision of a Cabinet Secretary, Administrator, or Commissioner appointed by the President or, at the State level, Governor, they are obliged to carry out the mandates of the legislative branch of government. This has not been a particular problem for much of our history, during which the two branches were under the control of the same political party at any given time. However, in recent years, the public has become increasingly distrustful of their elected officials, and has thus been increasingly disposed to split tickets, whereby we elect a President or Governor of one party and a Congress or legislature of the other, to guard against feared abuses. In such situations, agency personnel are subjected to dual pressures, and, in some cases, from partisan appointees in the agency itself.

The Regulation Adoption Process

Finally, let's look at the process whereby regulations are adopted. It ought to be noted at the outset that the legislators, in drafting their laws, themselves often delegate rule-making authority to one or more of the relevant administrative agencies. And just as with the assignment of legislative bills to standing reference committees as noted in the previous chapter, legislators may well pick "friendly" agencies to draw up the rules. It is an additional measure of control that legislators have over the implementation of their legislative proposals. The rules themselves are adopted in accordance with a process set forth in an umbrella statute known as the Administrative Procedure Act, enacted in 1946.[1]

The process generally works like this. The delegated agency first looks at the statute to get a clear picture of its policy objectives. A Steering Committee decides what is in the purview of its responsibilities, such as how wide a net to cast, what expertise is required, what decisions have to be made, what may need to be researched. It then assembles a Working Group of staffers who collectively have the range of expertise necessary to determine how best to implement the law. The Working Group talks to people in and out of the regulated communities to get a feel for the potential practical problems and the costs of their ultimate prescriptions, collects relevant data, and begins work on the proposal. Since the members of the Working Group represent a broad spectrum of perspectives and knowledge bases, their interaction is itself a political event of which publicly little is known, but which often has significant impact on the final product, as we shall see in our discussion of the EPA later in this chapter. Their work results in a "formal proposal" to be submitted to the public for comment. In some cases, there are pre-proposals on which there may be hearings prior to rulemaking. At the federal level, before proposed regulations can be submitted for public comment, however, they must be reviewed and approved by the Office of Management and Budget for fiscal impact, a requirement imposed by two Executive Orders.[2] The whole regulation-drafting process is extremely technical and complex, and, in the case of major legislation, takes months, sometimes years, to complete. The resulting draft is then submitted to public hearings at which anyone can testify and offer objections, produce compliance cost estimates, and warn of potential practical problems with implementation.

The regulatory agencies are legally required to submit their proposed regulations to this public review process so that the proposal can be distributed ahead of its taking effect for all to read and digest. But they are under no legal obligation to revise the regulation in response to anything brought up at these hearings, though they often have to prepare written responses to issues raised by the public. When the public hearing process on proposed regulations is complete, they formally "adopt and promulgate" the proposed regulations, which then have the force and effect of law.

Why Regulations are "Political"

With a clear conception of what regulations are, of the administrative position and role of those who develop them, and of the regulatory adoption process itself, it is now possible to see why regulations are at the center of environmental politics.

First, it should be apparent that regulations, for all the science that goes into them, are inevitably policy documents. The establishment of any particular standard, tolerance, or concentration of an air pollutant, for example, may well seem value neutral, but those same standards, tolerances or concentrations surely affect some populations more than others: children, the aged, asthmatics, pregnant women, or the chemically-sensitive, to name but a few. Similarly, the extent of buffer areas to protect wetlands will impact commercial builders differently from residential builders. Additionally, a regulation concerning the level of cleanup of existing sites or buildings of hazardous discharges, which is required as a precondition for construction or renovation, is a major factor in any decision about urban redevelopment and often the linchpin argument in the so-called "brownfields/greenfields" debate. This debate involves deciding whether to site a new facility on previously developed land and thus promote urban redevelopment ("brownfields") or on undeveloped land ("greenfields"). That is why the public hearing process on proposed regulations is at least as contentious as the legislative process. Interest groups of all manner and size take the opportunity to weigh in. In the case of issues with far-reaching consequences, public hearings are held in a number of geographical areas to afford maximum opportunity for input.

The policymaking potential increases substantially in the case of state regulations implementing federal laws. As discussed elsewhere, the federal government delegates the implementation of some of its major enactments, most notably in the areas of clean air and water, to the states. It does this principally because states have vastly different population densities, industrial profiles, geography, topography, and the like, and states are in the best position to determine the least economically and socially disruptive means for them to reach federal goals and targets. By shifting its regulatory burden to the states, the federal government also escapes the political wrangling necessarily involved. As a result, states have even more latitude than usual to apportion burdens among different interests, and incur, as a consequence, a good deal more political pressure. As we shall see later in this chapter, the EPA has recently gone even further in sharing rulemaking responsibility with other government agencies and lower levels of government.

The process of rule adoption, then, is ultimately a lawmaking endeavor. Most regulators would disdain such a notion and have no conscious inclination to serve as unelected legislators, but the nature of their work frequently makes them vulnerable to the charge of "making laws" without due authority, and this puts them in an uneasy political position.

The Roles of Legislators and Interest Groups

Next, let's look at legislators, and the regulatory politics they provoke. In our examination of the lawmaking process in the previous chapter, we noted that it was, characteristically, a balancing act. Legislators start with a proposed solution to a public problem, but to get their proposal passed, they must reconcile a variety of contending forces affected in various ways by that proposal. Compromise and tradeoffs with their fellow legislators are the norm. Since they are under the constant watch of their constituents, and function in a public forum with substantial media attention, they want to be, or at least want to *appear* to be, effective and reasonable as well as public-spirited. This often results in a passed bill with a complex and sometimes contradictory mix of provisions to accommodate, or placate, as many as possible of those interests. Their goal is to get the bill passed, and they often do whatever is necessary to accomplish that. In their single-minded pursuit of enactment, they often shift inherent problems and inconsistencies to the regulators, who are ultimately responsible for making it work.

Worse, legislators like to get credit for "doing good," even if their socially conscious proposals will have an adverse effect on powerful interest groups. While it is not often talked about, those inside the regulatory community can recount innumerable instances wherein a legislator won public plaudits for sponsoring a praiseworthy bill, and then, before the ink was dry on the President's or Governor's signature, began pressuring the regulatory agency to "go easy" in its implementation, in the service of an affected interest or constituent. Regulatory personnel, then, are unwittingly burdened with the "impurities" of the legislative process, and often find themselves trapped between the political pressures from sponsors and their own integrity. And even if legislators do not actively coerce the regulatory agency into moderating its rules, they blame "bureaucrats run amok" when constituents come to them with costs and burdens flowing from the legislation. Regulators are not uncommonly scapegoats for the "downside" of environmental statutes.

Finally, let's look at the interest groups whose activities would be directly affected by the law. Many of them, of course, have weighed in during the legislative process, particularly those with formal representation and a substantial presence in the halls of Congress or state legislatures. But some often find it unwise to press their opposition too fervently during the legislative process, particularly if, as is often the case, the bill purports to address a compelling public need or concern, or challenge the disposition of a politically powerful legislator. Such interest groups often wait until the rulemaking phase, when they can pursue their interests more effectively, and clandestinely, at the regulatory table. The regulatory process affords the full spectrum of interest groups the opportunity to recover what may have been compromised, or conveniently left vague, during the legislative process, or to cushion or undermine the impact of a given law on their activities. They may even use the regulatory process to achieve a competitive advantage in the marketplace by working to structure the regulations so that they hamper competitors more than themselves. Further, they can supplement their formal testimony with specific pleading to the supervisory administrators, who have the opportunity to incorporate provisions to accommodate them before approving a proposed draft. And all this takes place in a setting that is, for all practical purposes, "nonpublic," where they will suffer no bad publicity for appearing to challenge popular goals in the service of their self-interest. As a practical matter, the media are absent from, and largely unaware of, deliberations on regulatory matters. The process is too technical, too protracted, and too uneventful to be newsworthy.

A good example of interest group lobbying can be found in the regulatory atmosphere surrounding state legislation proposed in the wake of the

Bhopal catastrophe in India. The legislation granted the state of New Jersey's Department of Environmental Protection extraordinary powers in the service of preventing a recurrence of any such tragic event. The state chapter of the Chemical Industry Council was in no position to exercise its muscle to prevent its passage because the citizens of the state with the second largest concentration of chemical plants in the nation were understandably frightened by any possibility of a similar accident occurring near them. Opposing preventive measures would be, from a public relations standpoint, unthinkable. The legislature passed legislation without opposition, despite the fact that the powers it gave to the State to oversee chemical plant operations were unprecedented.[3]

Notably, it was only when the state's Department of Environmental Protection began to craft regulations to flesh out the legislation that the Chemical Industry Council became actively involved. The council "educated" the department on how chemicals were handled in sophisticated manufacturing plants, and in so doing was able to shape the regulations that plant operators had to follow henceforth. They were even consulted on which chemicals should be covered under the regulations, since the chemical released at Bhopal, methyl isocyanate, was by no means the only one that could have such an acute lethal effect on those exposed. But they did one better. The Council suggested and promoted protocols that had the effect of giving the major chemical companies with substantial expertise and financial resources disproportionately represented by it competitive advantage over so-called "mom and pop" operations. Smaller companies simply did not have the resources to comply with the regulations and had to terminate production of products that utilized them.

On the federal level, a similar strategy was employed by DuPont, the world's largest producer of chlorofluorocarbons (CFCs), the chemical compound associated with destruction of the ozone layer. For decades, DuPont aggressively opposed government action to eliminate the chemical. By the late 1980s, as evidence of the continuing destruction of the ozone hole mounted, DuPont reversed course. Seeing the prospect of strict regulation, the company had been working on substitutes. On the eve of the Montreal Protocol, the international treaty addressing ozone depletion, DuPont argued for, rather than against, the global policy to restrict them. No doubt perceiving that continued resistance would be fruitless and self-defeating, they judged that limiting future production on a strict schedule would, in the short run, raise prices and maximize profits, especially since a unilateral ban on the part of the U.S. would disadvantage them relative to European producers. More importantly, in the long run, it would give them a leg up on their substitute. Again, intra-industry competitive advantage guided the regulatory posture of DuPont.[4]

When interest groups fail in their efforts to eliminate the regulatory provisions they find most repugnant they can, and frequently do, seek redress in the courts, arguing that their particular situation was not contemplated by the Legislature in enacting the statute, and that the regulations are therefore beyond the scope or their authority and in violation of "legislative intent." This charge, the most common raised in legal challenges to rules, essentially affirms that the regulators, whom they disparagingly refer to as "bureaucrats," are really acting as legislators, making laws rather than rules. Of course, in many cases regulators do go well beyond the reasonable parameters of the statute. But, as we have seen, the process of rule adoption is, implicitly or explicitly, a policymaking activity, and it is for the courts to decide when regulators have crossed a critical line. Important to note, though, that even when interest groups lose their cases in court, they can take advantage of delayed implementation of the rules while the case was pending in the courts, and that is itself a victory, since cases and subsequent appeals can go on for years.

In sum, interest groups often participate more actively and aggressively in the regulatory arena than on the floors and committee rooms of the legislative bodies. The relative obscurity of the regulatory process allows parties adversely affected by popular legislation to pursue their self-interest without incurring public scorn, and the highly technical and sluggish pace of the regulatory process discourages media and public attention. The substantive expertise of many of these same players in highly specialized areas, however, also makes them valuable, sometimes necessary, partners in the rule-development process.

Further, the administrative personnel that develop regulations are easier targets than duly elected Representatives and Senators. While they may seem to be insulated from political pressure by reason of their job security and their ultimate power over the final form of regulations, they are politically vulnerable in other ways, especially to the wishes of legislators. First, the Legislature holds the power of the purse. Legislatures ultimately must approve the budgets of administrative agencies, and it takes little more than a threatened budget cut to get a "recalcitrant" agency to be "more responsive." The most pronounced exercise of this power was carried out by the Reagan administration, during which the budget of the EPA, until that time on a steadily upward rise in response to ever-increasing responsibilities, was sharply reduced. Similarly, the 104th Congress, personified by House Speaker Newt Gingrich, stalled one of President Clinton's major proposals—to raise EPA to cabinet level status, where it would have had more budgetary muscle.

Second, that same Congress, in a little-publicized measure, the Small Business Regulatory Enforcement Fairness Act of 1996, granted Congress legislative oversight powers.[5] Specifically, a provision in the act called the "Congressional Review of Agency Rulemaking" gave Congress 60 days to review major new regulations as a precondition to their taking effect, and facilitated the passage of resolutions to disapprove those which it did not think satisfied "legislative intent" or which cost disproportionately more than the benefits it promised. While such legislative authority has been called into question both on Constitutional grounds as violating the separation of powers doctrine, or on the practical consideration that it would just give lobbyists another bite of the apple, President Clinton signed it. Lawmakers have sought to limit the discretion of regulatory bodies in another way—by including provisions in the legislation circumscribing their options in setting standards, establishing criteria, or imposing fines and penalties for violations.

More recently, as discussed in detail in the previous chapter, members are increasingly responding to what they regard as a runaway EPA by including provisions as riders to unrelated legislation, many of which are regulations in all but name. In so doing, they can bypass the regulatory process entirely and provide low-profile relief to the regulated community.

Lastly, it should be noted that, in some ways, legislators themselves are, with respect to regulation, an interest group. They are justifiably concerned that rules adopted to carry out their bill's provisions, are, in fact, likely to fulfill its policy objectives. That is their obligation. They also have a stake in minimizing the costs and burdens such rules may impose on their constituents. In carrying out this function they add their voices and influence to the many interests that routinely descend upon environmental regulators.

Before closing this section, mention should be made of a refinement of the rulemaking process described above that came to the fore in the mid-1980s—"negotiated rulemaking," or "regneg" for short. Regulatory negotiation applies the principles of alternate dispute resolution to environmental rulemaking. Briefly, negotiated rulemaking replaces the inherently adversarial existing process with one that allows interest groups to participate in the process *before*, rather than after, regulations are drafted. In so doing, it reduces the "thrust and parry" that characterizes the traditional procedure, by allowing groups to put their concerns on the table early rather than their hardened positions later. Experience has shown that permitting affected parties to sit down with regulators at the initiation of rulemaking minimizes costs by allowing parties to combine research on agreed upon issues, improves compliance, promotes public acceptance, and in many cases obviates the need for adversely affected parties to seek judicial review. Notwithstanding these advantages and its successful employment at the Federal level in several environmental cases, the fact that it has not become more widely applied probably indicates that political give-and-take is more deeply embedded in the regulatory process than anyone would care to admit. But, as well shall see, the Clinton administration made a specific effort to institutionalize regulatory negotiation in its "reinvention" protocol.

The EPA and Institutional Politics

On March 16, 1995, President Bill Clinton and Vice-President Al Gore issued a detailed report called *Reinventing Environmental Regulation* as part of their National Performance Review.[6] In it they enumerated "10 Principles for Reinventing Environmental Regulation," by which EPA would be guided in carrying out its mission in the future:

1. Protecting public health and the environment are important national goals, and individuals, businesses and government must take responsibility for the impact of their actions.
2. Regulation must be designed to achieve environmental goals in a manner that minimizes costs to individuals, businesses, and other levels of government.
3. Environmental regulations must be performance-based, providing maximum flexibility in the means of achieving our environmental goals, but requiring accountability for the results.
4. Preventing pollution, not just controlling or cleaning it up, is preferred.
5. Market incentives should be used to achieve environmental goals, whenever appropriate.
6. Environmental regulation should be based on the best science and economics, subject to expert and public scrutiny, and grounded in values Americans share.
7. Government regulations must be understandable to those who are affected by them.
8. Decision making should be collaborative, not adversarial, and decision makers must inform and involve those who must live with the decisions.
9. Federal, state, tribal and local governments must work as partners to achieve common environmental goals, with non-federal partners taking the lead when appropriate.
10. No citizen should be subjected to unjust or disproportionate environmental impacts.

These principles respond specifically to the persistent attacks leveled against the EPA during the preceding decade by interests ranging from conservative and libertarian think tanks to environmental justice groups, as well as Congress and the White House. They call upon the EPA to make the cost of regulatory compliance as minimal as possible and to use the marketplace to do this: to adopt performance-based, rather than prescriptive, standards; to make rulemaking collaborative rather than autocratic; and to be sensitive to the effect of siting decisions on economically vulnerable populations. Collectively, they represent little short of a metamorphosis of the EPA's character, functions, and method of operation. Let's look at history, then, for it reveals much about the political struggles inherent in regulatory policymaking in general, and about the complex and turbulent politics to which the EPA has been subject during the almost five decades since its establishment.

Historical Pressures on EPA

The Environmental Protection Agency was formally established by Reorganization Plan No. 3, an Executive Order submitted by President Richard Nixon to Congress on July 9, 1970. The reorganization plan creating the EPA was the result of several year-long struggles. The first was between presidential aspirant Edmund Muskie of Maine, then Chairman of the Senate Public Works Committee, and President Richard Nixon, each of whom sought to enhance their election chances by corralling the newly emerging environmental constituency.

The compromise that prevailed involved the transfer to the newly minted EPA of a potpourri of programs, offices, and functions from other departments, a pair of councils, and a commission.[7] With that mixed bag of responsibilities came a diverse, and in some respects eclectic, constituency.

It should also be noted that in amalgamating existing agencies, the newly formed EPA absorbed managers and regulatory personnel from those agencies and, with them, an assortment of missions, working alliances, and perspectives. During previous years, staffers of those agencies had, of course, built up working relationships with the regulated entities under their respective jurisdictions and, inevitably, certain sympathies with their concerns and needs, which they took with them to their new "home."

The Executive Order's preamble clearly established pollution control as the new agency's central responsibility. It sought to break down the existing balkanized approach to pollution control by media, and implement more coordinated research, monitoring, standard-setting, and enforcement, while offering industry consistent standards and states the promise of financial and technical assistance. Environmental interests hoped finally to have a strong, consolidated advocate for their causes in the executive branch; the President and other federal officials saw in its creation a means to manage environmental protection in a way that accommodated the needs of business and industry. Thus began a debate over just how to raise the child, so to speak—how much independence to give it, how to meld the disparate influences on it, how to control its spending, and how to punish it for "misbehavior."

The early years, during which the agency sought to gain its footing, found it courting environmental interests. The EPA's first administrator,

William Ruckelshaus, initially focused on strict enforcement rather than organizational structure or technical and scientific resources. The EPA's early operational protocol is referred to as "command and control," whereby the agency established strict standards to be met and enforced. As realization of the many adverse environmental effects of the post-war industrial boom dawned on the public consciousness, a strong-armed regulatory approach by the EPA became necessary. The increased costs to the business and commercial activities that the approach inevitably entailed were by and large subsumed by the concomitant economic prosperity.

This authoritarian approach gave rise, however, to the first of what would become a succession of attempts to rein in the EPA as the economy weakened. The Nixon administration created a review group that established as preconditions to regulatory adoptions Quality of Life Reviews, a euphemism for a requirement that the EPA consider economic development and fiscal impacts in its regulatory process. The program's principal focus was to ease the regulatory burdens on business, not to conduct any balancing of costs and benefits to society. The most far-reaching impact of the program was, in fact, to initiate "debate about both Presidential review of regulations and the use of benefit–cost analysis," a debate that continues to this day.[8] Clearly, the cost of regulatory compliance was a central issue for the Administration and its business community constituents. It is important to note, however, that financial burdens are more empirically quantifiable than environmental benefits.

The Ford administration was similarly concerned about the effects of governmental acts on business. Among President Ford's actions was to issue Executive Order 11821 that required the preparation of "inflation impact statements" as a precondition to new regulations. These statements ultimately became an important precursor to cost-benefit analyses, which have, incrementally, become a staple of regulatory practice.

President Carter, despite his party's historic anti-business posture, was also interested in assuring that regulatory burdens on business were minimized and regulations were cost beneficial. One of his Executive Orders, 12044, issued in March 1978 and titled "Improving Government Regulations," also targeted rules that may have significant economic impact. Accordingly, he established the Regulatory Analysis Review Group, chaired by the Council of Economic Advisors and comprising representatives of the Office of Management and Budget (OMB) and the economic and regulatory agencies. The charge of the Group was to evaluate agency regulations and make them a part of the public record. Specifically, it mandated that all federal agencies conduct an economic analysis of each proposed regulation that had a projected cost of $100 million a year or more. Thus did President Carter "institutionalize both regulatory review by the Executive Office of the President and the utility of benefit-cost analysis for regulatory decision makers."[9]

It is important to note at this point that attempts to control the EPA were in large part a reflection of two countervailing factors. The first was the EPA's growing responsibility and authority. The 1960s and 1970s, and even much of the 1980s were, from an environmentalist's perspective, halcyon days; fueled by a series of environmental disasters—Times Beach, the oil spill off Santa Barbara, Love Canal, Times Beach, Three-Mile Island—public fears and anxieties impelled Congress to pass a score of major pieces of legislation, each requiring strict and far-reaching regulatory implementation. But with the EPA's growing power came a regulatory burden that was simply enormous—and unmanageable. The regulations implementing the laws passed by Congress required complicated and sophisticated technological and scientific determinations. To make matters more difficult for the EPA, the laws imposed strict timetables for their regulations' development and promulgation. The EPA fell months, even years, behind the statutory deadlines for their adoption, which disturbed Congress, the environmental community, and, in some cases, the business community. And so the pressure on the agency to perform increased as its budget, level of personnel, and flexibility decreased. Yet its power and authority over an ever-widening range of problems made it perhaps the most feared of federal agencies. It became an easy scapegoat for the economic malaise that marked the Carter years, and, thus, the centerpiece of Ronald Reagan's election platform.

The Reagan Assault and Its Aftermath

Ronald Reagan's comfortable victory over President Carter was viewed in part as an affirmation of the public's desire for smaller, less burdensome and less expensive government, and in large measure it was. The public, however, was not yet ready to reduce its commitment to environmental protection, as the Administration was soon to learn.

President Reagan's environmental strategy was crafted by conservative think-tanks—principally the Heritage Foundation—whose ideology is market-oriented. There were several components of that strategy, but perhaps the most significant and enduring was implemented pursuant to Executive Order 12291, "Federal Regulation," signed on February 17, 1981. In addition to requiring agencies to prepare cost–benefit analyses for major rules and issue only regulations that maximize net benefits (social benefits minus social costs), the Executive Order required draft regulations be sent to OMB for review before presentation to the public for their comments. It also created a Task Force on Regulatory Relief, chaired by the Vice-President, to supervise this process and referee disputes between the agency and OMB. While Reagan's predecessors had incrementally expanded the role of the OMB, Reagan made it a major obstacle before any proposed environmental regulation could go public. It was in the deliberations of the OMB that another component of the strategy—cost–benefit analysis and risk–benefit analysis, long sought by business interests—were integrated significantly into public policymaking. These were hurdles not easily cleared by EPA, since costs were readily calculable and most often empirical while benefits were characteristically long-term, to some extent speculative, and not infrequently incommensurable.

In the first year of his second term, Reagan issued Executive Order 12498, "Regulatory Planning Process," that increased OMB's oversight role. It required agencies to advise OMB, in advance, of all major rules they had under consideration, so that the Office could coordinate them with other agencies and recommend modifications.[10]

As has been frequently noted, the OMB was beyond the reach not only of administrative agencies, but of the courts and Congress, all of whom were loath to interfere in the work of the President. The tug of war over the EPA between Congress and the Administration, in this administration, clearly swung in favor of the White House. Consistent with the pro-business bias of the President, meetings of the OMB as well as the EPA were opened to the representatives of those who would be subject to any regulations, and substantially closed to the range of public interest groups who were commonly allowed to weigh in previous administrations. Many of the officials of the EPA previously worked in the private sector, and, perhaps more importantly, planned to return. They were thus unduly accommodating to business interests as policies were discussed.

A second component of the anti-environmental strategy was devolution. Reagan sought to limit the power of the EPA by transferring power and authority to State and local governments. Federalism, as this is commonly called, involved delegating the implementation of federal laws to State governments wherever possible and developing generic laws that States could implement in their own way.

Finally, President Reagan significantly reduced the budget of the EPA, despite the fact that, as noted, it was striving mightily to try to keep up with its delegated responsibilities. The sharply reduced funding available to it necessarily limited its research capacities, even as it was paradoxically required to justify its rules on sound science, turning it more into an enforcement agency. Some of these actions even rattled the Administrator of the EPA, Anne Gorsuch, and constituted one of a number of factors leading to her premature departure from the agency.

While President Reagan did not emasculate the EPA, he did leave it wounded and short on funding, low in employee morale, and subject to administrative encroachment by other agencies with different agendas and different constituencies. Even though, under the second stint of William Ruckelshaus, it regained some of the respectability it lost during the scandals and excesses of Reagan's first term, the EPA was still reeling during the Administration of George H. W. Bush. The late 1980s and early 1990s were a period of fiscal austerity for the nation, and the case was often made, if not always persuasively, that environmental regulation was a drain on jobs in particular and the profits of business in general. It was virtually without any public outcry that President Bush's Vice President, Dan Quayle, could chair a Council on Competitiveness comprising a group of business interests including the Secretaries of Treasury and Commerce, the Attorney General, the Director of the Budget, the Chairman of the Council of Economic Advisers, and the Chief of Staff. Behind closed doors and with no public record of proceedings, this council heard the complaints and concerns of private sector executives. During its tenure, it unilaterally overturned several regulations deemed by the Vice-President as excessive, burdensome, and unnecessary. The essential point is that the Council fundamentally ignored the established legal procedure for adopting regulations by simply vetoing regulations that felt imposed costs on business disproportionate to their anticipated benefits. An outraged Congress sought to contain the Council by reducing its budget, but it nevertheless continued until it was disbanded by President Bill Clinton.[11] Thus, during the administrations of Reagan and Bush, government became extraordinarily sympathetic to business interests, a shift facilitated by a struggling economy that was pinned to environmental excesses.

In an effort to survive, the EPA, during the latter years of the Reagan administration, began work on new initiatives, one of which was to prioritize its workload. In 1987, EPA's Office of Policy Analysis published *Unfinished Business—A Comparative Assessment of Environmental Priorities*, a compilation of task force reports establishing agency priorities based on risk. This represented the first major effort at coordinating the various programs in EPA, at once raising science to a higher level and providing some rationale for allocating limited money and resources in publicly defensible ways. It also involved, in a significant way, local units of government.

That work, however, failed to forestall the second major attack on the EPA launched by the Republican representatives in the 104th Congress that swept into office in the 1994 elections. There were at least two major prongs to that attack. The first was, at least superficially, benign. Congress commissioned the National Academy of Public Administration to determine if the EPA was allocating resources to the most pressing environmental concerns and to determine how and by whom these priorities were set. The charge was implicitly stimulated by an alleged loss of trust in the effectiveness of the EPA by the public, even in the face of continued public support for its mission. *Setting Priorities, Getting Results*, as the resulting 1995 report was called, was, as one might expect from its authors, a management study. Its conclusions, also not surprisingly, were strikingly similar to the direction that the Reagan and Bush administrations wanted to pursue: 1) a more defined mission, but with the flexibility to carry it out; 2) devolution of responsibility and decision making authority to the states and localities; 3) flexibility and accountability to the private sector and to local governments; 4) improvement of its management operations by establishing specific goals and strategies, using comparative risk analyses to inform priorities, and setting and tracking benchmarks of progress; 5) expanded use of risk analysis and cost-benefit analyses in making decisions; and 6) a breakdown of its media orientation in favor of a more integrated structure.

The Contract with America: Echoes of Reagan

The other prong of the attack was more clandestine. The Republican House candidates had campaigned collectively for election on a pre-announced program of legislative initiatives that it called "The Contract With America." One of the major components of that program was a bill they called the "Job Creation and Wage Enhancement Act." While that particular bill, as it was described in the "Contract," did not even mention the word environment, it contained three measures that would, if enacted, significantly undermine environmentalism by requiring: 1) that all federally mandated requirements on the states be funded by the federal government, the so-called "federal mandate, federal pay" provision; 2) that owners of land on which development is limited by environmental law be fully compensated for the loss of their economic value; and 3) that virtually all environmental regulations be based on sound science, to be implemented by EPA's disclosure of the scientific premises, studies, and conclusions on which the regulation was based to the public, including the regulated community, for complete review as a precondition to their promulgation. The obstacle that the Republican constituency sought to create was not only substantive, but virtually paralyzing: it would take enormous resources to collect, systematize, and distribute such voluminous data, and it would be prohibitively time-consuming to review the comments from the outside world. Actually, the House of Representatives, the driving force behind this provision in particular and the "Contract With America" in general, passed some version of each of the three provisions, but only the federal mandate/federal pay was passed by the Senate and ultimately signed by the President. Neither of the other two was passed by the Senate, presumably because its President, Robert Dole, was by then seriously considering a run for the U.S. Presidency, and couldn't brook a nationwide debate about such volatile and far-reaching issues.

It would have been reasonable to assume that the new stresses on EPA that the Reagan and Bush administrations exerted—stresses to be less autocratic and more cooperative, consumer friendly, and market-oriented—would abate with the election of Bill Clinton as President and long-time environmentalist Al Gore as Vice-President in 1992. But in a curious way, they did not. Indeed, they were generally sanctified and institutionalized more firmly in the government protocol than ever before. This was attributable to several factors.

First, the now almost decade long critique of government as bureaucratic, inefficient, indifferent, and costly, initiated by President Reagan was, by and large, shared by the general public. The average citizen did not see any inconsistency between this characterization of government and his confidence that this same government, in the name of the EPA, could protect him from toxic waste, polluted air and water, and urban sprawl.

President Clinton continued the tradition of shaping the regulatory process by Executive Order in issuing Executive Order 12866, "Regulatory Planning and Review." It retained cost–benefit analysis and the basic framework of existing regulatory review, but allowed OMB to review only the most significant proposals, set a 90-day time limit on their review, and restored openness and accountability to the process. The most significant acts of the Clinton administration in the regulatory sphere, though, responded substantively to the public's disenchantment with government, a disenchantment captured in two books that commanded nationwide attention.

The Regulatory Activism of the Clinton Administration

Reinventing Government: How the Entrepreneurial Spirit is Transforming the Public Sector, by David Osborne and Ted Gaebler, a carefully crafted prescription for better governance published in 1992, implicitly capitalized on the underlying public discontent with the federal government. Osborne and Gaebler presented a measured mission and protocol for a new kind of government, one that "steered" instead of "rowed," was collaborative with the private sector, mission-driven rather than rule oriented, customer friendly, preventive rather than remedial, decentralized, and market-oriented. While the authors seem to disdain political labeling, their recommendations were uncannily close to, if not congruent with those advocated by the anti-EPA forces of the previous several years. It also provided what was to become a significant term in the regulatory reform vocabulary, "reinvention."

Another book on the same theme was more unsparing and critical. *The Death of Common Sense* by Philip Howard, published in 1994, was an openly anti-regulatory tract that detailed a litany of the consequences of expensive, overly complicated, misguided, and ineffective government rules, many though by no means all of which were environmental. Though its thrust was purely negative and sarcastic—providing countless laugh lines for luncheon speakers at business gatherings nationwide—it clearly struck a chord. After all, how often does a book on government sit atop the *New*

York Times best-seller list for the better part of two years, as this one did? It too provided an important term in the regulatory reform vocabulary. The notion that the EPA's priorities and protocols often violated "common sense," the mantra until now of the anti-environmental community, was soon to be sanctified and institutionalized by the new Democratic administration. Democrats understandably bristled at the Republican's appropriation of the term for "regulatory overkill." In a battle of semantics, the Clinton administration began to associate their new regulatory protocol, embodied in the new "reinvention" principles, as a "common sense" initiative.

While the enemies of the EPA were eroding its credibility from the right, a long-standing issue, the disproportionate number of unwanted facilities whose siting was approved by the EPA in low-income and/or minority neighborhoods, came to the fore in the early 1990s. The EPA had been defending itself from charges of racism for over 20 years, but the environmental justice movement finally coalesced with the People of Color Leadership Summit in October of 1991, and the "Principles of Environmental Justice" document that it produced. The event made environmental justice a potential political land mine for the EPA, impelling it to modify its previous self-righteous stand as a dispassionate scientific agency to one that would henceforth be sensitive to equity concerns. But it was not until President Clinton issued Executive Order 12898 in 1994, directing all federal agencies to incorporate environmental justice concerns into their decision making process, that that interest was given formal recognition.

Pressure not only from partisan forces and environmental justice advocates, but from the popular media, including a steady stream of articles in newspapers and magazines literally charting the disparity between what the experts thought were the most serious threats to public health and the environment and the EPA's agenda, impelled President Clinton and Vice-President Gore to embrace the 10 principles enumerated above, implicit in the regulatory philosophy embodied in *Reinventing Government*, and recast EPA. The previously mentioned March 1995 report announced a new era in environmental regulation. Henceforth, the EPA was to seek "common sense" (the phrase is repeated countless times in the report) solutions to environmental problems, keep an eye to cost-effectiveness, and, perhaps most important of all, share decision making with those affected by its actions. EPA would henceforth focus its regulations on performance and market factors; base priorities on sound science; build stronger partnerships with the private sector as well as state and local governments; reduce paperwork; improve accountability, compliance and enforcement; and, in general, become more user-friendly.

Specifically, the report presaged the initiation of nearly two dozen new experimental programs, one important piece of which was called, not incidentally, the Common Sense Initiative (CSI). In the words of EPA Administrator Carol Browner, the CSI is an "effort to make good on what business and environmentalists have been telling us for two decades— that we must look at whole facilities, whole industries, and their overall impact on the environment. We must do a better job of cleaning up the environment and do it cheaper." Accordingly, the CSI pilot program convened teams of representatives from all levels of government, environmental interests, labor, industry, and environmental justice groups to study existing regulations in six industries. The teams were charged with developing regulatory protocols that would promote pollution prevention rather than "end of the pipe" controls, were flexible, would focus on whole industries rather than individual pollutants, and were consensus-based. Thus, the media-based, pollutant-focused "one-size-fits-all" regulator was to begin its transformation into a collaborative, results-oriented facilitator.

In succeeding years, the CSI program waned but a companion program, Project XL (Excellence and Leadership) that offered the regulated community a straight swap of regulatory flexibility for improved environmental performance, became the centerpiece of EPA reform. The program invited facility operators, industry sectors, communities, and even government agencies regulated by the EPA to submit proposals for exceeding environmental standards using strategies that would otherwise violate existing regulations. The primary criteria for approval of an XL project including better results, cost and paperwork reduction, promotion of multi-media or pollution prevention effect, and stakeholder support were established by the EPA but the central purpose of the effort was to decentralize regulation. The EPA's role was limited to establishing the program's criteria, to working with the states to negotiate the projects, to monitor the results, and to extract lessons that may be applied in other regulatory contexts. While environmental interests were concerned with a potential lack of accountability, less public participation, and a circumvention of judicial review, they did, for the moment, hold their fire until definitive results came in.

George W. Bush and the "Capture" of EPA

Once the EPA's strict "command and control" regimen secured a measure of control over rampant pollution, the economic consequences of their regulations resurfaced as a major issue. We have seen that every President from Richard Nixon to Bill Clinton tinkered with the regulatory process to suit his own disposition. Whether through the creation of review groups, economic impact statements, cost–benefit or risk–benefit analyses, or OMB priority setting, all tried to accommodate economic considerations in the rulemaking process.

As noted earlier, the EPA, like other administrative agencies, is in a difficult position. Its formal responsibility is to carry out the mandates of Congress, the Legislative branch of government, yet it is supervised by, and reports directly to, its chief officers who are cabinet secretaries and administrators and, ultimately to the President of the United States, at the top of the Executive Branch. Regulatory practice thus displays an uneasy tension between Congress' stated goals and the President's political objectives. In one way or another, Presidents have sought to establish a balance between social benefit and economic cost, though the Democratic Presidents—Carter and Clinton—have generally accorded wider berth and deference to the EPA and its sister agencies' social missions than have Nixon, Ford, Reagan, and George H.W. Bush.

Anything like a balance, though, has been destroyed in two different ways by the George W. Bush administration. First, while it is, of course, commonplace for Presidents to appoint people sympathetic to their own policies and views, seldom, if ever, has decision-making authority been so uniformly put in the hands of former officers or lobbyists of the corporations or industries it is their responsibility to regulate.[12]

Appointing representatives of interest groups to head administrative agencies is a perilous practice at best, as President Ronald Reagan learned in appointing Anne Gorsuch as Administrator of EPA and James Watt as Secretary of Interior, both of whom were forced to resign under public fire. At worst, it calls into question the integrity of all decisions handed down by those agencies. In the present case, no fewer than 18 appointees to environment or energy related positions have arguable conflicts of interest, and many formerly lobbied against laws and regulations they now administer.

Second, in an act more significant and far reaching, the President issued amendments to President Clinton's Executive Order 12866 (Regulatory Planning and Review). As discussed earlier, Clinton's Order retained the basic parameters of regulatory practices while only modestly circumscribing OMB's role. But the newly issued amendments to that Order not only dramatically reverse course, but transparently politicize rulemaking. Whereas it had become established practice to *accommodate* economic concerns in deciding what issues to take up and how to address them, President Bush's amendments permit the EPA and other agencies such as the Occupational Safety and Health Administration (OSHA) and the Food and Drug Administration (FDA) to act only when they can identify "the specific market failure" that justifies government action. In effect, the EPA is deprived of most discretion in interpreting the law and determining how to implement it; in the absence of specific statutory direction, regulatory action can be initiated only when the marketplace cannot, or refuses to solve a perceived problem or need.[13] To take a hypothetical case, as one media source did, the EPA could not issue regulations protecting workers subject to hazardous materials exposure in their workplace unless employers failed to address the problem on their own.[14]

In addition, the amendments provide that guidance documents issued by the EPA be subject to the same scrutiny by OMB as draft regulations themselves. The EPA prepares guidance documents on how it will enforce its prospective regulations to respond proactively to OMB's challenging reviews. The combined effect of this provision and the one previously mentioned leave the EPA virtually incapable of regulating with anything like scientific independence.[15] Further, the amendments make the EPA's Regulatory Policy Officer a presidential appointment with specific approval authority for any rulemaking, and supervisory responsibilities over their development. That Officer puts the EPA's work directly into the White House, to which business interests have ready access.[16] This clearly jeopardizes environmentally friendly policies.

Finally, the amendments require the EPA to estimate the "combined aggregate costs and benefits of all its regulations planned for that calendar year to assist with the identification of priorities."[17] The cost–benefit balancing test now conducted for each proposed regulation is to be applied for EPA's entire annual workload.

These amendments clearly shift power from an ostensibly politically neutral, science-based regulatory agency to an instrument of the Office of the President. The EPA has been "captured."

And so the more than 35-year history of the EPA has seen it transformed from an authoritarian, rigidly bureaucratic, centralized power to a more flexible, pro-business, cost-conscious, power-sharing facilitator. That transformation, embodied in microcosm in the "10 Principles for Reinventing Environmental Regulation," was spurred by battles between successive Congresses and Presidents and the constituencies each branch of government wanted to use the EPA to cultivate. It was fostered as well by public attitudes toward government in general and its impact on the economy in particular; by consistent pressures from the regulated community exerted directly and indirectly through legislative and regulatory agents; by the insistent and compelling claims of economically disadvantaged and minority ethnic populations; by the various needs and situations of individual states and municipalities; and by forces within the agency itself. It is important to note that the George W. Bush administration is shaping the EPA in a manner consistent with the larger political goal of strengthening the Executive branch at the expense of Congress. The history of the EPA is, finally, a mirror of the complex mix of political forces at work virtually since the inception of modern environmentalism.

Central Ideas

For a variety of reasons, the administrative agencies in the executive branch play as pivotal a role in making environmental policy as legislators. The EPA, the agency principally responsible for developing, implementing, and enforcing environmental law has, over time, transformed itself from an authoritarian, centralized bureaucracy to a flexible, collaborative facilitator. Along the way, it has been required to balance environmental protection with cost considerations. Notwithstanding its more measured posture, it has been "captured" by a highly partisan Office of the President that makes it more of a handmaiden of politics than an environmental watchdog.

Chapter 4

The Burgeoning Role of State and Local Governments

This agreement [wherein Virginia Electric agrees to cut emissions to avoid suits by NY] is a critical affirmation of the role that states can play in not only environmental enforcement, but also the broader range of enforcement issues where states have compelling interests that are not always pursued by other levels of government.

(Eliot L. Spitzer)

There are few places on the planet where the federal government does . . . what the public would like it to do, and the sub-sovereign states step up to do it. In every state, to at least some extent, climate change is now being addressed.

(James Holtkamp)

Earlier, we looked at the ways in which Congress, the federal government's lawmaking body, undertakes the business of making environmental policy. We noted that Congress, by reason of its diverse representation, does not, indeed cannot, set down policies in autocratic fashion. Instead, Congress must acknowledge and reconcile a wide variety of interests in order to achieve the consensus necessary to make law. We also noted that that process is played out on a very public stage. So comprehensively do national affairs dominate media coverage that in the minds of most people, Congress and "government" are synonymous, and all other agencies and instrumentalities are all but invisible. A 1998 report underwritten by The Project on the State of the American Newspaper documents diminishing coverage of state government affairs, and a decline in staffing at the state-house level in more than half the states. The decrease in attention and staff at the local level helped create the public perception that virtually all-important policies were forged at the federal level.[1]

But the evolving and increasingly significant role for state and local governments in national environmental policymaking has over time been capturing headlines and garnering public attention. It is, of course, well known that states implement and enforce national policies in a number of areas, a function that has been delegated to them in statutes enacted over the last half of the 20th century. Aside from serving these administrative functions, or, more accurately, how and to what extent they are expected to carry out these functions, states, counties, and municipalities have compelling concerns with the nature of those federal policies, and feel motivated to participate in their formulation. Though they are generally represented by their Congressional delegations, the particular problems of individual states and municipalities were often ignored or sacrificed in the mass of issues and forces that dominate national political discourse. For these reasons it was important for states and municipalities to play an advocacy role in the formulation of environmental policy. But the widely acknowledged abdication of environmental responsibility by the George W. Bush administration galvanized local governments and spurred a veritable explosion of actions, initiatives, and lawsuits by states and municipalities that has transformed the political landscape by shifting the influence from federal to state and local governments. In fact, what has happened since the onset of the 21st century has been nothing less than a tectonic shift of policy influence downstream.

State Governments and Federal Policy

To fully appreciate this shift, some historic perspective is useful. Until the early 1970s, responsibility for protecting the environment and for addressing ecological threats came principally from state and local governments, and state courts. Environmental issues were regarded generally as local issues, and the federal presence in such matters was meager. Individuals who claimed to be harmed by irresponsible environmental behavior had to seek redress in state courts, and overcome difficult burdens of proof.[2] But in the 1970s, a flood of national legislation established the federal government as the dominant player in environmental protection. Laws regulating water quality, pesticides, noise, coastal management, endangered species protection, toxic substances, waste management and air quality were passed, and the EPA was charged with establishing national standards in most of these areas. Congress delegated to the states and municipalities, responsibility for implementing and enforcing most of the EPA's standards, and provided much, though not all of the funding necessary to do so. Such an arrangement made a certain amount of practical sense. Since states and local governments are closer to the problems, they had a better grasp of their sources, and of the available options for addressing those issues. They can thus tackle them in the most efficient and effective way and in a manner that minimizes adverse economic and social consequences, especially important since most of these laws have quite different impacts on the various jurisdictions. To that extent, devolution of implementation to levels of government closer to the people is a practical allocation of authority and action, but such power sharing is not without its challenges—and its politics.

The Reagan administration made a concerted effort to return power to the states when it assumed office in 1981. This effort was called the "New Federalism," and it sought to restore what it regarded as the proper balance by shifting programs dominated by the federal government to state and local governments. The policy issues with respect to conservation and land use are different, so it is best to look at them separately later. In the area of pollution control, the so-called "devolution" of authority envisioned by President Reagan became complicated, for the line between regulatory implementation and policymaking is complex and political.[3]

It is complex and political for a variety of reasons. First, politically conservative interests that would relax if not eliminate much environmental regulation have heretofore preferred that authority be exercised at the most local level possible. State and local governments have traditionally lagged behind the federal government in financial resources and in expertise, and are weaker "opponents" of those potentially regulated. Most states have Constitutional mandates to balance their budgets, so that they are often forced to prioritize their efforts rather than fully satisfy federal requirements. In recent years, one of the rallying cries of states has been "federal mandate, federal pay," a call that has had significant resonance. In fact, a measure to require the federal government to fund new initiatives that would impose significant new costs on states was the only one of the environmental bills in the Republican platform package, "Contract With America," to be enacted.[4]

With respect to expertise, much the same is true. With a few notable exceptions, state governments generally do not have the levels of technical and scientific expertise in their administrative agencies that the federal government does, and the growing trend to impose term limits on their legislators has acted to further dilute subject matter knowledge and experience. The situation is even truer at the municipal level, where a great percentage of officials are laypeople acting in temporary, often voluntary, capacities. It goes without saying that all these factors provide a sufficient incentive for anti-environmental interests to move environmental regulation down the government ladder.

Beyond budgetary and technical concerns, the reality is that state and local governments have particular and influential constituencies. Major industries, e.g. the pharmaceutical industry in New Jersey, the auto industry in Michigan, the oil industry in Texas, the tourist industry in Florida, and the agriculture industry in Iowa exercise enormous political influence on their governments by virtue of the vast numbers of people they employ and the substantial contribution to their states' tax bases they make. However indifferent federal policymakers can be to these industrial interests, the states must not only be sensitive to the disproportionate impact a national policy may have on them, but literally do battle on the federal legislative and regulatory fronts to minimize their adverse impacts. Good environmental policy may well be an important value for state governments and their residents, but economic viability is equally, if not more, important. That is why one so often finds business and state government as allies in lobbying efforts to defeat, or shape, federal policy.

If particular commercial and industrial interests can exert pressures on the states, it requires even lesser commercial and industrial interests to influence municipalities, whose tax bases are even more fragile. Certain public functions such as solid waste collection, wastewater treatment, drinking water quality, and growth management are generally carried out by local jurisdictions—counties and municipalities. These functions are indeed much affected by federal legislation, but municipalities have little opportunity to affect policy in these areas. They only rarely try to work out their problems caused by federal mandates with Congress, but they do lobby their state governments, not only for help with Washington, but also for direct assistance. Their situations are analogous to the state/federal relationship. Adjacent municipalities can adversely affect each other by their commercial or industrial activities or land use plans, the impetus for which are almost invariably economic benefits. But municipalities also marshal their individually modest political powers when it is in their mutual interest to do so.

Quite aside from specific constituent interests, states and municipalities have more general interests to reconcile, for states are not themselves internally homogeneous. Pennsylvania, a largely rural state, nevertheless has two major urban pockets—Philadelphia and Pittsburgh. Colorado's vast skiing and park areas that attract tourists are often at odds with Denver's urban character, where air quality is a major problem. Much the same can be said with respect to the relationship between Illinois and Chicago. A similar, though more expansive, split is that between the densely populated inner cities of northern New Jersey and the rural and agricultural areas of south New Jersey. Urban areas, as one might expect, have very different needs, and are subject to different pressures, than rural areas. The population shifts toward urban areas that the 2000 Census documents resulted in a corresponding shift in interests.

To deal with these kinds of problems, municipalities increasingly line up with sister municipalities in the same state to promote or protect their "territory" from towns with different industrial and population profiles. Issues like the siting of potentially hazardous facilities, traditionally a local decision, are becoming increasingly rancorous, especially as federal efforts to promote economic opportunity in urban areas clashes with local concerns about healthy neighborhoods.

State and local governments, then, must participate directly or indirectly in the federal policymaking process in order to protect the interest groups upon which their own economic viability depends, as well the more general interests they represent by virtue of their populations and geography. They often do this collectively, through national associations and organizations with similar problems. The National Council of State Legislatures, the Council of State Governments, the National Governors' Association, the United States Conference of Mayors, the National League of Cities, and the National Association of County Officials are among the more prominent of the alliances that they have entered into to help them meet their special challenges. Most of these were formed relatively early in the 20th century, essentially to facilitate information sharing and communication. But while they are not lobbies in the usual sense, these organizations played increasingly important advocacy roles as well, and afford smaller units of government more clout in Washington. More clearly political are the permanent offices in Washington that many states have established. It is the mission of these offices to stay abreast of legislation, regulation, and other policy initiatives that may affect the state, and maintain a vigilant presence so that prompt action to defend that state's interests can be undertaken before more politically complicated responses are required.

The increasing role of states in environmental policymaking, for all these reasons, has been considerable. The conservatives' attack on environmental activism in general, and the EPA in particular, since the Reagan ascendancy has had its effect. Environmental policymaking has devolved to where the states now issue most of the permits, initiate most of the enforcement actions, and fund most of the programs. EPA seems more willing, if not eager, to turn over a decision-making function to the states, as the discussion of regulation in Chapter 3 suggests. Most notably, the two parties have effected a broad shift in regulatory policy. The EPA imposed prescriptive standards, dictating not only *what* standards were to be met, but also specifically *how* they will be met; now they would impose performance standards, whereby states are accorded the flexibility to satisfy the standards in the manner they see fit. In the 1990s, there was increasing cooperation between the EPA and the states. In 1995, three dozen states entered into a National Environmental Performance Partnership System (NEPPS) with EPA to establish dialogue, planning, and priority coordination between the states and EPA. The participating states negotiated Performance Partnership Agreements (PPAs) to foster effective environmental protection to the people. While the name for these partnerships suggests that the state contribution is limited to the realm of how to implement federal mandates, states are, in fact, making policy along the way.[5]

Policy initiatives are also growing out of cooperation between the EPA and an association formed in 1993 by state commissioners of environmental protection called the Environmental Council of the States (ECOS).

In 1998, ECOS and EPA forged the Joint EPA/State Agreement to Pursue Regulatory Innovation that established a foundation whereby the states could submit innovative ideas to EPA and expect their expedited review.[6] Such new initiatives enable state and local governments to better accommodate their constituents' interests without violating federal strictures, or at least modifying them with federal blessing.

As states gain parity with the EPA, major regulated industries seem more willing to negotiate with them, sometimes acceding to higher permit fees for a streamlined permit process and more reasonable regulatory decisions. Over the latter years of the 20th century, states became more important players in the game, not just implementers of policy imposed from above. Neither EPA nor other federal agencies, though, was prepared to abdicate responsibility for environmental threats and conditions that cross state boundaries. That is, indeed, the salient issue of federalism. The cliché is that "pollution knows no political boundaries," so that while states and municipalities may attempt to meet the standards in ways most favorable to them at the expense of other jurisdictions downwind or downstream, the federal government must remain a vigilant protector of regional and national populations, and assure that no jurisdiction—no state, county, or municipality—can improperly burden other jurisdictions in the course of cultivating its own interests. That has set up any number of battles both on the floors of Congress and in the courts.

Other Roles

The balance of interests and responsibilities between states and the nation in many areas is delicate, and constantly shifting, but environmental issues pose especially thorny problems because so many of them involve phenomena that embrace, or cross, state or regional boundaries. After all, the Mississippi River flows from the Canadian border to the Gulf of Mexico, inevitably carrying pollutants with it, while Ohio River Valley air pollution migrates to the Northeast. Regional associations among states—like the Coalition of Northeast Governors (CONEG)—have been formed to anticipate such problems and address them collectively. They have had some real successes, but battles continue.

New York State, along with other Northeastern states, for example, have had perennial difficulty meeting federal Clean Air Act standards due in substantial measure to the air pollution carried by prevailing winds eastward from other parts of the country. Emissions from coal-fired power plants in the Midwest and South undermine the efforts of northeastern states to comply with federal requirements and to minimize acid rain by imposing stringent regulations on their own industries and citizens. Because of the Commerce Clause, states are sometimes constrained to go to court to protect their interests and meet their needs.

Conservation Issues

It is readily apparent how the ambient nature of pollution creates special problems for states and municipalities and the industries for which they serve as hosts, requiring them to become aggressive advocates for these interests in policymaking forums. It is less obvious, though just as true, that land use issues impose corresponding obligations on them. Though lands and the resources they contain remain "in place," of course, the resources themselves are not, and cannot be regarded as, the private property of the jurisdiction in which they are located. They are, rather, national resources owned by the federal government for the use and enjoyment of present and future generations of Americans.

At the heart of this clash between state and federal interests is the fact that much, in some western states most, of the land is owned by the federal government. In the 1800s, in an effort to settle the West, the federal government offered economic incentives to states and private interests to settle them. Some of these incentives took the form of extremely attractive leases to graze lands, extract minerals and natural gas, and log woodlands.[7] But the federal government, perhaps overly generous in these initiatives in the light of history, has maintained some degree of control over the commercialization of these resources, and this has persistently rankled both the western states and their extractive industries, who have regarded the federal government as a cruel, if not illegitimate, landlord. More than 100 years later, in the late 1970s and 1980s, there was an organized effort by western Senators to wrest control of these lands from the federal government in what was to become known as the Sagebrush Rebellion. When their own efforts fell short, they were pledged support from the Reagan administration in general and from Secretary of the Interior James Watt in particular.[8]

But an interesting twist of irony was instrumental in the failure of this effort. While western Senators and their constituents were trying to effect the transfer of federal lands from the control and regulation of agencies like the Bureau of Land Management, the Fish and Wildlife Service, and the U.S. Forest Service to the states, the conservative Washington establishment was promoting the "privatization" of these lands, under the fear that state governments were perfectly capable of exercising almost as much unreasonable authority as the federal government. The interests who stood to gain commercially from relaxation of federal control feared that privatization would mean that they would have to buy these lands in the open market, and pay appropriate taxes on them. Since they were presently enjoying "sweetheart" deals under which they paid virtually nothing for the rights to graze, drill, mine and log, privatizing these lands might well be worse for them. Thus there developed a split in goals between the private sector industries and the federal government that caused the whole effort to lose focus and flounder. Still, there are perennial legislative and judicial initiatives by the states and their industrial constituents to secure more freedom to commodify what they regard as their rightful possession. While conservation issues in other parts of the United States have shorter roots and are generally less contentious, activities as diverse as logging in Maine's forests to sugar production in Florida's Everglades to ethanol production in Iowa's cornfields (at least until recently) find the states in active advocacy roles to promote, protect, and defend the interests important to them and their constituents that may not otherwise be acknowledged or negotiated by the political system.

At the close of the Clinton administration and the onset of the George W. Bush administration, state and local interests seemed to be gaining political strength. Three events during this brief interface support this conclusion. First, the Clinton administration's FY 2000 budget included an increase of 5% over the amount Congress approved for environmental aid to state and local governments. The monies were to be used for expanded grants to states for purchasing ecologically sensitive lands; to assist cities in reducing air pollutants associated with global warming; for tax credits to subsidize local bonds for environmental purposes; and for contributions to state revolving funds for municipal wastewater treatment facilities. While these funds are, in and of themselves, insufficient to fundamentally change the political calculus, they did represent an effort to minimize the adverse impact on states of federal environmental mandates, thus making state and local governments less economically dependent on their private sector constituents.

Second, President Bush appointed Gale Norton as his Secretary of Interior. Norton is a protégé of James Watt, the Reagan administration's Interior Secretary who, as noted earlier, was at the center of the Sagebrush Rebellion of two decades ago. Like Watt, she was an attorney for the Mountain States Legal Foundation, a legal advocacy group that fought against the land management policies of the federal government. Most significant, however, she was an outspoken proponent of more local, state, and private involvement in crafting the nation's land use programs. Just how strong her views were could be drawn from a 1996 speech in which she analogized the struggles between states and Washington to the Cold War: "Just as free markets triumphed over Communism . . . we are in a time when we can be part of the intellectual battle that shifts power from Washington back to states and local communities."[9] Clearly, states and local communities had an uncompromising supporter in Washington as environmental policies were debated.

Finally, in January, 2001, the United States Supreme Court, in a landmark decision, limited the scope of the federal Clean Water Act of 1990. Specifically, it prevents the federal government from regulating small, local bodies of water even though, collectively, they represent 20% of the area that could fall under the jurisdiction of the Act. The Supreme Court argued that such regulation would represent a significant infringement on the states' traditional primary power over land and water use, and thus curtails to some extent Congress' right to regulate commerce between the states.[10] While narrowly tailored to the specific situation before them, it does represent the disposition of the court's majority to favor state and local regulation over federal regulation whenever credible.

Thus, at the turn of the century, state and local governments were in a stronger advocacy position than perhaps they had ever been. With the courts, the executive branch, and a substantial percentage of the general population leaning in their direction, they were expected to be increasingly vocal in pursuing their interests. But the explosion of state and municipal programs and initiatives, individual and collective, over the first half dozen years or so of the 21st century, could not have been anticipated.

The factors igniting this explosion are two. First is the now almost universal acknowledgement by the public, by policymakers, and by the business community that global climate change represents a real, significant, and potentially irreversible threat to our health, our economy, and many of our planet's resources. Second, is the George W. Bush administration's explicit refusal to participate in the Kyoto Treaty, signifying its unwillingness to accept the prevailing concerns about climate change, or, at least, its unwillingness to act forcefully and comprehensively to combat it. This administration has, to date, preferred to leave mitigation, as well as preemptive action, to voluntary activities. Clearly, as we shall see, the states and local governments feel a sense of urgency absent in Washington. Their many and varied actions will address, however modestly, some of the root causes and generate some of the remedies of climate change. But hopefully, and most likely, this explosion will serve as a catalyst for a massive policy change at the federal level.

California and the States

While Arizona, Florida, and Vermont have each developed statewide greenhouse gas control or clean energy strategies, it was California that jumpstarted the movement. In July of 2002, California enacted a law requiring that the greenhouse gas emissions of all passenger vehicles sold in the state be reduced to the "maximum" economically feasible extent, starting in model year 2009. The state's Air Resources Board adopted implementing regulations. Because the Board predates the U.S. EPA, the state is able to set its own, more stringent air quality regulations. Once the state does so, the Clean Air Act of 1990 authorizes other states to adopt them. By Fall, 2007, 17 other states had. In 2004, the California legislature adopted a law called the Pavley Amendment, which mandated rules limiting greenhouse gas emissions from new motor vehicles sold in

California beginning in the 2009 model year. It, too, has become a model for other states. If the measures survive pending legal challenges, they will exert substantial pressure on auto manufacturers to build a single, conforming vehicle. Finally, Governor Schwarzenegger continued his leadership in reducing greenhouse gas emissions when he signed an Executive Order in January, 2007 establishing the world's first low-carbon standard for transportation fuels. It will reduce dependence on oil, boost clean technology efforts, and reduce greenhouse gas emissions by at least 10%. Groundbreaking as these strictures are, their ultimate effect will depend largely upon the extent to which they are adopted elsewhere, since the effect of states acting alone, both on net greenhouse gas reductions and on national policy, is limited.

What multiplies the influence of states is the spate of regional alliances and cooperative initiatives they forged in the first decade of the 21st century. On December 20, 2005, seven northeast and Mid-Atlantic states— Connecticut, Delaware, Maine, New Hampshire, New Jersey, New York, and Vermont—joined in the Regional Greenhouse Gas Initiative (RGGI). The participating states are committed to implementing a market-driven, multi-state cap-and-trade program designed to limit CO_2 emissions. The right to emit the gas becomes a tradable commodity on January 1, 2009.[11] Massachusetts, Maryland, and California have all expressed an intention to join. RGGI was the first of several coalitions of states to set up a regional market for CO_2 emissions.

In August of 2007, a coalition of six western states—Arizona, California, New Mexico, Oregon, Washington, and Utah—and two Canadian provinces, Manitoba and British Columbia—finalized their own regional climate pact, The Western Climate Initiative (WCI) to cut greenhouse gas emissions to 15% below 2005 levels by 2020. The members aim to have a cap-and-trade system in place by August, 2008.[12] The Initiative follows up on a West Coast Governors' Global Warming Initiative announced in November of 2004. At that time the Governors of Washington, Oregon, and California approved a series of recommendations to reduce global warming pollution in recognition of their mutual acknowledgement of the potential adverse consequences on the economy, health, and environment. They also expressed the belief that the regions could enjoy economic benefits by importing less fossil fuel and making greater investment in clean energy.[13]

A third regional climate initiative, the Midwestern Regional Gas Reduction Accord, was signed in November, 2007 by nine Midwestern governors and Manitoba. The states committing to the accord are Wisconsin, Minnesota, Illinois, Indiana, Iowa, Michigan, Kansas, Ohio, and South Dakota. The Accord aims to establish greenhouse gas reduction targets, and develop a cap-and-trade system to meet them. The targets are to track the 60–80% recommended by the Intergovernmental Panel on Climate Change (IPCC).[14]

Municipal Actions

The initiatives undertaken by municipalities in the past several years to combat global climate change have been, in their own way, as remarkable as those of the states, since local levels of government have little legal authority to enforce them outside their limited jurisdictions. These efforts by municipalities are much more than token or symbolic efforts. Mayors, particularly in collaboration, can have a formidable influence on members of state legislators and Congress, and the initiatives themselves, while individually modest, have cumulatively achieved measurable gains.

Such a collaboration was initiated on February 16, 2005, the day that the Kyoto Protocol, the international agreement for signatories to meet reduced CO_2 emissions, took effect. On this day, Seattle Mayor Greg Nickels, under the umbrella of the U.S. Conference of Mayors, launched a campaign to encourage cities around the country to take it upon themselves to achieve the goals of the Kyoto Protocol, a collective effort responding to the failure of the United States to ratify it.

2005 Adopted Resolutions—*Environment*

Endorsing the U.S. Mayors Climate Protection Agreement

WHEREAS, the U.S. Conference of Mayors has previously adopted strong policy resolutions calling for cities, communities and the federal government to take actions to reduce global warming pollution; and

WHEREAS, the Inter-Governmental Panel on Climate Change (IPCC), the international community's most respected assemblage of scientists, has found that climate disruption is a reality and that human activities are largely responsible for increasing concentrations of global warming pollution; and

WHEREAS, recent, well-documented impacts of climate disruption include average global sea level increases of four to eight inches during the 20th century; a 40% decline in Arctic sea-ice thickness; and nine of the ten hottest years on record occurring in the past decade; and

WHEREAS, climate disruption of the magnitude now predicted by the scientific community will cause extremely costly disruption of human and natural systems throughout the world including: increased risk of floods or droughts; sea level rises that interact with coastal storms to erode beaches, inundate land, and damage structures; more frequent and extreme heat waves; more frequent and greater concentrations of smog; and

WHEREAS, on February 16, 2005, the Kyoto Protocol, an international agreement to address climate disruption, went into effect in the 141 countries that have ratified it to date; 38 of those countries are now legally required to reduce greenhouse gas emissions on average 5.2% below 1990 levels by 2012; and

WHEREAS, the United States of America, with less than 5% of the world's population, is responsible for producing approximately 25% of the world's global warming pollutants; and

WHEREAS, the Kyoto Protocol emissions reduction target for the U.S. would have been 7% below 1990 levels by 2012; and

WHEREAS, many leading U.S. companies that have adopted greenhouse gas reduction programs to demonstrate corporate social responsibility have also publicly expressed preference for the U.S. to adopt precise and mandatory emissions targets and timetables as a means by which to remain competitive in the international marketplace, to mitigate financial risk and to promote sound investment decisions; and

WHEREAS, state and local governments throughout the United States are adopting emission reduction targets and programs and that this leadership is bipartisan, coming from Republican and Democratic governors and mayors alike; and

WHEREAS, many cities throughout the nation, both large and small, are reducing global warming pollutants through programs that provide economic and quality of life benefits such as reduced energy bills, green space preservation, air quality improvements, reduced traffic congestion, improved transportation choices, and economic development and job creation through energy conservation and new energy technologies; and

WHEREAS, mayors from around the nation have signed the U.S. Mayors Climate Protection Agreement which, as amended at the 73rd Annual U.S. Conference of Mayors meeting, reads: The U.S. Mayors Climate Protection Agreement A. We urge the federal government and state governments to enact policies and programs to meet or beat the target of reducing global warming pollution levels to 7% below 1990 levels by 2012, including efforts to: reduce the United States' dependence on fossil fuels and accelerate the development of clean, economical energy resources and fuel-efficient technologies such as conservation, methane recovery for energy generation, waste to energy, wind and solar energy, fuel cells, efficient motor vehicles, and biofuels; B. We urge the U.S. Congress to pass bipartisan greenhouse gas reduction legislation that includes 1) clear timetables and emissions limits and 2) a flexible, market-based system of tradable allowances among emitting industries; and C. We will strive to meet or exceed Kyoto Protocol targets for reducing global warming pollution by taking actions in our own operations and communities such as: 1) Inventory global warming emissions in City operations and in the community, set reduction targets and create an action plan. 2) Adopt and enforce land-use policies that reduce sprawl, preserve open space, and create compact, walkable urban communities; 3) Promote transportation options such as bicycle trails, commute trip reduction programs, incentives for car pooling and public transit; 4) Increase the use of clean, alternative energy by, for example, investing in "green tags", advocating for the development of renewable energy resources, recovering landfill methane for energy production, and supporting the use of waste to energy technology; 5) Make energy efficiency a priority through building code improvements, retrofitting city facilities with energy-efficient lighting and urging employees to conserve energy and save money; 6) Purchase only Energy Star equipment and appliances for City use; 7) Practice and promote sustainable building practices using the U.S. Green Building Council's LEED program or a similar system; 8) Increase the average fuel efficiency of municipal fleet vehicles; reduce the number of vehicles; launch an employee education program including anti-idling messages; convert diesel vehicles to bio-diesel; 9) Evaluate opportunities to increase pump efficiency in water and wastewater systems; recover wastewater treatment methane for energy production; 10) Increase recycling rates in City operations and in the community; 11) Maintain healthy urban forests; promote tree planting to increase shading and to absorb CO_2; and 12) Help educate the public, schools, other jurisdictions, professional associations, business and industry about reducing global warming pollution.

NOW, THEREFORE, BE IT RESOLVED that The U.S. Conference of Mayors endorses the U.S. Mayors Climate Protection Agreement as amended by the 73rd annual U.S. Conference of Mayors meeting and urges mayors from around the nation to join this effort.

BE IT FURTHER RESOLVED, The U.S. Conference of Mayors will work in conjunction with ICLEI Local Governments for Sustainability and other appropriate organizations to track progress and implementation of the U.S. Mayors Climate Protection Agreement as amended by the 73rd annual U.S. Conference of Mayors meeting.

Specifically, municipalities signing the agreement commit to meeting or beating the Kyoto targets in their own communities. They will also urge their state and the federal government to enact policies and programs to achieve or exceed the greenhouse gas emission targets set out for the United States in the Kyoto Protocol, i.e. 7% reductions from 1990 levels by 2012. Lastly, municipalities will petition the U.S. Congress to pass the bipartisan greenhouse gas reduction legislation, which would establish a national emission trading system.[15]

The campaign has been enormously successful; by the end of 2007, over 750 mayors, representing a quarter of the nation's population, have signed the Agreement. Signers can expect assistance from a number of groups. The Sierra Club has pursued a supportive "Cool Cities" program that not only recruits new participants, but also helps to develop and identify practices that cities can enact to meet their obligations.[16] Technical support is also provided by ICLEI—Local Governments for Sustainability, an association of local governments and national and regional local governmental organizations that provides technical consulting, training, and informational services.[17] Support is also provided by the Institute for Local Self-Reliance that, among other services, evaluates the success of these measures.[18]

The scope, number, and diversity of strategies individual cities adopted to deal with climate change are impressive, and merit at least a representative enumeration:

• New York City now requires the replacement of its fleet of Crown Victoria "Yellow" cabs with hybrid vehicles over the next five years. Carmel, Indiana, a suburb of Indianapolis, has similarly required the shift of its entire city fleet to hybrids or plant-sourced biofuels;

• Boulder, Colorado has imposed the nation's first "climate tax" on electricity use, the proceeds of which are dedicated to fight global warming;

• Fargo, North Dakota is reclaiming methane emissions from its landfill and selling them to a soybean processing plant for use in its boilers. It is also changing all its traffic light bulbs to LEDs, which use 80% less energy;

• Salt Lake City, San Antonio, and New Haven are among a number of cities offering free parking for hybrids or other cars that have earned EPA's Smart Way or Smart Way Elite designations;

• A number of cities have committed to exploiting the greenhouse capturing capacities of plants. Denver, Colorado has committed to planting 140 trees a day for the next 20 years; Los Angeles has undertaken an initiative it calls Million Trees LA, whereby the city, in cooperation with community groups, businesses, and individuals will plant one million trees; and Chicago is promoting the planting of rooftop gardens, which cool the buildings below and cut the need for air-conditioning;

• Berkeley is subsidizing the cost of solar installations by allowing participating homeowners to enjoy reduced property taxes.

More far-reaching strategies employed by cities include the adoption and enforcement of land-use policies that reduce sprawl, preserve open space, and create walkable communities; the promotion of transportation alternatives to cars: bicycle trails, commute trip reduction programs, and car pooling and public transit; the prioritizing of energy efficiency in building codes and the retrofitting of city facilities with energy-efficient lighting; and the exclusive purchase of Energy Star equipment and appliances for city use. And the mayors have created a website, www.greenplaybook.org, to suggest measures that cities can adopt.

For all their enthusiasm and commitment, local governments are, by and large, not on track to meet the numerical goals of the Agreement, and most have demonstrated no empirical improvement in emissions. The reasons are several: they lack the tools to accurately measure their CO_2 emissions, and do not even have an accurate reading of their 1990 baseline. Also, their success is dependent to some extent on federal actions, such as the imposition of fuel efficiency standards for autos, and on actions by many of their states, such as the enactment of renewable energy standards, that have not been forthcoming. Highly populated and heavily industrial urban areas would benefit from a broad national policy to control greenhouse emissions that does not force them to take actions that would jeopardize their relationships with their economic bases.

Nevertheless, the initiatives, programs, and strategies adopted by the states and municipalities betoken a commitment to dealing promptly and comprehensively with global climate change, and reflect significant public concern about its adverse consequences. Together they cannot help shaking national policymakers out of their lethargy, and are equally as certain to motivate business and the general public to become integral parts of the solution. The states have historically been characterized as "laboratories of democracy," where solutions to problems are tested before becoming nationalized if their experiments prove promising. It appears that with respect to the challenge of climate change, these "laboratories" are working full time, and the stakes have never been higher.

Central Ideas

State and local governments, generally thought to be merely extensions of the federal government, are significant interest groups themselves. Their economic viability and their environmental conditions depend upon constituencies not always served by federal policies. Accordingly, they have lobbied Congress much as other interest groups do. But most recently states have formed alliances, coalitions, and associations to substantively address greenhouse gas emissions and promote appropriate energy policies, and hundreds of municipalities have committed to myriad practices to address climate change. Thus, these lower levels of government have sought to fill the policy vacuum created by the abdication of responsibility by the federal government.

Chapter 5

The Growing Sophistication of Environmental Advocacy

Saving the earth has never seemed so important, or so confusing. Not only do we have to deal with holes in our ozone layer, toxic seepage in our homes, vanishing lemurs in our burning rain forests, and too damn many copies of "999 Simple Things You Can Do to Save the Planet," we have also got to hack our way through a jungle of environmental organizations that's thick and getting thicker.

(Bill Gifford)

Our aim is to change the discussion within the boardrooms of major corporations. . . . That's where we will win ultimately, not in government agencies or Congress. Our strategy is basically like plugging up the toilet—by stopping them from opening up new landfills, incinerators, deep-well injections systems, and hazardous waste sites.

(Lois Gibbs)

The major organizations that have constituted the backbone of the environmental movement for almost the whole of the 20th century are names familiar to almost all Americans. With the founding of the Sierra Club in 1892, the National Audubon Society in 1905, the National Parks and Conservation Association in 1919, the Izaak Walton League of America in 1922, the Wilderness Society in 1935, the National Wildlife Federation in 1936, the Defenders of Wildlife in 1937, and The Conservation Foundation in 1938, the environmental establishment incrementally became a major political force in American society. Collectively these groups became virtually synonymous with what were generally referred to in the media as "the environmentalists." Individually or jointly, they participated in virtually all the major battles that were fought over conservation issues at least since the struggle over Hetch Hetchy in the wake of the San Francisco earthquake of 1906. In so doing, for almost a half-century they effectively defined environmentalism and no discussion of environmental politics can even begin without acknowledging the value, nature, and extent of their involvement.

But *how* they have defined environmentalism, and the constituencies that they represented in their advocacy over that time, provide important lessons in the history of environmental politics, and a window on how environmentalism developed. Moreover, the new groups that have grown up alongside the major organizations since the latter years of the 1960s, groups that have challenged the establishment for public attention, commitment and funding, are causing the establishment to rethink and revise their missions, carving out new directions for environmental policy, and forcing governments at all levels to review their policies and procedures.

Over roughly the first half of 20th century, the conservationist agenda of the major environmental organizations was clear and focused—to protect and preserve the natural resources of this country. They fostered the association of environmentalism with nature—with wilderness, with coastlines and lakes and streams, with mountains and canyons, with birds and wildlife, and with exotic flora and fauna. They did so in the service of a constituency of outdoor enthusiasts and travelers who were wealthy and politically savvy. They were fearful of losing something precious and irreplaceable to "civilization" and its technologies. Their overriding interest was to maintain a clear line between the pristine and the polluted.

The period between, say, the 1940s and the 1960s, represented a transition period; conservationists found themselves involved in political struggles when their "wilderness values" were threatened by society's technologies, most conspicuously by dam projects. It was over a series of battles to forestall and defeat such projects that the established environmental organizations cut their political teeth, and "learned the tactics of political advocacy." The organizations themselves did not undergo any substantive structural change during this period, nor did their missions require reevaluation, because dams had always violated the aesthetic and spiritual values they preached. The signing of The Wilderness Act in 1964 marked their success in fighting off the first wave of challenges to their essential identity.[1]

As the environmental agenda evolved, to focus increasingly on air and water pollution, on the generation of wastes and their irresponsible disposal, on pesticide applications and their effects on human health, and on the impacts of energy production and development on the ecosystem, the environmental movement began to feel a need to address the increasingly sophisticated legal, scientific, and economic issues. Mainstream organizations felt constrained to attract a wider membership base and to adopt new political strategies and expand their missions beyond their core conservationism. Changes were necessary to advance the expanded environmental agenda that developed in the 1960s and 1970s. To meet the new challenges, a new generation of organizations was established that brought an array of specialized professional disciplines to the environmental effort. The

Environmental Defense Fund (1967), Friends of the Earth (1969), the Natural Resources Defense Council (1970), and the Earth Justice Legal Defense Fund (originally the Sierra Legal Defense Fund) (1971) among others were founded to provide the litigation and the scientific and economic expertise required to enforce the scores of new laws and regulations passed by Congress and the administrative agencies. By the end of the century, literally hundreds of new environmental groups of a whole new order sprang up all over the country. These organizational developments mirror the significantly altered policy posture that environmentalism has had to take on over the past several decades.

The evolution began to occur at about mid-century, when the country discovered the environmental degradations associated with the burgeoning industrial activity that followed World War II. Though their memberships remained largely white, male and upper class, and their goals accordingly preservationist, the national organizations began to take a more activist political stance. They lent their influence to the more general push for a quality environment, mainly through increased lobbying of Congress. Many established offices in Washington and testified on the full range of issues, some unrelated, or only peripherally related, to conservation. They also took on a public education role, and, increasingly, filed court suits against both private sector violators of environmental laws or regulations and governments who failed to fully enforce them.

We can see this evolution in microcosm—its accomplishments, its internal strains, and a foreshadowing of its new directions—in the work of the seminal environmentalist of the 20th century, David Brower, who served as Executive Director of the Sierra Club from 1952 to 1969. A successor and ideological twin of John Muir, founder of the Sierra Club, Brower dedicated his early career to making it a force in forging environmental policy. He maintained pursuit of its historical mission in a series of successful battles to preserve Dinosaur Monument and Point Reyes, establish North Cascades and Redwoods National Parks, block the construction of two hydroelectric dams in the Grand Canyon and, most notably, promote the enactment of the Wilderness Act of 1964. But the tactics he employed in these efforts were distinctly more political than the Sierra Club's old guard were comfortable with. His unsuccessful attempt to halt the construction of the Diablo Canyon nuclear reactor in California was only the last in a series of aggressive political activities that alienated him from his more traditional colleagues in the Club, and was instrumental in paving the way for his resignation.[2]

During his tenure, however, the Sierra Club increased its membership more than ten-fold, making its constituency obviously broader and more diverse, as well as more politically active. This new dynamic helped the Sierra Club take their first steps, however tentative, toward an expanded environmental presence. Brower also refined two other political tactics that would become common in succeeding years. He made direct personal appeals to influential government officials with jurisdiction over the matters he was concerned about. He raised to a fine art the persuasive power of the coffee-table size books with spectacular photographic depictions of the natural beauty and wildlife that would be violated or even threatened with extinction, if proposed developments went forward. Conceived and utilized as inanimate lobbyists, such books became popular among the general public as well, and reinforced the conservationist message. He also used another technique that has now become a staple of environmental politics—full page "letters to the public" in the *New York Times*, making the case and encouraging readers to petition their representatives in Congress for help.[3]

After leaving the Sierra Club, Brower continued to anticipate where the viability of the environmental movement lay. He became more conscious of the relationship between conservation and urban issues like traffic, polluted water, and consumerism. He also involved himself in the broader ecological crisis. For example, he fought (though unsuccessfully) federal approval to lay the Alaska pipeline at the risk of damage to the surrounding landscape and wildlife habitat, and the development of the Supersonic Transport aircraft battles, which would cause, among other consequences, a significant noise impact. Friends of the Earth and the Earth Island Institute, both of which he founded, took on problems that had global dimensions, issues like atomic arsenals and nuclear proliferation. His instinct that environmentalism would have to embrace concerns related to the arms race and social justice was uncannily prophetic, for that was precisely where environmentalism was going, as we have seen. In the last years of his life, he helped organize the Alliance for Sustainable Jobs and the Environment, bringing together environmentalists and steelworkers in what has become one of a new breed of environmental collaborative, an alliance that is discussed in detail in Chapter 8.

As noted, Brower's career serves as a template for environmental organizational development after mid-century. Even as the major groups continued to pursue their own agendas, consistent with their respective missions and memberships, they became increasingly involved in the growing political battles over environmental, as well as conservationist, issues. In fact, to put it more precisely, they began making the connection between environmentalism and conservation, thus building a bridge from the established natural resource protection constituencies to the developing anti-pollution and public health advocates. That involvement, however, was initially through the traditional channels—active participation in the legislative and regulatory processes, in a manner that was polite and civil. They sought to influence policy by influencing policymakers directly, as befits the disposition of their traditional core constituencies.

Law and Science Incorporated

As discussed earlier, the movement's newly emergent political activism spawned new allies. The Environmental Defense Fund (since renamed "Environmental Defense") brings science, economics, law and private sector partnership initiatives to the solution of environmental problems. Environmental Defense (ED) was launched on the wings of its successful legal effort to prevent the spraying of DDT on lands on Long Island, which led to a nationwide ban on DDT. In marrying law and science, the case announced a bold new force for environmental protection. While ED continues to participate in the policymaking activities of government, it also works to secure its goals by corporate partnerships and community involvements. Similarly, The Natural Resources Defense Council (NRDC) brings science and law to pursue its broad mission, and, like ED, works directly with states and the business and financial sectors to achieve environmental goals. NRDC has, most recently and significantly, brought its scientific and regulatory expertise to help California draft its widely heralded law limiting greenhouse emissions.

The collaboration of environmental groups on the most high profile case in 2007 is emblematic of several of the new elements in environmental advocacy, and thus merits closer attention. The TXU Corporation, a Texas utility, had proposed the construction of no fewer than 11 coal plants to meet what it regarded as anticipated demand for electric power. Moreover, the utility had petitioned to have its application for the plants "fast tracked," a request to which the state seemed initially receptive. But the Sierra Club joined ED in a legal action opposing acceleration of the administrative hearings on the petition. As the legal case was pending, Environmental Defense, appalled at the prospect of a spate of new coal-fired plants, created a website, Stoptxu.com, publicizing TXU's plans and building a national constituency in opposition. No doubt partially in response to unfavorable publicity and the unease of many of its stockholders, TXU entered into negotiations with a group of equity firms who sought to buy it. But the prospective purchasers wanted assurance that ED and its allies would bless the arrangement and bring the environmental community along. For such assurances, environmentalists wanted substantial environmental concessions. Negotiations resulted in the following arrangement: the new owners would commit to the cancellation of eight of the 11 proposed plants, support federal legislation to require reductions in CO_2 emissions through a cap-and-trade system, double TXU spending to promote energy efficiency to \$80 million a year for five years, and reduce TXU's own carbon emissions to 1990 levels by 2020.[4]

The arrangement was the result of a remarkable combination of factors, circumstances, and players that would have been unthinkable earlier. Most prominently, the concerns over the prospective financial consequences of global warming hung over TXU and its shareholders, and predisposed them to seek preemptive economic relief. Those same concerns, shared by the public at large, were readily marshaled by ED through its website and imposed further pressure on the utility. The willingness of ED and NRDC to work with a corporate entity in seeking a mutually satisfactory result for all, rather than invite confrontation, was another characteristic of this new breed of environmentalists. And, finally, ED's and NRDC's employment of a high-profile Wall Street firm to help conduct negotiations with the equity firms purchasing TXU was also precedent-setting. The environmental community has, indeed, come a long way from marching in the streets carrying signs and enlisting support for their causes. They are carving out a wholly new protocol.

Environmental Defense and the Natural Resources Defense Council are perhaps the most prominent of the new generation of environmental advocacy groups, but they are by no means alone. As indicated earlier, Friends of the Earth was founded in 1969 by David Brower. It is the U.S. component of what is now an international network of grassroots groups in 70 countries. Its recent merger with Bluewater Network has enabled it to work on a diverse agenda, from public lands protection to genetically engineered food, from improved fuel efficiency of standards for automobiles to guaranteeing the safety of cosmetics. In most of these cases, it has achieved its goal by direct appeal to the relevant business concern. It secured the commitments of over 400 companies to avoid the use of chemicals known or strongly suspected of causing cancer; it has lobbied the World Bank to increase financing for renewable energy projects; and pressured the Ford Motor Company to improve their fleet's fuel economy.

Rainforest Action Network (RAN) was founded in 1985. Its principal tactic is the grassroots market campaign that seeks to force major corporations to consider the larger social and environmental consequences of their actions in their business practices. While RAN may exaggerate its role in causing some of the major corporations—Home Depot, Citigroup, Boise Cascade, and Goldman Sachs—to change their way of doing business, they have an estimable reputation for involvement in the concessions of business concerns.[5] As global climate change has grown as a more widely perceived threat, so have its "victims." In perhaps its most aggressive campaign yet, it targeted the leading funders of coal plant construction projects—Citi and Bank of America. In almost eco-terrorist mode, RAN shut down a Citi branch in Washington, D.C., and one of its local chapters closed Bank of America ATM locations throughout Charlotte, North Carolina, declaring them "global warming crime scenes."

New advocacy groups with increasing relevant expertise joined the effort. Earthjustice, which has carried much of the litigation burden for the environmental community, had its origins in the Sierra Club's legal action in 1969 to prevent a project to develop Mine King, a valley in Nevada.

The legal team was established in 1971 as the Sierra Club Legal Defense Fund, which used the law to level the playing field in battles against a whole host of commercial and industrial interests. It has provided *pro bono* legal representation to hundreds of clients, environmental organizations, and state and community coalitions. To reflect the diversity of its clients, it changed its name to Earthjustice in 1997.

Two new scientific groups joined the cause as well. The Union of Concerned Scientists (UCSUSA) has grown from a collaboration of students and faculty at the Massachusetts Institute of Technology in 1969 to what is now a formidable organization providing independent scientific information and perspective on a whole host of issues to legislators, the media, and other non-profit organizations. Since a number of Nobel laureates and noted academicians are included on its roster, it stands as an authoritative source. Similarly, Physicians for Social Responsibility (PSR), which originated in 1961 as an opponent of nuclear development and a supporter of disarmament, formally enlarged its mission in 1992 in recognition that the dangers of climate change, toxic proliferation, and atmospheric pollution were also threats to the nation's health and social and economic welfare. However specialized, each of these organizations partakes in policy deliberations as well, applying the law and science to reinforce environmental gains. Taken together, this assemblage of advocacy groups rendered the environmental community vastly more capable of dealing with the increasingly sophisticated problems and threats our society was now facing.

During the 1960s and 1970s, the major organizations and their more litigious brethren, though they took somewhat different tacks, assumed the responsibility to make the environmental gains secured in the governmental arena stick—a period during which they represented the broad public interest against the encroachments of the corporate polluters. These were the decades during which their reputation as "the environmentalists" was solidified, and the time when environmentalism became an accepted national value. The environmental community and the broad general public were essentially in sync.

But things were to change significantly in the 1980s. The principal event was the election of Ronald Reagan, whose agenda targeted environmental regulation directly, and promoted the mining, logging, drilling, and grazing of land, as well as increased state ownership of federal lands. So threatening was the prospect of his successful implementation of this agenda that the public responded enthusiastically to the environmental organizations' calls for help, swelling their membership rolls dramatically. During the 1970s, their growth was modest, in some cases flat, the exception being the National Audubon Society, which more than tripled its membership, from a little over 100,000 to almost 400,000. During the 1980s however, memberships in environmental organizations made quantum leaps. The Sierra Club, the National Parks and Conservation Association, the Environmental

Defense Fund, and the Natural Resources Defense Council each more than tripled in size, and the Wilderness Society increased more than ten-fold.

Such numbers reflected the growing public interest in environmental matters to be sure, but they also reflected both a new confidence in these organizations as well as a public concern that the Reagan administration would roll back environmental gains of the past decade. In particular, Interior Secretary James Watt pursued land use policies that encouraged commercial development in many of the natural areas these groups regarded as sacred. Such land use policies became one of the environmentalists' best fundraising tools. Publicizing these policies created a general anti-regulatory climate, were probably the environmentalists' best fundraising tool, as Americans looked to these groups for protection from an unfriendly Executive branch.[6]

Most of the environmental cutbacks contemplated by the Reagan administration were forestalled by a strengthened alliance between the major environmental organizations and the environmentally progressive members of Congress and the federal agencies. But there were problems. The level of political involvement engaged in by the mainstream organizations demanded new levels of funding well beyond what membership dues could provide. Increasingly, they had to seek a number of new sources of financial support. One has been foundations, most of which, of course, are genuinely philanthropic and politically neutral, but some of which have their own political agendas.

Additional sources of revenue were (and remain) large corporate donors, who have a variety of motives to share their wealth with the "enemy." Some try to build environmentally-friendly images for themselves in the minds of a public for whom environmentalism has become next to Godliness, but many donate to round off the adversarial edge between them. Still another source of revenue are national mass mailings, in which requests for money are accompanied by vivid descriptions of the violence that would be done to one or another of our most precious natural resources or endangered species, or human health, by a present condition or policy that needs a champion. More recently, as the influence of the public on policymakers has become unmistakable, the typical single-page format of such mass mailings has taken on a three-part character: a brief lobbying statement about some problem or threat that the organization will fight to alleviate; a prepared form letter to the recipient's Congressional representatives, or to the President entreating the policymaker to address the issue legislatively; and, finally, the obligatory request for a donation. These are quite familiar to any regular contributor to mainstream organizations.

The increasing need for funding and the growing reliance on business interests to supply that funding have, in the minds of some observers, compromised the integrity of the major organizations. Some have even gone so far as to suggest that the environmental lobby, except in its broad parameters, is now almost indistinguishable from its business counter-parts.[7] For confirmation, the critics look not only at the environmentalists' plush and commodious offices in Washington, but also to the business-friendly compromises that they have too often made to address problems. Specifically they point to accommodations they have made with polluting industries. One example is the pollution tax credit, wherein businesses are provided a tax incentive to reduce pollution rather than face penalties for violating established standards. Another is the so-called "bubble-policy," which treats an industrial facility as one large emission source that must satisfy a cumulative standard rather than as, under trad-itional regulation, a number of separate sources, each of which must meet standards. Another contentious accommodation is the incorporation of cost–benefit analysis, which introduces economic burdens as qualifying factors in setting emission limits.[8] Less subtle are the clubby relationships between business and the organizations, fostered by the fact that promin-ent corporate officials are not infrequently on the boards of these organiza-tions, which surely facilitates the securing of grants and other financial help, but just as surely calls into question the ideological purity of the organizations' commitments.

Another factor that affected the mainstream's political posture until recently is the concentration of their offices and activities in Washington and New York, and their focus on national issues, often at the expense of local ones. Local chapters of the national organizations, by and large, decreased in number and significance as power moved to the Northeast. This relocation trend, together with their effort to work pragmatically from within the system rather than from without, had substantial con-sequences, and some achievements.

The Rise of Environmental Justice

Whether certain segments of the general public felt abandoned by the organizations or whether they felt comfortable that the overall environ-ment was adequately protected by them, is a matter of speculation. What is clear is that, concurrent with the growth and corporatization of the national environmental organizations in the 1980s, there appeared the budding of another, quite different movement. The early signs took the form of citizen action groups that assembled to address a particular con-cern or problem, or accomplish a single purpose. There were, for example, volunteer groups that "adopted" a beach, a highway, or some other public tract, taking upon themselves the responsibility to keep it clear of litter and debris. There were other groups—"friends of open space" or "citizens united to prevent urban sprawl"—that kept watch over local planning and zoning boards to assure that development is consistent with land use plans that protect the environment. There emerged ad hoc coalitions of local citizens who organized themselves to protect specific wetlands, beach areas, or woodlands. These community activists focused less on policy and more on addressing specific problems or threats that affected their daily lives in their own neighborhoods. It should be noted, however, that these early groups were concerned principally with amenities—like litter—rather than significant environmental threat.

But while a small segment of civilian activists were engaging in efforts to save their beaches, their lawns, and their property values, a far more significant, militant, far-reaching and diverse movement was taking hold. It shared with these local groups an interest in the environment of their daily lives and a commitment to action rather than policymaking. But there the similarities end. This new movement concerned itself not with amenities but with health—with exposure to toxic pollution and radiation in their workplaces, homes, and communities.

The constituents of this movement, unlike those of the national groups and even the "friends" groups, occupy the middle or lower economic strata, and are constituted disproportionately of people of color, aggrieved minorities, and women. They see themselves as victims of environmental degradation rather than as guardians of environmental integrity. To put it more bluntly, they feel "dumped on," with the "dumpers" as often governments as they are corporate institutions. They are angry because, as they see it, their civil rights as well as their homes have been violated.

While over time some organizational structures have developed to provide education, technical assistance, and networking capacity to the individual groups, the movement is fundamentally decentralized, disparate, and grassroots in character. The individual groups see it as their mission to take control of their own destinies rather than trust government, or even supposedly environmentally-friendly organizations and institutions, to protect their homes, neighborhoods, and workplaces. They distrust, as well, the formal processes of lawmaking and thus do not lobby or seek financial support from special interest groups.

It's hard to determine just when and how grassroots movements began, but it's safe to say that there was a latent, if amorphous, concern about the health dangers posed by toxic chemicals that threatened Americans in many quarters. Reports about the dangers of Agent Orange, PCBs, radioactive waste, and dioxin had been reported in the press time and again during the 1970s. And some highly publicized events like the discovery of dioxin at Times Beach, the children's cancer cluster at Woburn, and, of course, the malfunction of the nuclear power plant at Three Mile Island, only reinforced public unease and made these threats more than hypothetical matters. The discovery of hazardous chemicals in the Love Canal neighborhood of Niagara Falls, NY served as the critical spark that ignited a firestorm of protest.

Though by no means unique, the situation at Love Canal came to be regarded as the pivotal event in the birth of this new grassroots movement. This is attributable in large part to Lois Gibbs, one of the resident victims, who channeled her outrage first into a successful effort to require the government to relocate the hundreds of families potentially affected, and then into the founding of the Citizens Clearinghouse for Hazardous Waste (CCHW). CCHW galvanized the existing unease in hundreds of communities nationwide into a genuine environmental protest movement. In the more than three decades since its creation, the CCHW has grown into a substantially larger network of local groups, now numbering more than 8,000, with a new name—the Center for Health, Environment and Justice. The new name is not just public relations; rather it is emblematic of the enlarged set of values underpinning the movement. Though initiated to help respond effectively to specific local concerns, the myriad efforts are animated by a sense that not only the environment, but social justice, is being threatened. But marrying good environmental policy and social justice has proven to be a daunting task indeed.

Before getting to that, it is instructive to see how the federal government and the national environmental organizations responded to those who were vigorously opposed to the practice of locating heavy industrial operations and waste disposal facilities in low-income and minority neighborhoods. Also of importance is to see how their concerns were integrated into environmental policymaking. These forces developed into what became known as the "environmental justice" movement, a movement that soon gained momentum and influence. It embodied and reflected much of what had happened to mainstream environmentalism, not least in that the public was becoming more involved, and most major environmental organizations embraced it and welcomed its constituents into their tent. But for a number of complex reasons, a substantial segment of the environmental justice community not only insisted on its own identity, but has actively opposed some of the initiatives of the EPA and other traditional environmental forces. That tension grows out of the related but by no means congruent interests of social justice and environmentalism, a conflict that serves as a veritable paradigm of environmental politics as it stands at the onset of the 21st century.

Principles of Environmental Justice
Adopted October 27, 1991
1st People of Color Environmental Leadership Summit
Washington, D.C.

Delegates to the First National People of Color Environmental Leadership Summit held on October 24–27, 1991, in Washington D.C., drafted and adopted 17 principles of Environmental Justice. Since then, *The Principles* have served as a defining document for the growing grassroots movement for environmental justice.

Preamble

WE, THE PEOPLE OF COLOR, gathered together at this multinational People of Color Environmental Leadership Summit, to begin to build a national and international movement of all peoples of color to fight the destruction and taking of our lands and communities, do hereby re-establish our spiritual interdependence to the sacredness of our Mother Earth; to respect and celebrate each of our cultures, languages and beliefs about the natural world and our roles in healing ourselves; to insure environmental justice; to promote economic alternatives which would contribute to the development of environmentally safe livelihoods; and, to secure our political, economic and cultural liberation that has been denied for over 500 years of colonization and oppression, resulting in the poisoning of our communities and land and the genocide of our peoples, do affirm and adopt these Principles of Environmental Justice:

1. **Environmental Justice** affirms the sacredness of Mother Earth, ecological unity and the interdependence of all species, and the right to be free from ecological destruction.
2. **Environmental Justice** demands that public policy be based on mutual respect and justice for all peoples, free from any form of discrimination or bias.
3. **Environmental Justice** mandates the right to ethical, balanced and responsible uses of land and renewable resources in the interest of a sustainable planet for humans and other living things.
4. **Environmental Justice** calls for universal protection from nuclear testing, extraction, production and disposal of toxic/hazardous wastes and poisons and nuclear testing that threaten the fundamental right to clean air, land, water, and food.
5. **Environmental Justice** affirms the fundamental right to political, economic, cultural and environmental self-determination of all peoples.
6. **Environmental Justice** demands the cessation of the production of all toxins, hazardous wastes, and radioactive materials, and that all past and current producers be held strictly accountable to the people for detoxification and the containment at the point of production.
7. **Environmental Justice** demands the right to participate as equal partners at every level of decisionmaking, including needs assessment, planning, implementation, enforcement and evaluation.
8. **Environmental Justice** affirms the right of all workers to a safe and healthy work environment without being forced to choose between an

unsafe livelihood and unemployment. It also affirms the right of those who work at home to be free from environmental hazards.

9. Environmental Justice protects the right of victims of environmental injustice to receive full compensation and reparations for damages as well as quality health care.

10. Environmental Justice considers governmental acts of environmental injustice a violation of international law, the Universal Declaration On Human Rights, and the United Nations Convention on Genocide.

11. Environmental Justice must recognize a special legal and natural relationship of Native Peoples to the U.S. government through treaties, agreements, compacts, and covenants affirming sovereignty and self-determination.

12. Environmental Justice affirms the need for urban and rural ecological policies to clean up and rebuild our cities and rural areas in balance with nature, honoring the cultural integrity of all our communities, and provided fair access for all to the full range of resources.

13. Environmental Justice calls for the strict enforcement of principles of informed consent, and a halt to the testing of experimental reproductive and medical procedures and vaccinations on people of color.

14. Environmental Justice opposes the destructive operations of multinational corporations.

15. Environmental Justice opposes military occupation, repression and exploitation of lands, peoples and cultures, and other life forms.

16. Environmental Justice calls for the education of present and future generations which emphasizes social and environmental issues, based on our experience and an appreciation of our diverse cultural perspectives.

17. Environmental Justice requires that we, as individuals, make personal and consumer choices to consume as little of Mother Earth's resources and to produce as little waste as possible; and make the conscious decision to challenge and reprioritize our lifestyles to insure the health of the natural world for present and future generations.

As a clear demonstration of the social and political success and influence that the environmental justice movement had attained, President Clinton issued an order directing each federal agency to "make achieving environmental justice part of its mission by identifying and addressing . . . disproportionately high and adverse human health or environmental effects of its programs, policies, and activities on minority populations and low-income populations . . ."[9] The Order was extraordinarily broad and deep—extending specifically not only to the United States, but as well to its territories and possessions, to Puerto Rico, and to the Commonwealth of the Mariana Islands. Furthermore, the Interagency Working Group on

Environmental Justice created by the Order comprised representatives not only from EPA, but from 10 executive departments, as well as from the Offices of Management and Budget, Science and Technology Policy, the Assistants to the President for Environmental Policy and for Domestic Policy, and from the National Economic Council and the Council of Economic Advisors. The Group's delegated responsibilities were to assist these Federal departments and agencies in developing criteria to identify the disadvantaged populations, coordinate research and data collection, and, in general, help them prepare, administer, and enforce the individual strategies that the Order required each to develop to address the problem.

The problem, as the Order suggests, is that people of color and those in the lower economic strata of our society are subject to a disproportionate health risk from environmental pollutants and conditions associated with the industrial plants and waste facilities that are too commonly sited in their neighborhoods. Often they, as a class, are unreasonably subject to adverse health consequences from some of these activities and circumstances. The evidence for this conclusion was collected in a definitive national study sponsored by the United Church of Christ. Its report, *Toxic Waste and Race: A National Report on the Racial and Socioeconomic Characteristics of Communities with Hazardous Waste Sites*, was published in 1987. In lending substance to the claims of the growing environmental justice movement, the study represented a watershed in its supporters' efforts to get public recognition of these inequities and government action to redress and compensate them.

The next couple of years saw renewed attention to the issue from Congress, government agencies, and scholars at conferences nationwide. In July of 1990, EPA Administrator William Reilly established the Environmental Equity Workgroup to review the evidence of these alleged inequities. The Group's confirmation of the charge led in turn to the formation of an Environmental Equity Office to provide technical assistance, outreach, and communication to the movement. By 1991, the First National People of Color Environmental Leadership Summit was held in Washington, D.C., at which its principles were first codified. October 1992 marked the first significant efforts on the part of EPA to actively address the problem through a series of memos circulated to staff. Meanwhile, the reinvigorated grass roots activism of the supporters resulted in the formation of an Environmental Justice Transition Group, a diverse consortium of interests whose recommendations to President Clinton's transition team culminated in the Executive Order.

This Order represents a major milestone in the environmental politics of this country because it was a pioneering initiative on the part of the Federal government to enlist its combined resources in a systematic, proactive effort to protect and promote the health and environmental circumstances of a particular segment of the population. In this sense, this segment of the population represents a group of interests related by their mutual victimization. Because that interest group is defined principally by its racial and ethnic backgrounds and income, the Order effectively brings together the environmental movement and the civil rights movement that immediately preceded it, and from which it drew many of its first recruits.

The movement's roots are to be found, unsurprisingly, in the Civil Rights Act of 1964 and, particularly in Title VI of that Act, that accords minority populations equal protection under the law, and specifically prohibits discrimination against people based on their race, color, or national origin; or denies them benefits from, or participation in, any government activity that receives federal funding. That fundamental principle was extended to environmental programs in 1973 by EPA's issuance of a regulation to implement Title VI in their programs, and again in 1984 by another regulation prohibiting any recipient of EPA financial assistance from undertaking any policy that has a discriminatory effect under the Civil Rights Act of 1964. These legal authorities were specifically invoked by President Clinton in his Executive Order.

There is, then, a clear statutory and regulatory foundation on which to base action to redress "environmental racism," as it has been called, and to empower low income, minority, and ethnic people to participate in policy decisions that otherwise might have been made in the traditional institutional ways, thus depriving them of basic human rights. At the turn of the century, both the Executive Branch and EPA embarked on such an effort and the environmental establishment embraced it.

Yet both the government and the environmental advocacy groups have found that initiatives to promote a safe and healthy environment for the targeted populations identified in the Order are complicated by the mandates of other federal programs and policies, and by a long and complex social and cultural history. They are also presenting new challenges not only for the EPA, but for environmental policymaking in general. We will discuss these one at a time.

The effective implementation of the Order in any number of cases has met with strong opposition—and from precisely those whose interests it was specifically designed to protect. There can be no justification for disproportionately subjecting any group of citizens to the ill effects of environmental degradation, much less those who are politically least able to defend themselves. That is the unimpeachable basis for the scores of protest marches, policy papers and books, and conferences condemning the situation. Yet officials in local and state governments, much of the business community, and a not insignificant percentage of the allegedly aggrieved populations themselves see those initiatives as impeding federal programs. Some examples of those instances are cases in which establishing "empowerment" or "enterprise zones," that offer business financial incentives to bring economic development into poverty areas and create jobs for minorities and the poor.

Environmental justice principles are also at odds with what was called the "brownfields" program, whereby the federal government is promoting the cleanup and reuse of abandoned industrial sites in urban areas rather than the siting of new plants in pristine areas, again to advance the redevelopment of blighted areas and create jobs for those most in need. Environmental justice advocates argue forcibly that clean jobs can be created in minority communities as well, and that one should not have to make the choice between health and work. But Harry Alford, President and CEO of the National Black Chamber of Commerce characterized the effect of environmental justice policy as "preserving the economic blight of urban communities."[10] Years earlier, urbanologist Anthony Downs commented that what to the elite is environmental degradation is standard of living to the common man.[11]

The EPA is thus legally mandated to concurrently carry out two policies that have differing, in some cases competing, effects on the same population. More particularly, the clear mandate to safeguard the health of populations whose homes, neighborhoods, and workplaces are often threatened by siting decisions, sometimes clashes with another need of these populations such as jobs and economic opportunity. Residents of such places are often willing to live with the risks in exchange for economic opportunities that accompany those risks. Thus, EPA often finds itself trying to reconcile competing interests. This conundrum has pitted government agency against government agency, social justice group against social justice group, and minority citizen against minority citizen. The mainstream environmental organizations have been sympathetic to the plight of the poor, to be sure, but they too are torn between their central mission and some of the unintended effects of its blind pursuit.

In a larger social and cultural context, the strife occasioned by the ascendant environmental justice movement is only a recent manifestation of a broader ideological clash between environmentalism and social justice that goes back more than a quarter-century. For reasons suggested earlier in this chapter, environmentalists have historically been seen by minority activists as blue-collar workers, and political scientists and sociologists as a social elite. Both in their eyes are predominantly white, upper or upper-middle class, professional suburbanites whose basic living needs have long since been satisfied and who can now indulge in a privileged lifestyle that values environmental quality without regard to the price it may exact on the economy, government, or other human welfare concerns. Its harshest critics have even charged environmentalism with bigotry and racism in its attempt to protect the lifestyle of the comfortable at the expense of the poor and underprivileged. These critics point to environmentalists' support of such policies as population control, open space preservation, large-lot zoning and other growth-control strategies as evidence of a thinly veiled effort to impede the upward mobility of the have-nots and thus protect their own homes, neighborhoods, and recreational areas from the encroachment of urban pressures. However environmentally desirable, such policies have the effect of segregating economic classes, and minimizing, if not eliminating, industrial activity in the most affluent areas.

Indeed, it was in such a context that the label "NIMBY" (not in my back yard) was coined to refer to those suburbanites who oppose the siting of "LULU's," (locally undesirable land uses) in their neighborhoods. Their political and economic might often effectively stymies the location of industrial plants and waste facilities in their upscale surroundings. While the motivation for their protests is often the protection of property values, too many of their efforts are to improve quality of life by promoting clean air, clean water, and responsible toxic management for them to be written off as self-serving.

Whereas, given the broad political profile and voting history of mainstream environmentalists, it would be difficult to label them as deliberately anti-poor and racist, we have seen that environmentalism was, at least in its origins, the province of the more well-to-do and politically active. Statistics on membership in environmental organizations; on visitations to parks, forests, and other such recreational areas; and on participation in activities like hunting, fishing, backpacking, bird-watching, and hiking all attest to an interest group served by a conservation agenda, and distinctly unrelated, if not indifferent, to urban needs and concerns. It is an identity that has historically dogged the movement.

These kinds of charges have persistently stung the environmental community, who rightly insist that all citizens, regardless of their station in life, are equal beneficiaries of clean water, clean air, open space, and parks, forests, and wilderness areas, and thus take comfort that they are serving a solemn mission. But even more galling to them is that the business and construction interests, their principal political adversaries, have exploited the "elitist" identity, and have proudly proclaimed—with varying degrees of integrity and effectiveness—that their industrial and commercial activities in fact serve the genuine interests of people instead of animals, trees, and flowers, and that the so-called altruism of the environmental groups is narrow and self-interested. In the recent dispute over the application of environmental justice policy, the not uncommon alliance of business and environmental justice protesters gives credence to the claim.

Against this historic backdrop, one can see that the clash over implementation of the Executive Order reflects a longstanding and fundamental tension between the interests served by programs to promote environmental quality and those served by programs that advance economic opportunity and social justice. It could, and hopefully will, lead to better environmental policies for everyone. That is, after all, the intent. Much of what the environmental justice movement has brought to environmental advocacy is desirable. It redefined citizen empowerment, demanded the wider public distribution of pollution data, strengthened the push for pollution prevention, influenced consumer and business behavior, and, perhaps most important of all, broadened and democratized the environmental constituency.

On the other hand, the environmental justice movement poses formidable problems for environmental policymaking, and for the national organizations. First, it effectively asks for environmental policy to redress other social and public health inequities, a lot of baggage for essentially siting decisions to carry. It interposes a new element in a whole range of policy options that emerged from EPA's reinvention, and thus creates as much policy confusion as it may illuminate. It further complicates the relationship between the federal government, which is charged with carrying out this new mandate, and state and local governments, in whose authority reside many of the siting decisions. Perhaps most threatening of all, it challenges the ability of the governmental establishment itself to solve these problems, an establishment that mainstream organizations have worked with for years and in which they retain considerable stake. The environmental justice movement obscures the very real accomplishments of the mainstream organizations, accomplishments attributable to their spirit of practical compromise. Environmental justice groups have taken a role in the political drama, but they must share the stage with an establishment that continues to accord environmentalism an established place among the general public and in Congress. The incorporation of the lofty social goals of environmental justice has unquestionably strengthened the environmental movement at a time when it needed it most.

The Critique of Culture

In the 1980s, the national environmental organizations and the nascent environmental justice movement claimed segments of the population and, in their respective ways, tried to shape policy to satisfy their respective constituents. The 1990s, however, witnessed a tilt away from traditional environmental advocacy towards a diversification of causes. The membership gains enjoyed by the mainstream organizations during the 1980s that were likely in response to concerns about the policies of the Reagan administration eroded in the 1990s. Most observers attribute this to a revived level of comfort about the environmental stewardship expected from an environmentally-friendly administration, particularly Vice-President Gore, long an outspoken environmental advocate and author of *Earth in the Balance*, a book setting forth an extraordinarily activist agenda.

But the inroads made by environmental justice reformers have manifested their influence. Facility siting decisions now undergo unprecedented scrutiny. In addition to questioning the will, if not the capacity, of the mainstream organizations to attend to the specific problems of specific people in specific places in respect to national policy concerns, the environmental justice reformers introduced social and economic issues into the discussion, opening up the national environmental advocacy groups to criticism from the other quarters, and paving the way for another redefinition of environmentalism. In the 1990s, environmentalism became not only a cause in itself, but an element of a broad panoply of social concerns.

The linking of social justice and environmentalism brought with it labor, peace, arms control, population control, immigration policy, globalization, industrial agriculture, poverty and a host of other related constituencies, again as Brower anticipated. The critique of our deteriorating environmental condition became a critique of the culture at large, not only nationally but globally as well. This gave rise to a number of alliances between previously separate groups and alliances that began to lobby not so much as interest groups but as global saviors.

The Confrontational Politics of Eco-Terrorism

If the environmental justice movement called on environmentalism to shed its elitist character, expand its agenda to include urban issues, and, in general, demonstrate as much concern for human welfare as for natural resources, the so-called eco-terrorists militantly pressed for just the opposite. Though known as much for their tactics as their mission, they represent an ideology more in tune with the historical conservationism of a John Muir than with any modern day environmentalist. Eco-terrorists unashamedly place trees, wild animals, and sea mammals on equal footing with humans. As such, they represent a modest counterforce to those exerted by environmental justice and other social and public health interests on the environmental establishment.

"Eco-terrorism," sometimes known as "ecotage," is the direct action that individuals take to protect animals, trees, and other natural resources from what they regard as an outrageous assault by industrial and commercial society. Their actions include spiking trees destined for cutting, "decommissioning" construction equipment, lying down in front of bulldozers, "tree-sitting" in old growth forests, throwing paint on fur coats, freeing animals from research laboratories, and sinking whaling ships. They call their disruptive tactics "monkeywrenching," and argue that the real terrorists are those who would destroy a redwood to make a picnic table. They depart from the essential character of the mainstream organizations from which many of their leaders came both in their exaltation of nature and in their reliance on direct citizen action rather than lobbying to promote their cause. They decry the "corporatization" of the major environmental groups who, in their view, have become indistinguishable from their business counterparts, and chide them for selling out their principles under the guise of reasonable compromise.

Despite their embrace of a lofty mission, the eco-terrorists represent a radical fringe of the environmental movement. While the most prominent of their groups, Earth First!, disdained violence, guns, and explosives, they traded in guerrilla tactics. Most recently, they engaged in dramatic, headline-grabbing acts, like taking up long-term residence in old-growth trees to forestall their "clearing." But its progeny, groups like the Earth Liberation Front, who were behind the most costly single act of eco-terrorism—the 1998 burning of a development in Vail, Colorado—the Animal Liberation Front, and similar groups have been more destructive, if not more violent, in the service of stopping what they regard as the exploitation of the environment. One hesitates to call these groups organizations; rather they are highly committed, loosely connected activists motivated by an old-style naturalism. The low profile and clandestine character of their network is no doubt attributable to the fact that their activities are illegal and prosecutable. Still, the consequences of these acts are significant. By 1998, no fewer than 1,500 acts of domestic eco-terrorism had been documented.

Eco-terrorist groups, of course, did not invent environmental citizen activism. That is a legacy most recently of those who saw themselves as victims of the environmental degradation visited on their homes, schools, and workplaces. But the eco-saboteurs brought the spirit of citizen action to the service not of the new environmental agenda, but of the old. In that, they represent an interesting political anomaly. Their political effectiveness has been, and remains, marginal at best, however. Unlike the new breed of citizen activists who seek to put new pressures on politicians to address the environmental conditions they feel threatened by, eco-terrorists seek to circumvent or, more accurately, ignore rather than influence, institutional policymakers. It is, then, their dependence on intimidation rather than persuasion that makes them radical and, no doubt, keeps them from being anything other than an antagonist not only to those in the mainstream who share some of their values, but even to many of their fellow co-conspirators, who see them as undermining their own more tempered strategies. In a curious way, they have served the larger, long-term interests of the traditional environmental organizations by making them look more moderate and rational even as they remind them of what they see as the mainstream's abdication of their central mission.

Earlier in this chapter, and elsewhere in this book, I have spoken of the gradual "domestication" of the environmental agenda, the evolution from "conservation" to "environmentalism," and the increasing attention paid to public health and urban concerns in a revised environmental agenda. As indicated earlier, Rachel Carson's *Silent Spring* was instrumental in initiating that evolution. In bringing public health to the public consciousness, it unwittingly unleashed a host of other social justice concerns. To be sure, the established environmental organizations have maintained their conservationist core, but others were created, reinvented, and expanded at least in part to accommodate urban pollution issues.

Some have argued that the 1990s represented a "dry season" for a movement "on the run" from business, local officials, and angry citizens.[12] It suffered decreases in revenue and membership, and intramural disputes over goals and tactics.[13] But with the ascendancy in this century of global climate change, and its attendant energy and air pollution dimensions as overriding public concerns, the broad range of environmental advocacy organizations has been impelled to march in common cause. All their diverse missions have been subsumed by this singular ecological phenomenon, unprecedented in scope and threat. Wilderness and wildlife organizations publicize the role of climate change in exacerbating wildfires, floods, droughts, and the prospective extinction of polar bears. The national Sierra Club has subordinated its many goals in favor of forging a national strategy to implement a revolutionary energy policy designed to combat global warming. The Natural Resources Defense Council and Environmental Defense are working on protocols to minimize CO_2 emissions from transportation vehicles and industrial facilities, and legislation and litigation to enforce them. Friends of the Earth and the Rainforest Action Network are developing and implementing campaigns to make the corporate world more climate-friendly. And there are new soldiers in the climate battle. More than 10,000 EPA scientists, under the banner of a new organization, Public Employees for Environmental Responsibility (PEER), filed a petition calling on Congress to take immediate action against global warming, stressing that "time is running out to prevent environmental changes induced by human-caused pollution."[14] And so, in an odd twist of irony, the environmental mission, having narrowed its focus from a set of broadly national concerns to a more local and domestic agenda, has totally reversed course and gone global.

Central Ideas

National conservation organizations carried the environmental agenda to Congress and the nation for the first half of the last century. But as conservation issues gave way to environmental threats, a new generation of organizations with scientific, legal, and economic expertise joined the mainstream. The appearance of a profusion of grassroots groups, concerned more with the conditions in their own communities than with the broader goals of the traditional environmental movement, brought new social issues and dimensions to the environmental wars. They become a formidable political force, and have goaded government as well as the mainstream organizations into addressing new issues in new ways. Less formidable though newsworthy have been the destructive activities of a band of eco-terrorists who, in ideology though not in practice, recall the philosophy of John Muir. But the advent of global climate change as an almost universally recognized ecological threat has brought not only the wide array of environmental advocacy groups together, but has given them common cause with other interest groups, notably though not exclusively, the business community.

Chapter 6

The Greening of Business

Challenging existing environmental programs and priorities is not anti-environment. . . . The free market provides the basis for a superior approach to environmental policy. . . .
(The Competitive Enterprise Institute)

The business of business is business . . . but it ought to be legitimate business, and not at the expense of future generations.
(Ray Anderson, Interface, Inc.)

If environmental advocacy groups have been the public's chief defenders against threats to the environment and the ecosystem, it is the business community whose activities have historically been seen as principally responsible for those threats. Industrial operations inevitably generate significant levels of air and water pollution and a steady stream of wastes; and building and infrastructure construction projects impose burdens on land and reduce its capacity to control flooding, drought, and soil and beach erosion. The products they provide for a consumer-oriented society exhaust natural resources faster than they can be replenished, when they can be replenished at all, and the energy supplies upon which these activities depend impose their own risks to public health and safety, such as accidents like those at the Three Mile Island nuclear facility and the oil spill from the Exxon Valdez tanker at Prince William Sound. Because business operations pose such risks to the environment, they have been subject to increasingly stringent and comprehensive regulation by government. As the biggest stakeholder in how environmental policy is framed, business has always been an aggressive and prominent participant in the policymaking process.

Businesses have continued to pursue their rational self-interest in the halls of Congress and with the administrative agencies, and have, over the past several decades, found a need to adopt new strategies and allies in an effort to respond to the public's growing environmental concerns. The result has been a complex, many-faceted effort to soften their image, break down the adversarial relationship between themselves and environmental activists, and advance the notion that a thriving economy and a healthy environment are not mutually exclusive. Further, they have promoted the idea that environmentally responsible corporate behavior can make business as much a part of the solution as part of the problem, an effort that has been ratcheted up dramatically in recent years. Let's look first at the evolution of business' posture over the last decades of the 20th century. We will then look at the more comprehensive, aggressive, and substantive initiatives they have undertaken since 2000.

The business community represents a formidable force in policymaking. First, it has vastly greater financial resources than the environmental community, resources that have routinely been employed not only in support of the electoral campaigns of business-friendly candidates, but in maintaining a nationwide cadre of lobbyists pacing the halls of state and federal capitols, armed with voluminous information and detailed position papers on all issues that affect them. They have established national networks in the form of professional and trade associations designed originally to communicate with each other on the full range of common concerns, but which have been directed in recent years to perform a lobbying function. The U.S. Chamber of Commerce, the National Association of Manufacturers, and the Small Business Association are but three of the largest and most influential overarching business alliances, but literally hundreds of other groups representing individual industries and commercial activities, for example, the Chemical Manufacturers Association, the American Petroleum Institute, the Association of American Railroads, the Alliance of Automobile Manufacturers, the American Farm Bureau Federation, the American Electric Power Service Corporation, all play significant lobbying roles in Washington, as well as in state capitals.

But more important even than these organizational assets of business is one that no environmental organization or any other pro-environmental interest can claim: its fundamental relationship to the economy generally and to employment in particular. Historically, they have cultivated the notion in the public mind—with much success—that unreasonably regulating them will adversely affect the nation's economic well-being, and cause job loss and dislocation. Thus, the debate has historically been framed as "the economy vs. the environment."

Historical Background: Business and the Reagan Agenda

During the 1960s and the early 1970s, the political give-and-take between the environmentalists and business interests was not especially contentious. The post-World War II economic boom rendered the costs of meeting environmental concerns relatively manageable, particularly since the Environmental Protection Agency (EPA) was having difficulty meeting the regulatory obligations imposed on it by an activist Congress. But the regulatory burdens on industrial and commercial activities began to take hold by the middle 1970s; the mainstream environmental organizations established a more dominant presence in Washington and, accordingly, took a more active and aggressive role in seeing that environmental standards were sufficiently strong and enforced. The amount of money spent annually on pollution abatement by the public and private sectors between 1972 and 1980, by conservative estimates, virtually doubled.

These accelerating costs motivated the business community to match the environmentalists' increasingly active advocacy role in shaping environmental policy and practice. Regulatory reform became their rallying cry. But they did not direct their efforts at the Congress; rather they focused on the executive branch, and found a willing and powerful ally. Ronald Reagan, the avowedly pro-business President that they had waited for since the 1920s, was intent on curtailing what he saw as a federal government that was too large and intrusive, and a body of environmental law that was wasteful and excessive. In his view, when government was needed, it should be administered at the state and municipal levels that are closest to the people; federal spending should be limited essentially to entitlement programs. In environmental law in particular, he found a quintessential example of bloated government, over-regulation, and resources squandered in the name of social theories, collectively stifling free enterprise.

President Reagan's effort to remedy the situation was supported from the outset by the National Republican Party Platform of 1980 (which he, of course, had a role in shaping) that "declare(d) war on government regulation," and expressed the belief that "the marketplace, rather than bureaucrats, should regulate management decisions."[1] Within weeks of taking office, he signed Executive Order No. 12291 that gave the Office of Management and Budget the authority and responsibility to review all rules for their *economic* consequences. It also required a cost–benefit analysis[2]—a process of weighing the costs and benefits of a project in dollar terms even when they are not directly monetary—be conducted as a precondition to the adoption of new regulations, to inform review of existing regulations, and to be considered in proposed new legislation. The Order also required administrative agencies to justify the need for the regulations, and the consequences that they may have on those most affected by their implementation. With respect to potential harm, the probability of risk must outweigh the benefits of government non-interference in private activities.[3] At the very least, the mandates of the Order would have the effect of slowing down the rule adoption process. A moratorium was imposed on many regulations to provide the opportunity to review them.

In addition to this "dream agenda," business had a virtual open door to the offices of the U.S. Environmental Protection Agency under Administrator Anne Gorsuch Burford, who came with strong connections to the business community. Not only were the agency's rolls filled with former employees from regulated companies, but also, industry representatives most affected by proposed regulations were admitted freely into decision-making proceedings to give "advice" during their development. On the other hand, environmental organizations were generally excluded and public participation in environmental policy sessions virtually disappeared.

With respect to land use issues, Interior Secretary James Watt, who equated government regulation with socialism, was given a mandate to promote growth. Bringing strong western ties to the office, he supported an effort by a number of western states, dubbed the "Sagebrush Rebellion," that lobbied for a return of federal lands to local hands and the restoration of what it regarded as their lost property rights. Together they sought to open up public lands to mining, drilling, grazing, timber harvesting, and natural gas exploration. Extractive industries had high hopes of turning the corner on the "tyrannical" rule of the Bureau of Land Management, and to gain a measure of parity with the federal government in managing their lands.[4]

All this was, of course, music to the ears of business, who welcomed an administration that would promote their agenda vigorously and unapologetically. Economic factors were, once again, a major part of the mix, and the environmentalists were seemingly at bay. But, fortunately for the environmentalists, both Burford and Watt overplayed their hands, got entangled in scandal, and left the administration prematurely in disgrace.[5] With them went any hope of fully realizing the agenda on President Reagan's desk as he took office, although the principal elements of that agenda—the decentralization of environmental power, the adoption of cost–benefit analyses as integral parts of rulemaking, and the privatization of government functions—affect environmental policy to this day.

Though the scandals surrounding Anne Gorsuch Burford and James Watt set business' ambitions back to some extent, a series of major real life events—most significantly the release of a lethal chemicals at a plant in Bhopal, India in 1984 and the massive oil spill in Alaska's Prince William Sound from the Exxon Valdez tanker in 1989, with the distant echoes of the near disastrous nuclear accident at Three Mile Island of 1979 still in memory—forced them to change direction more significantly. These events, of course, captured prominent media attention, reinvigorated the environmental consciousness of the public, and validated much of what the environmentalists had been saying about the risks posed by industrial activities. It became clear to the business community that they had to focus more of their lobbying efforts on the public, who were understandably imploring their representatives to take stronger action to protect them from the risks to which they saw themselves increasingly subject. If big business was to head off a new round of even stricter regulations, clearly public concerns had to be addressed and negative attitudes toward them modified.

Corporate Codes of Conduct

One of the initial elements of a new business strategy to accomplish this goal was to convince the public that they were as distressed by environmental accidents as the public, and that they would take every responsible measure to assure a safe and clean environment. Thus, around the middle of the 1980s, a number of corporate interests began to adopt voluntary codes of environmental management practice. Though different in a number of particulars, all of these codes committed companies to adopt internal systems of environmentally conscious management and to track their progress toward goals they set for themselves at the outset. Three of these codes merit brief discussion.

The first of these codes, Responsible Care, was conceived in Canada, but adopted by the U.S. Chemical Manufacturers Association (CMA) in the wake of the worst industrial accident in history, the leak at a chemical plant in Bhopal, India in 1984, and a fortunately less serious explosion that followed a year later at a plant in Institute, West Virginia. These accidents tarnished the chemical industry's image and put communities hosting chemical facilities on edge. Recommended by CMA's Public Perception Committee, the openly admitted objective of Responsible Care was to improve their members' environmental, health, and safety performance in order to quiet critical public audiences. Responsible Care is a comprehensive program, implemented by the American Chemical Council, comprising a range of elements covering everything from community education and emergency response to pollution prevention, process safety, and employee health.[6]

A second major code to be adopted was that devised by the Coalition for Environmentally Responsible Economies (CERES), formed to address environmental problems from the perspective of the marketplace. Its narrow purpose was to provide investors with environmental performance data that they could use along with other indices of performance in making their investment decisions. Its founder, Joan Bavaria, was insightful enough to realize that the availability of such data would foster greater trust between the member companies and the public. The core belief was that by paying attention to the quality of the environment, ecological and public health disasters like the Bhopal accident and the Exxon Valdez spill that could threaten the economic viability of corporations could be avoided. The CERES coalition was more diverse than Responsible Care, comprising not only investors and investment professionals, but environmental advocacy groups, labor unions, and even the State of

California Controller. The Coalition's initial project was, tellingly, the "Valdez Principles" (though it was later renamed the "CERES" principles), a set of rules affirming the responsibility of corporations to conduct business mindful of their stewardship of the environment. Specifically, the principles commit endorsers to many things.

PRINCIPLES TO WHICH ENDORSERS COMMIT

- Protect the biosphere;
- Use natural resources in a sustainable manner;
- Reduce wastes and minimize their adverse impacts;
- Use energy wisely;
- Reduce risk;
- Market only safe products;
- Fully compensate any damages for which they are responsible;
- Fully disclose risks to employees and the public;
- Appoint environmental managers or directors;
- Annually audit environmental performance.

Though the CERES principles were not widely endorsed, they did initially secure the participation of several major corporations, e.g. Sun Company, General Motors, and Polaroid, when the principles were modified. The "Valdez Principles" got much publicity, and surely raised corporate consciences even as they helped restore public confidence.[7]

A year after the founding of CERES, the Global Environmental Management Initiative (GEMI) was born. It was the product of discussions among the environmental managers of chemical, pharmaceutical, electronic, and consumer product manufacturers motivated by concerns over potential environmental liability. They sought a forum for dialogue among themselves and with the public. GEMI developed the Business Charter for Sustainable Development in conjunction with the Chamber of Commerce, which, like the previously mentioned codes, invoked members to track environmental progress through self-audits, one result of which was the concept of "total quality environmental management." Through national conferences that the Charter sponsors, it publicizes its work to the public and the wider business community.[8]

From Corporate Codes to Corporate Actions

These codes of conduct were the initial and largely defensive responses of those industries targeted by the environmental community. That the codes of conduct remain in force is important to note. But more important is that each of these codes of conduct and their principles have increased the number of their signatories exponentially and, more significantly, undertaken more substantive activities since 2000.

Responsible Care has grown into a 50-nation international group, comprising more than 90% of the world's chemical industry capacity. If the initiative was at first vulnerable to the charge that it was fundamentally a public relations effort, it has since been fitted with teeth. The consortium now lays claim to a variety of accomplishments ranging from reduction of toxic emissions to reductions in energy consumption and greenhouse gas intensity.

Correspondingly, since its inception, CERES has developed dramatically, both in numbers and influence. It now constitutes a national network of investors, environmentalists, and social organizations focusing, in the past several years, on the potential economic and environmental risks of global warming. Specifically, CERES has assembled an Investor Network on Climate Risk (INCR), joined recently by the American Insurance's Global Investment Group that comprises investment organizations managing trillions of dollars in assets; organized more than two dozen investor, Wall Street, and corporate interests to develop an action plan to address global warming; and conducted and published research on the possible effects on the business of climate change. These programs are testament to the genuine concern among investors about climate change and its economic consequences.

And finally, in 2003, the Equator Principles, a framework promoting environmental and socially responsible investment by financial institutions worldwide, was established. Specifically, the Equator Principles govern the financing of projects to mitigate risk factors, from forest protection to emissions reductions. Major U.S. corporations such as Wachovia, Wells Fargo, Bank of America, Citigroup, and JP Morgan have committed to comply with its standards in their lending practices.[9]

Other Industry Initiatives

The financial sector in particular has stepped forward with new initiatives. For example, an interesting variation on corporate behavior guides is being developed by investment research houses. Conceding that global warming regulation is virtually certain to soon be part of U.S. environmental policy, and that some form of carbon trading scheme will be a key component of that regulation, these financial advisers are putting together an investment-rating scheme based on how much individual companies would be affected. Those who would profit from a carbon trading protocol are rated high on the investment scale, while those who would be adversely affected, low.

The guide's criteria are unabashedly economic; no other environmental (or social) factors are considered in making investment recommendations. In fact, by focusing on greenhouse gas emissions, nuclear power generators would secure high ratings. Putting nuclear power at the top of any priority list would, no doubt, rankle most environmental advocates, though they are not comfortable with fossil-fueled power generation either, and some prefer nuclear generation as the lesser of two evils.[10]

Economic self-interest is at the center of the efforts of a sister industry —insurance. In addition to joining the INCR network, The American Insurance Group has established an Office of Environment and Climate Change to develop an appropriate policy to deal with the potential problems resulting from climate change. Another major insurance firm, Travelers, is offering hybrid car owners in more than 40 states discounts on their auto insurance premiums. Similarly, Fireman's Fund is reducing premiums on more energy-efficient "green buildings" that emit fewer greenhouse gases. As well, it will provide financial incentives to encourage clients to install more energy-efficient features in their houses. JP Morgan and Citigroup have adopted their own environmental protocols that are responsive to not only climate change but to social and community needs as well. Insurers are protecting themselves in more direct ways. Risk Management Solutions, a risk forecasting company, has predicted a substantial increase in coastal turbulence in the years ahead attributable to climate change. Several insurers are increasing rates and limiting coverage of coastal areas, where more than half the U.S. population lives.[11]

Finally, Marsh, the country's largest insurance broker, is collaborating with Yale University on a program of sustainable government forums to provide corporate board members with a broad perspective on the potential financial and legal consequences of climate change. Clearly, the insurance industry, which will bear the lion's share of climate change's economic damages, is taking a serious new look at risk. Indeed, the new perspective of the insurance industry is perhaps best summed up by the title of the Lloyd's of London's report: "Climate Change: Adapt or Bust" as part of its comprehensive 360 Risk Project.[12]

Another industry that has become more "green" is the ski industry. Directly affected by climate change, more than four dozen U.S. ski resorts are purchasing wind-power credits as an offset of their emissions. The purchase of wind-power credits involves a company's donating an amount equal to that that they pay for fossil-fueled power to wind generators elsewhere. Notably, Vail Resorts' purchase of wind power credits from Renewable Choice Energy makes the company the second largest corporate buyer of wind power in the country.[13]

But perhaps the most dramatic and telling initiative is the United States Climate Action Partnership (USCAP), a consortium of 10 major corporations and major environmental advocacy groups calling on the federal government to enact legislation to require significant reductions of greenhouse gas emissions. USCAP's founding document, *A Call for Action*, sets forth a set of principles and recommendations that it offers as a blueprint for a comprehensive, market-driven plan to address climate change.[14] Some participants concede that the effort is motivated in part by concerns that state action might fashion a patch quilt of regulations, some perhaps harsher and less responsive to business interests. Peter Darbee, chief executive of PG&E candidly said, ". . . we have the opportunity to construct something more pragmatic and realistic while President Bush is in office. A future political climate after 2008 might produce solutions less sensitive to the needs of business."[15] Still, such a program represents something of a sea change in business/environmental relations.

Altruism or Manipulation?

It must be reiterated that all these efforts address the potential economic consequences of global climate change, not any broader range of environmental threats. They are borne of self-interest, as well as social conscience. They have thus been undertaken voluntarily rather than in response to government mandates that would have been vigorously opposed a decade ago. At least in this area, the private sector implicitly concedes that addressing environmental threats—most particularly global climate change—is simply good economics.

That is a message now being reinforced by still another group of stakeholders—investors. Increasingly, investor interests, for example the New York City Comptroller, the Service Employees International Union, CERES, the Energy and Environment Program at the Interfaith Center on Corporate Responsibility, and INCR have been pressing their corporate principals to prepare for climate change and its potential risks. According to CERES, the coalition of investors and environmental groups, shareholders have already filed more than 40 resolutions in 2007 (up more than 30% from 2006) asking for information on how their corporations' business decisions are minimizing risk to their investments.[16] Energy companies such as utilities and oil companies are prime targets, but the "hit list" includes such corporations as Wells Fargo, Bed, Bath and Beyond, and Exxon.[17] Investors are threatening to file class action lawsuits if their corporations' failure to accommodate global warming threatens to make their investments vulnerable. Support for such resolutions at annual shareholder meetings is growing exponentially.

Perhaps more telling than the newly adopted policies, programs, and communications efforts of industries directly or indirectly affected by environmental conditions are the initiatives of companies whose activities and profits have only a marginal relationship to environmental factors. The broadest group of these has voluntarily joined the Green Power

Partnership, an initiative of the U.S. EPA. Organizations that sign on agree to purchase all, or a portion, of their electricity consumption with green power, principally though not exclusively wind power, as a way to minimize the adverse environmental impacts of power generated from fossil fuels. A diverse group of national corporations, including Wells Fargo, Coldwater Creek, Whole Foods, Starbucks, FedEx Kinko's, Safeway, and Staples are among the ranks of the more than 500 partners.[18]

While Wal-Mart is but a single corporate entity, the world's largest retailer is a veritable industry in itself, with the reach and market power to effect significant change, and dramatically so in collaboration with other transnational corporations. In the past several years Wal-Mart has undertaken an impressive range of environmental and energy initiatives:

- a commitment to double the efficiency of its truck fleet, ultimately saving an estimated 6% of U.S. petroleum;
- a program to provide incentives to their 60,000 suppliers to phase out hazardous ingredients from consumer products and to reward those that replace the suspect chemicals with benign alternatives;
- the establishment of a goal to reduce packaging generated by their suppliers by 5% by 2013, to be administered through a scorecard that will allow manufacturers to evaluate their packaging practices for volume, greenhouse gas emissions, raw materials use, and recycled content, which scores will guide Wal-Mart's purchasing decisions;
- the investment of $500 million in technologies to reduce greenhouse gases from stores and distribution centers by 20% in less than 10 years;
- participation in a collaborative campaign with General Electric to promote the sale of compact fluorescent light bulbs by drastically discounting them, supplemented by in-store promotions and associate and customer education;
- a commitment that all the wild-caught fish its sells will come from sustainability-certified fisheries; and to market a line of organic foods.[19]

It also has on the drawing board large scale solar power installations,[20] wind generation powering its own electric company in Texas,[21] and plans to incentivize the production and sale of sustainable electronics.[22]

These are among the most far-reaching of the actions taken by business to mitigate environmental threats and promote environmental goals. Perhaps raising corporate consciousness of the public's environmental concerns in the early 90s was responsible for the subsequent activities. But these activities should not be taken as an ideological shift toward green advocacy. First, most of these business measures are related to the core group of related environmental challenges—global climate change, air

pollution, and energy—and, thus, promise demonstrable economic benefits while responding to public concerns. These businesses continue to
oppose government regulation of their operations. Specifically, the petroleum industry, while saturating the media with a campaign to convince
the public that it is mindful of global warming and of the need to find
alternative fuels in face of the very real limits on the world's oil reserves,
nevertheless lobbies for increased oil and gas development in pristine areas.
Similarly, automobile manufacturers tout the environmental characteristics of their vehicles even as they continue to oppose mandates for
increased fuel efficiency. Industry giant, General Electric, with an historic spotty environmental record, attempts to soften its image with its
"Ecomagination" campaign. And, most notable, Wal-Mart's environmental and energy initiatives are seen by many as a thinly-veiled effort to
reshape an image among progressive groups openly critical of its questionable human rights, personnel, and community development practices. A
study conducted by Corporate Ethics International exposes what it regards
as Wal-Mart's "green" hypocrisy. It documents that Wal-Mart's PACs
make generous campaign contributions to members of Congress with poor
environmental voting records, supporting over 150 who voted against fuel
efficiency standards and more than 200 who voted for the National Energy
Act of 2005, decidedly anti-environmental legislation.[23]

In sum, from their nature and timing, there seems little doubt that
codes of conduct were undertaken in recognition of the need to regain
public confidence. Environmentalists saw them as just a public relations
effort, largely because their strictures were voluntary and because the
public has only limited access to the performance data they track. Some
hard-core environmentalists remain skeptical. Yet actions to which these
codes commit their signers went beyond the specific standards that would
be required by regulation to the management of their internal systems.
And in promoting the appointment of environmental managers to high-
level positions in their corporate organizational structure, they brought
environmental issues into the boardrooms and the policy deliberations
of big business. Ultimately, these modest early efforts morphed into
more far-reaching measures that, whatever their motive, are securing real
environmental benefits. In the last two decades, the corporate world has
changed from an opponent of environmentalists to their working partner.

Business Lobbying Through Surrogates

While corporations were directly taking on eroding public attitudes
toward them by implementing these codes of conduct, their portfolios
were carried by two sets of front groups. Though very different in strategy,
posture, and character, the two shared a common agenda, favorable to, and
endorsed and largely funded by, corporations, but acting independently, at

least superficially. Together they constituted a genuine anti-environmental movement, or environmental "backlash", as it was called. Major forces in environmental politics a decade ago, their roles have been modified in recent years.

This anti-environmental movement worked and reworked a number of themes:

- economic regulation imposes costs on both the private and public sectors, crippling the economy and taxpayers, and are disproportionate to the benefits it promotes;
- natural resources are better protected and maintained by private ownership than by government regulation;
- environmental regulations are not aimed at real, substantial health risks, but are rather keyed to the political agendas of environmental advocacy groups and the budgetary needs and aspirations of government regulators;
- virtually all of the allegedly catastrophic environmental threats— ozone depletion, overpopulation, acid rain, global climate change—are based on faulty, if not fraudulent science; and
- environmental concerns are most effectively and economically addressed by laissez-faire government and a free market economy.

Its adherents routinely asserted not only that the sky hasn't fallen, but that the environment, including our natural resources, is in better condition today than in years past.

One of these front groups, called "Wise Use," was a loose coalition of 400 or so small groups of ranchers, representatives of extractive industries, property rights activists, people who use off-road vehicles recreationally, farmers, and right wing ideologues. They coalesced in August of 1988 at a national conference, the Multiple Use Strategy Conference, sponsored by the Center for the Defense of Free Enterprise, at which they set down a formal agenda. "Wise Use" was a term coined early in the 20th century by Gifford Pinchot, the nation's first forester and Chief of the U.S. Forest Service, to describe responsible conservation—the balancing of preservation and the productive use of land in a manner that accomplishes both. But the modern anti-environmental alliance that used the phrase for its name goes well beyond what Pinchot would have endorsed, advocating the virtually free and unfettered exploitation of land for people's needs.

Though Wise Use presented itself as a "down home, just plain folks" organization, it enlisted the substantial support of corporations like Chevron and Exxon, and the American Farm Bureau, as well as the expected help from national lobbies of the extractive industries. Picking up from the failures of James Watt and the Sagebrush Rebellion, it started out as a western property rights movement intent on repealing the

Endangered Species Act of 1973, opposing the repeal of the 1972 Mining Act, and, generally, opening up federal lands to development. But since the late 1980s, it expanded to much of the country, challenging not only the wisdom, but also the very Constitutional validity of government regulation of land. Wise Use became a force that tapped into popular sentiments—the sanctity of individual freedom and the evils of big government that compromise it. It is interesting to note that the movement rose to prominence at precisely the same time that a counterpart populist movement, called "environmental justice" (discussed in Chapter 5) was also developing into a national political force. In Wise Use, business had its own grassroots organization.[24]

But times have changed. For a variety of reasons, Wise Use has moderated its public posture and its provocative rhetoric. But it is no less powerful. It has insinuated itself into mainstream government; many of its former leaders have assumed positions of authority in the present administration, most notably Gale Norton as Secretary of the Interior and Ann Veneman as Secretary of Agriculture.[25] And many of its legislative goals, like authorizing drilling in the Arctic National Refuge and logging in Alaska's Tongass National Forest, and scaling back the Endangered Species Act of 1973, remain on Congress' agenda.

Think-Tanks

Different from Wise Use in many ways, but pursuing the same mission is a group of conservative and libertarian think-tanks that began taking an active role in shaping environmental policy in the 1980s, though most were established in the 1970s to address other economic and political issues. Whereas Wise Use was essentially western, these think-tanks are headquartered principally in Washington, D.C., and while the focus of Wise Use is on land use and property rights, the focus of the think-tanks is more often on the regulation of industrial and commercial activities. Bound together by the shared core conviction that the environment is best protected by the marketplace rather than government, the promotion of free-enterprise and limited government is their common mantra.

Unlike Wise Use, the think-tanks are funded principally by the corporate giants, though most frequently through their sponsored foundations rather than directly. This indirect method of funding and their careful avoidance of direct political action allow them to maintain tax-exempt status as educational institutions, despite the undeniable fact that they aggressively pursue a distinctly political agenda and seek to influence not only the public but also lawmakers.

The most influential of these think-tanks, and the one most responsible for orchestrating the efforts of the group, was, and remains, the Heritage Foundation, founded by Joseph Coors in 1973. It was, in fact, the Heritage

Foundation that prepared *Mandate for Leadership*, a formal policy statement and agenda presented to Ronald Reagan as he entered office. Other major think-tanks often working in tandem with Heritage and other sister organizations, and always in sympathy with them, are the Cato Institute, founded in 1977; Consumer Alert, founded in 1977; the Reason Foundation, founded in 1978; the Political Economy Research Center, founded in 1980; the Competitive Enterprise Institute, founded in 1984; the Foundation for Research on Economics and the Environment, founded in 1986; and the Citizens for the Environment and the Science and Environment Policy Project, both founded in 1990. Almost all these are financed by the country's major corporate industrial groups such as petroleum, pharmaceuticals, automobile manufacturing, tobacco, and chemicals. Others are funded by independent corporate giants like Coca-Cola, Monsanto, IBM, Lockheed, and Alcoa; and other conservative foundations like Scaife, Olin, Carthage, and Bradley.[26]

These foundations promote their market-driven environmental policy prescription, and, at the same time, undermine the efforts of advocates for governmental regulation of the environment through a number of diverse activities. Perhaps the most effective of their strategies is to literally flood the popular media, especially in editorials and "letters to the editor" in rapid response to any legislative initiative or environmental event likely to generate a call for government action, or research finding alleging a new environmental threat or risk. It would be impossible to calculate the number of stories, columns, letters, and editorials the groups have collectively published in the last several years in newspapers and periodicals debunking global warming, for example, or chiding public fears of genetically modified food. Many of their own research reports became the subjects of newspaper "news" pieces. The Heritage Foundation, for example, once claimed to have secured 200 media "hits" from one of its reports. The foundations also gain access to the public through radio and TV talk shows, for which they make their representatives freely available. The spokespeople for these think-tanks have academic degrees, and their foundation affiliations seem impressive to citizens unaware of their sponsors.

The foundations have supported the authorship and publication of popular science books that ridicule what they regard as the exaggerated claims of the environmentalists. Ronald Bailey's *Ecoscam: The False Prophets of Ecological Apocalypse*, sponsored by the Cato Institute; *The True State of the Planet*, an anthology of pieces challenging the environmental positions on everything from global warming, to pesticides, to biodiversity, a project of the Competitive Enterprise Institute; and *Environmental Gore: A Constructive Response to Earth in the Balance*, published by the Pacific Institute for Public Policy, are but three of a score of books that were prominently displayed in bookstores throughout the country. As their titles suggest, these books chide the environmental community for fear-mongering through bad science and bad economics.

Finally, the foundations support their own legal foundations that challenge regulations for their Constitutionality, consistency with legislative intent, or appropriateness of application. The Mountain States Legal Foundation, whose President formerly served James Watt in the Department of Interior, is funded almost exclusively by a consortium of oil interests, while the Pacific Legal Foundation is financed by chemical manufacturers, power companies, real estate developers, and oil and timber companies. Even when these suits fail, they significantly delay the implementation of adopted regulations and divert government agency revenues from substantive work to legal fees, both of which serve their agenda, albeit indirectly.

If anything, these foundations have become more strident. The Competitive Enterprise Institute continues, with success, to lobby against federal standards requiring automakers to improve the gasoline mileage of their automobiles on the ground that such standards would result in smaller, more dangerous vehicles. Even more provocatively, the Henry M. Stimson Center has urged government to close down websites that publish information about hazardous materials in local communities on the grounds that such information could be used by terrorists. And the National Center for Public Policy Research maintains a website, tellingly titled "envirotruth.org," attacking the "jihad" that environmental activists are waging against corporations and pursuing its mission to combat "eco-terrorism." Of greater reach is a network of think-tanks sponsored and funded by ExxonMobil called the Frontiers of Freedom and a group of others that aim directly at discrediting the science behind global warming in general and at sinking the Kyoto Treaty specifically. Frontiers of Freedom is only one of literally hundreds of lobby groups masquerading as educational institutions.[27]

Wise Use and corporate think-tanks, then, both advance a business agenda with respect to environmental policy. They allow the business community to appear to stand apart from the political fray while their intermediaries work to shape public opinion on the issues most relevant to them. Meanwhile, the nationally prominent corporations have been able to project an aura of responsibility and good environmental citizenship.

Back to Congress

The sluggish economy of the late 1980s and early 1990s made it difficult for the government to defend the strict environmental standards and rules adopted over the previous decade or two, and business' claims that they were responsible for job losses, plant relocations, and higher taxes were received with more sympathy. The climate was ripe for regulatory reform, and the so-called Republican revolution that swept into Congress in 1994 was prepared to provide it. Ironically, it presented the reverse situation from the one that prevailed in 1980; this time the Congress was pro-business and the President and Vice-President were sympathetic to environmental regulation. So business redirected at least some of its efforts once again toward Washington, though, as we shall see, it did not by any means abandon its direct appeals to the public.

In 1994, Republican Congressional candidates ran on a broad program of reform that they called the Contract with America. Embedded in one of its bills, the deceptively titled "Job Creation and Wage Enhancement Act," were three measures that would have significant environmental consequences, all of which were unsuccessfully advanced by President Reagan: to establish a procedure to analyze proposed regulations for their scientific soundness and cost-benefit ratios; to require compensation (up to 10% of market value) to property owners whose land use potential is reduced by environmental regulations; and to require the federal government to evaluate all costs imposed on state and local governments of implementing new environmental programs, and of capping those costs to the level of the preceding year.[28]

Each of these provisions would have, in its own way, devastated environmental protection policies. And that was likely their intent. The business community saw in the Contract's environmental strictures another opportunity to enact at least a significant portion of the Reagan agenda. But though the measures were passed by the House of Representatives, only the "federal mandate" measure passed the Senate and found its way into law, though in amended form. The other measures failed, in all likelihood, because then Senate President Robert Dole envisioned a run for the White House, and couldn't brook what promised to be a bitter political battle.

Still, the very same business-friendly principles that President Reagan struggled to enact remained on the Congressional agenda, and continued to inform policy, even if not enacted. Persistent conservative opposition to rigorous environmental regulation, supplemented by a deteriorating economy, began to take their toll on the EPA, and the maligned and expensive "command and control" protocol of the 1970s and 1980s began to give way to a more conciliatory and collaborative relationship between business and government, as discussed in Chapter 3.

Going Green: New Dimensions in Public Relations

Though they made gains with the EPA, business came increasingly to the conviction that it was the public, not government, that would drive policy, and that an even more comprehensive public relations effort was in order. The codes were developed out of the recognition that good environmental behavior is good public relations. But clearly more had to be done.

And so, as noted earlier, the late 1990s ushered in a period of "corporate environmentalism." The clarion call was sounded by a cover story in the prominent business magazine *Fortune* called "The Environment: Business Joins the New Crusade."[29] Identifying the environment as the "biggest business issue of the 1990s," it goes on to detail the many initiatives major corporate concerns were already undertaking to position themselves favorably with the public and capitalize on their environmental consciousness. During the next several years, daily newspapers, mass circulation magazines, and industry publications alike were trumpeting business' newfound environmental stewardship and the economic, health, and social gains to be derived from the incorporation of environmental thinking into corporate planning. Even *Science*, the weekly publication of the American Association for the Advancement of Science, included an extensive, multi-part section specifically devoted to "Environment and the Economy."[30]

That business and the environment are not only compatible but symbiotic was to become the core message of a national public relations blitz: "green" is practical *and* profitable. Other ways that business publicized this message was to enter cooperative agreements with environmental advocacy groups. One that got much publicity was the 1992 accord fashioned between McDonald's and the Environmental Defense Fund (EDF) to phase out the Styrofoam clamshell packages in which hamburgers were served, but General Motors also signed an agreement with EDF to work together on a much broader range of issues, including the scrapping of old vehicles, fuel efficiency standards, pollution reduction credits, and urban smog, to name a few. Later, British Petroleum, one of the world's largest oil firms, undertook a joint project with EDF to address the emissions of greenhouse gases at the source of global warming.

But EDF was not the only mainstream environmental organization willing to work with, rather than against, big business. Chevron enlisted the World Wildlife Fund to advise it on environmental issues, and the Rainforest Action Network, an environmental group focused, as its name suggests, on achieving specific goals rather than effecting policy changes. It forced Home Depot to phase out the sale of wood products from environmentally sensitive areas by 2002, and give preference to wood "certified" to have been the product of environmentally sound logging practices developed by a Forest Stewardship Council established in 1993. Three years later, Unilever, a major fish marketer, joined with the World Wildlife Fund to create a Marine Stewardship Council, which would address the dwindling world fish stocks by helping to ensure sustainable industry practices. More common is the practice among the corporate world to simply donate to environmental groups, arguably to present themselves as "good guys" but, more realistically, to endear themselves to their policy "opponents."

Conclusion

These were but a few of the countless efforts entered into jointly by business concerns and environmental organizations in the 1990s, efforts that have been extended and expanded into this century. As we have seen above, many and more substantive cooperative efforts have been undertaken. Such efforts serve the interests of both. Business has the money to fund these efforts, and profits from association with environmental groups. For their part, the environmental groups secure the cooperation and assistance, to say nothing of funding, of the private sector, and, at the same time, dispel the perception of inflexibility of attitude and indifference to economics that dog them. Whatever their propaganda value, most of even the early cooperative arrangements accomplished meaningful purposes. Those undertaken since 2000 have been substantially more productive.

Of more questionable value was the explosion of "green products" that industry flooded the market with during the early 1990s, products touted as "biodegradable," "ozone friendly," "recyclable," "environmentally safe," "natural," "phosphate free," even "reusable." Aimed at ecology-sensitive baby boomers, these "new" products multiplied by orders of magnitude during the early 1990s, and products sporting environment-friendly labels reached nearly $9 billion in sales by mid-decade. But the trend trailed off as public skepticism about them grew, and as consumer protection agencies and government watchdogs exposed many of their claims as meaningless at best, spurious at worst.

These products were but one of a number of promotional efforts conceived by a burgeoning sector of advertising specifically focused on maximizing their clients' economic benefit from a favorable environmental image. These agencies served as consultants to companies, helping them target audiences, train their workforces, and "green" their operations. As business has grown to appreciate the policy impact that the general public exerts, they have devoted more of their time to attending the conferences, reading the newsletters, and studying the polls that these agencies sell them. In short, during the 1990s, the environment itself became an industry.

Though the influx of new "green" products has only modestly abated, its advertising themes and products have altered. For example, auto manufacturers' ads that formerly pictured their vehicles against mountainous crests or picturesque landscapes now boast of their energy efficiency; oil companies that proudly publicized programs they fund to demonstrate that the rare birds, turtles, or wildlife they depict can live in perfect harmony with a habitat that has been the site of recent "development" now express their concern with global warming and the onset of peak oil. Closer to the consumer, Home Depot, the nation's second largest retailer, recently unveiled plans to market an environmentally gentler line of products under an "Eco Options" label.

The environmentalists, at least the most uncompromising of them, have a name for the kind of image polishing that so-called green products, green advertising, and even some green projects, trade in. They call it "green-washing" and it is essentially a new industry posturing to pursue the same old profit motive, a transparent attempt to pose as a friend of the environment without changing practices or procedures that would actually improve it. Harsh critiques of these practices have regularly appeared in a number of environmental journals, and Greenpeace, the most strident critic of all, has published an updated report, *Greenwash: The Reality Behind Corporate Environmentalism*, excoriating such practices principally by transnational corporations.[31] While the ultimate consequence of the pro-environment business initiatives now being carried out may well be exaggerated, it is impossible to dismiss them as pure public relations.[32]

As we view business in the 21st century, the characterization of decades ago of business as the implacable enemy of environmentalism is no longer justifiable. The current picture is more complex. A generation of CEOs with a more sophisticated notion of financial self-interest, an activist cohort of shareholders, a more cooperative government, an increasingly practical environmental community, and a more restive public are confronting environmental issues that require solutions that demand to be mutually addressed. Thus has the business community become an important ally of environmentalists. Even more ironic, business is seeking to solve problems, most notably climate change, left largely unaddressed by the federal government, which has abdicated its responsibilities for the energy and air policies that would mitigate that global problem.

Central Ideas

Historically the business community and environmentalists have been at odds over national policy, principally because industrial, and certain commercial, activities impose burdens on the environment. When several dramatic events, most prominently the Exxon oil spill, Love Canal, and Three Mile Island, raised substantial public concern over environmental threats, business expressed its concern by undertaking several largely public relations efforts and developing corporate codes of conduct. These were soon followed by the introduction of a number of "green product" promotions and shared programs with environmental organizations. But as the potentially catastrophic effects of global climate change on their bottom lines became clear, major corporations have undertaken a number of substantive policies to reduce the emissions of CO_2 and, perhaps more importantly, have joined the environmental community in calling on the federal government to establish and implement a national policy to deal with the new threat.

Chapter 7

Re-Emerging Activists

While business has been moving steadily toward more environmentally sensitive practices over the past two decades largely, though not exclusively, out of recognition that it is in its economic interest to do so, segments of two other stakeholder groups—organized labor and organized religion—are now joining with environmentalists in alliances and actions that aggressively advance environmental causes. Neither of these stakeholder groups is new to politics; the participation of both in public affairs goes back many decades, but their re-emergence in recent years is broadening and deepening the forces of environmental advocacy. Let's look at their different paths to the same place at the policy table.

I Organized Labor

> We are not promoting some kind of fuzzy, left-wing, feel-good stuff that Rush Limbaugh will love to attack . . . This is sound social and economic policy. This gives my grandkids a shot.
>
> (Leo Gerard
> United Steelworkers President)

> In the old days, we thought that smoke meant jobs. That pollution was a byproduct of prosperity. And that if the air smelled funny, and the mill killed all the fish in the river, such was the price of progress.
>
> ("Our Children's World"
> USW Environmental Task Force Report)

The historic relationship between union labor and environmental activists has been complicated and uneven; policy battles over the past three or four decades have found them alternately as allies and opponents. A number of factors account for this. Most broadly, the workplace safety and public health benefits of rigorous environmental policies have always been important to blue collar workers but their costs potentially threatened employment security. Those competing concerns have been reflected in labor's varying positions on specific environmental initiatives that would have differentially affected their members. Organized labor is, after all, not a monolith; the various unions represent a wide diversity of constituencies. The industries and activities the members of some unions engage in are more vulnerable to environmental risks in the course of their work than others and less vulnerable to economic dislocation. Workers in manufacturing and industrial trades such as the United Steelworkers (USW) and the Oil, Chemical and Atomic Workers (OCAW) are concerned not only with workplace safety but with a whole range of environmental threats and, accordingly, have been historically more sympathetic to environmental regulation. On the other hand, the Teamsters are involved principally, though not exclusively, in transportation and freight-related jobs, and are consequently more sensitive to economic issues, and workers involved in oil drilling or construction have understandably opposed constraints on commercial and industrial projects supported by environmentalists.

But environmentalists are not a monolith either. Over the years, the environmental community itself has broken along scientific, legal, social and geographical lines, each group with a somewhat different mission. The broadest demarcation of environmental concerns is that between land use issues and natural resource protection on the one hand and pollution control and waste reduction issues on the other. Industries associated with extractive activities—oil and gas drilling, coal mining, timber harvesting—are the focus of a different subset of environmental groups. Workers in those industries are more geographically concentrated and have more specialized skills. They are, accordingly, more concerned with the economic consequences of the regulation of their industries than with reducing their health and safety risks.[1] We shall see how the diversity of labor constituencies has accounted for their opposition to some significant environmental priorities and their support of others.

A second factor has been the state of the economy in general at various times over the past several decades. As noted in Chapter 6, during periods when the economy was thriving, environmental costs could be almost invisibly subsumed by business. At other times, when the nation's economy slumped and high-profile environmental threats veritably disappeared, the "jobs v. environment" debate tilted toward the former. More recently, globalization has caused a tectonic shift of the economic ground in favor of corporate interests and away from worker concerns. The importance of this development cannot be overestimated as a catalyst for the newfound cooperation of labor and environmentalists.

Finally, the developing public attitudes toward unions and environmentalists themselves have served as a catalyst for the merging of the two into alliances over the past half dozen years. For a variety of reasons, membership in organized labor unions has steadily fallen over the past decade or so. While the aggregate number of members in environmental organizations remains strong, environmental concerns, until very recently, have not been a factor in national electoral politics. Their partnership promises to help restore their important roles in shaping public policy in the service of their respective missions. Let's look at how all these factors, individually and collectively, have played out over the past 30 years or so, and why the newly reinforced relationship between the two may well dramatically increase the political influence of both.

While the OCAW's political activism began with its opposition to nuclear testing in the mid-1950s, organized labor's formal recognition of the ecological consequences of man's behavior dates back at least to 1970, when a special issue of *The American Federationist*, the monthly magazine of the American Federation of Labor (AFL) and the Congress of Industrial Organizations (CIO) was devoted to a "Man & Earth: Adjusting the Balance" theme. The issue laments the deterioration of the environment and calls on us all to take the "effort and sacrifice to address it." On a broader note, it acknowledges the introduction of the science of ecology into the American vocabulary and prophetically warns of the problems in "adjusting the balance between man and his environment."[2]

Not incidentally, 1970 marked the first mutually supportive political effort of environmentalists and labor; environmentalists strongly supported labor's campaign in support of the pending Occupational Safety and Health Act (OSHA) while labor lent its influence to passage of the Clean Air Act of 1990. Even so, the 1970s and 1980s were challenging times for the relationship. Increasingly stringent environmental regulation clashed with the energy crisis, the conflict over nuclear power, the phase-out of lead as a gasoline additive, and the stricter control of other toxic chemicals and pesticides. Employers exploited union fears of job losses to garner their support in these areas. The 1980s also saw an anti-union administration and an empowered corporate presence engaging in union busting and lockouts. They chilled activist OCAW efforts by threatening "the elimination of many of the products they manufacture, from chlorinated chemicals and nuclear fuels to carbon-based fuels."[3]

On the other hand, "right to know" legislation that requires workers and members of the community to be apprised of hazards used in production processes again found labor and environmentalists on common ground. And the explosion at a chemical plant in Bhopal, India, in 1984 caused labor to again join environmental interests in insisting on tighter safety standards. Again, when health and safety concerns are at issue, the two sectors willingly collaborated but when jobs were at stake, those unions most significantly affected retreated from their environmental allies.

This principle accounts for the issues that have most divided the two stakeholder groups. The widely publicized clash over preservation of old-growth forests, simplified in the media as a trade-off between jobs and spotted owls, alienated the timber industry. Meanwhile, proposed federal mandates for improved fuel efficiency of American car fleets were perennially opposed by the United Auto Workers, and the protracted environmental campaign to prevent drilling in the Arctic National Wildlife Refuge was vigorously opposed by the Teamsters, resulting in what many regard as the nadir of labor/environmental relations. Further, the reauthorization of the Clean Air Act of 1990 brought the United Mine Workers (UMW) into the political fray. The UAW, like their counterparts in extractive industries, feared that support of the legislation would cost them jobs.

But if individual unions during the 1980s opposed some major environmental initiatives, global trade issues brought into bold relief their overarching mutual interests in the 1990s. Their aggressive opposition to the North American Free Trade Agreement (NAFTA) early in the decade galvanized them as no other issue could have. That treaty subordinates labor *and* environmental protections to corporate profit. While the labor/environmental coalition failed to defeat U.S. participation in the treaty, their mutual antipathy to it initiated an impulse to partnership that has ushered in a whole new era of cooperation against their common enemy. Shortly after his election as AFL-CIO President in 1995, John Sweeney acted to promote the newly energized coalition by naming Jane Perkins, a former labor leader and president of Friends of the Earth, as the federation's first liaison to the environmental movement. He also created an environmental policy committee on the AFL-CIO executive council.[4] Their 1999 battle against globalization at the protests in Seattle against the World Trade Association (created by NAFTA) cemented their relationship.

Perkins' charge was to address climate change in general and seek compliance with the Kyoto Accords committing signatory nations to limiting greenhouse gas emission specific levels in particular. At least initially, such an effort would seem to undermine the work of some of the older, more established unions, like coal mining and automobile manufacturing. Change always unsettles employment patterns, and the nature and level of change that would be required in such a fundamental sector as energy would almost certainly result in losses in some job categories, even though, over time, many new jobs will be created to replace them.

But by the early years of this century, it became apparent to the leadership of the more progressive unions, like the Steelworkers and the Service Employees International Union (SEIU), that a successful response to the challenges posed by global warming involved a retooling of America, a transition away from a carbon-based economy and toward a new energy paradigm based on efficiency, alternate and renewable sources, and "green" architecture. To ease that transition is the objective of the Apollo Project, an extensive alliance comprising 17 major labor unions and many major environmental organizations, working alongside a range of economic, social justice, faith-based, and state and local partners. The Apollo Alliance is dedicated to creating "the next generation of American industrial jobs and treating clean energy as an economic and security mandate to rebuild America."[5] It is supported by a $300 billion investment in clean-energy infrastructure that would create an estimated 3.3 million union jobs. It has active chapters in at least a half dozen states.

The significance of the Apollo Alliance to labor/environmentalist relations cannot be overestimated. The goals now at the top of the environmental agenda—energy independence and global climate change mitigation—are now being pursued hand-in-hand with organized labor. They are doing this not at the expense of jobs but, on the contrary, through the development of millions of new, high-level, high-paying "green" jobs, all of which makes the latest labor/environmental alliance the unlikely result of more than 30 years of often contentious debates over a variety of core environmental issues, most notably auto fuel efficiency standards.

In early June of 2006, the United Steelworkers (USW), the nation's largest manufacturing union, boasting 850,000 members in the U.S., and the Sierra Club, the nation's largest environmental organization, with a membership of 750,000, formed a strategic alliance to jointly advance a policy agenda under the banner of "Good Jobs, A Clean Environment, and a Safer World." The formalization of the Alliance followed the publication of the second of two policy reports underlying it: "Our Children's World" (1990) and "Securing Our Children's World" (2006). "Our Children's World" was developed by the USW Environmental Task Force and adopted at its 25th Constitutional Convention. After enumerating a litany of environmental challenges—hazardous waste, air pollution, ozone depletion, global warming, deforestation—it argues, as its title suggests, that "the greatest threat to our children's future may lie in the destruction of their environment," and that "[F]or that reason alone, environment must be an issue for our union." Further, it debunks the notion that addressing environmental problems will economically threaten worker security: "we cannot protect Steelworker jobs by ignoring environmental problems." Even more starkly, it warns that the power of our population and technology to alter our environment irreversibly "seems out of control, creating enormous conflicts between human activities and the natural world . . . All of them are critical to our survival."[6]

Sixteen years later, the USW International Executive Board adopted "Securing Our Children's World," a follow-up to the 1990 report. In addition to reinforcing the importance of environmental protection to labor clearly affirmed in the earlier document, the 2006 policy statement broadens the union charge to address global poverty, economic justice, and human rights and the catastrophic consequences of global warming. The synergy between unions and environmentalists that the Steelworkers tout was fundamental to their new collaborative efforts:

"Without the two movements acting in concert, neither movement can succeed."[7]

In light of this call to action, the sealing of a "Blue/Green Alliance" between the Steelworkers and the Sierra Club in 2006 was virtually inevitable. Like the Steelworkers, the Sierra Club along with other environmental organizations were themselves engaged in some soul-searching. Despite robust membership in environmental organizations and favorable poll numbers, major environmental issues have failed in recent years to influence electoral politics. The triumph of an anti-environmental administration in 2004 even at a time when air pollution regulation and oil drilling in the Arctic National Wildlife Refuge were highly publicized national issues is evidence of this. Those results seemed to confirm the dramatic pronouncement of two environmental activists in a paper they presented at a meeting of the Environmental Grantmakers' Association in October, 2004 entitled "The Death of Environmentalism." Holding up environmentalism's failure to generate national policy to address the sources of global warming, the paper castigates environmentalists as "just another special interest" whose technocentric policy prescriptions no longer resonate with Congress or the public. More pointedly, it criticizes the movement for failing to find common ground with potential allies like labor. In short, the environmental community is invoked to divest itself of its elitist image and work more closely with the grassroots.[8]

The Alliance, then, represents a natural fit between the two often competing interest groups. It brings together blue and green collar members under a common agenda—"Good Jobs, A Clean Environment, and a Safer World." In collaborating on programs promoting energy independence and mitigating global warming, it takes up the nation's most urgent issues. Its mission, as the joint resolution establishing it asserts, is more holistic: "This alliance will focus its resources on those issues that have the greatest potential to unite the American people in pursuit of a global economy that is more just and equitable and founded on principles of environmental and economic sustainability."[9]

Not only does the Blue-Green Alliance double the members they individually represent, but it also allows them to bring very different audiences under the same umbrella. Bridging the working class and upper-middle class constituencies they represent independently gives them a louder bullhorn and broader reach.

But as well as serving to advance their different, but newly rediscovered synergistic interests, the Alliance is committed to restoring what the AFL/CIO acknowledged 36 years earlier was necessary for planetary survival —the "balance between earth and man." That balance resides, principally though not exclusively, in the mitigation of global climate change, the overarching threat to global economic equity, social justice, and international security, as well as ecosystem integrity.

II   The Theological Community

> We are not greens in collars . . . We are not the environmental move-
> ment at prayer . . . We are religious people responding to a new
> challenge by being faithful to our teachings and traditions.
>
> (Paul Gorman
> Director, National Religious Partnership for the Environment)

> God created it. We tend it. That settles it.
>
> (Bumper Sticker
> Evangelical Christian College Students)

The relationship between faith and ecology goes back at least four decades,
when Lynn White, a University of California Professor of History, wrote a
provocative essay, "The Historical Roots of our Ecological Crisis," in which
he attributes our deteriorating environmental condition to Christianity's
view that man is superior to nature and that nature is man's to use and
exploit. He finds this anthropocentric view in Genesis, 1:28, 29, where
God invokes Adam and Eve to "Be fruitful and multiply, fill the earth and
subdue it, and have dominion over the fish of the sea and over the birds of
the air and over every other living thing that moves upon the earth."[10]
White's thesis, as might be expected, generated a spate of challenges and
rebuttals advancing the alternative view that God made us the stewards,
not the masters, of Nature, a view anchored in Genesis as well (see, for
example, Genesis, 2.15). Soon, White himself backed off from the full
implications of his argument.

While the issue lay dormant for several years, by the onset of the 1990s,
testaments to humankind's responsibility to creation were being made by
literally scores of religious groups and leaders from all parts of the world.
British Prime Minister Margaret Thatcher explained her concern over
global warming by declaring that "We have a full repairing lease on the
Earth,"[11] and Pope John Paul II devoted his entire World Day of Peace
message on January 1, 1990 to that same human obligation.[12] These
affirmations reflected a tide of new attention to the physical state of the
world and the burgeoning of new relationships between the religious and
scientific communities.

In an *Open Letter to the Religious Community* issued in 1990, more than 30
world-renowned scientists, many Nobel Laureates, issued a call to the
religious community to join with them in an effort to save the world from
impending ecological catastrophe.[13] The religious community answered
the call. In 1991, at The Summit on the Environment, prominent
religious leaders across the spectrum of faiths and many of the world's
most notable scientists joined forces in *An Appeal for Joint Commitment in
Science & Religion*.[14] Painting an apocalyptic picture of the state of the

planet—from depletion of the ozone layer to global warming, from deforestation to extinction of species and the prospect of nuclear war—it sought to develop an holistic and comprehensive response: "Problems of such magnitude and solutions demanding so broad a perspective must be recognized from the outset as having a religious as well as a scientific dimension." As far back as the early 1990s, then, a partnership between the scientific and religious communities put human stewardship of God's works at the top of the social and political agenda and laid the foundation for what was to develop into fully-fledged environmental activism by faith-based groups in the U.S. That activism was given urgency by a growing anxiety that God's creation was under unprecedented threat.

Thus, scores of religious coalitions across the denominations, faiths, and sects formed and began to synthesize their mutually shared commitment to earth's protection and to address environmental problems. It should be noted at the outset, however, that it is under the banner of "creation care," not environmentalism, that these groups march. Traditional Christians especially maintain some distance from what they regard as the environment's core constituency, much of whose social and political agenda they regard as singularly secular, even, in some cases, pantheistic. They do find common cause in the preservation and protection of God's creation however, which both see as under assault. For all their social and political differences, both see deteriorating ecological conditions as a greater threat to the poor and vulnerable than to the rich and powerful. In this way, faith groups see environmental protection as simply an extension of their humanitarian mission.

A paradigm of the collaborations inspired by the Summit on the Environment is the National Religious Partnership for the Environment, a consortium of independent faith groups formed in 1992. The Partnership comprises the Coalition on the Environment and Jewish Life, the Council of Churches of Christ, the U.S. Conference of Catholic Churches, and the Evangelical Environmental Network. The core conviction of the Partnership is that the "environment" is fundamentally a religious issue where the "environment" is but a "pale reflection of a much richer word: Creation." Each partner, consistent with its own teachings and traditions, brings scholarship, leadership training, initiative, and public policy education to the protection of mankind's common home and well-being on Earth.[15]

One constituent of the National Religious Partnership for the Environment, the Coalition on the Environment and Jewish Life: Protecting Creation, Generation to Generation, seeks to put environmental protection on the agenda of the Jewish community and convince government officials that protection of the environment is a moral and religious obligation. It is the voice of 29 national Jewish organizations across the spectrum of Jewish communal life. It seeks to take fundamental Jewish values such as "repair of the world" and "performing deeds of loving kindness" into the public arena. Consistent with this mission, it participated in the mid-1990s opposition to proposals to undermine the Endangered Species Act of 1973.[16]

Perhaps the most extensive and diverse of the Partnership group is the Evangelical Environmental Network and Creation Care.[17] Comprising two dozen affiliates with scientific, academic, religious, and social action agendas, it was founded out of the recognition that "many environmental problems are fundamentally spiritual problems." Its *Declaration on the Care of Creation*, a biblical call to reduce pollution and environmental degradation, has been widely adopted by members of the evangelical community.[18]

Two other collaboratives pursue ministerial missions but were born out of specific issues and circumstances. The Noah Alliance, comprising the Academy of Evangelical Scientists and Ethicists, COEJL, and Restoring Eden, was inspired by the threat to creation and its many creatures posed by reform or repeal of the Endangered Species Act of 1973. In fact, its name derives from the belief that the Endangered Species Act is a modern Noah's Ark: "(w)e call upon US policymakers to emulate the forethought, self-restraint, and prodigious effort modeled by the biblical Noah—'a righteous man . . . blameless in his age' (Genesis 6:9)."[19]

Another interdenominational alliance, the Regeneration Project established in 1998, is devoted to deepening the connection between ecology and faith, but it began as an aggregation of Episcopal churches in California dedicated to deal with California's energy crisis. It now embraces not only Christian and Jewish but Muslim groups as well. The program, ingeniously named Interfaith Power and Light, has grown into what is now an extensive and active force promoting environmental change around renewable energy, conservation, and energy efficiency. They help their congregations buy energy-efficient lights and appliances, provide energy audits and implement their recommendations, encourage the purchase of fuel-efficient vehicles, and pursue renewable energy projects such as rooftop solar installation. There are now affiliates in 23 states. Like its sister organizations, it has more recently taken on the fight against global warming as a major cause.[20]

These are merely the most prominent and broad-based of the literally scores of theological alliances and organizations that discovered in Scriptural texts and teachings a mandate to preserve and nourish what God created and entrusted to Man. But more local and/or focused groups collectively display an impressive diversity of goals:

- Christians for the Mountains identifies as its highest priority the termination of mountaintop removal extraction of coal;
- the Religious Campaign for Forest Conservation seeks a cessation of

logging of old growth forests, commercial logging on public lands, and the redirection of timber industry taxpayer subsidies to forest restoration efforts;

- Alternatives for Simple Living seeks to equip people of faith to challenge consumerism. Begun as a protest against the commercialization of Christmas, it encourages celebrations that reflect conscientious practices;
- Target Earth, a national movement of Christian activists based in 15 countries, purchases endangered lands, preserves the jaguar, feeds the hungry and reforests ravaged terrain;
- the Unitarian Universalist Church Seventh Principle Project promotes the eco-spirituality implicit in the Church's Seventh Principle— respect for the interdependent web of all existence of which we are a part;
- the U.S. Catholic Conference Environmental Justice Program engages parishes in activities aimed at dealing with environmental problems, especially as they affect the poor;
- the Forum on Religion and Ecology, Harvard University Center for the Environment brings religious studies together with academic and activist discourse on the environment; and
- the World Stewardship Institute undertakes projects that link the business, science, and faith communities in the cultivation of environmental stewardship.[21]

While occasionally mentioned in their mission statements, the participation of these affiliations in direct political advocacy was modest, and, until the turn of the century, confined largely to opposing efforts to weaken the Endangered Species Act of 1973. They sought principally to educate their congregants, broaden their vistas, and engage them in grass roots activities that would introduce them to new responsibilities. Nevertheless they unwittingly embraced much of the environmental agenda and prepared the ground for a new relationship with environmentalists. First, of course, care for God's creation—preservation of the land's diversity, protection of God's creatures, and maintenance of the land, water, and air—became a deliberate and expressly stated commitment, congruent with the goals of environmentalism. Second was the considerable social capital they brought to the cause. The networks of institutionalized relationships they developed with each other and with the environmental community would come to play a significant role when, in the first decade of the 21st century, they assumed a much more vocal and aggressively political posture.

If endangered species, wetlands loss, deforestation, and ozone depletion were of general concern to these groups in their early years, it was the threats posed by global climate change—and air quality degradation specifically—that proved to be the driving force that motivated them to engage more directly in political advocacy. On Earth Day 2004, 95 national and state Christian leaders representing as many as 30 million congregants affiliated with the National Council of Churches, sent a letter to President Bush. That letter is arguably the most forceful, comprehensive, and explicit environmental policy statement ever issued by a religious coalition. Reprinted in a full-page ad in the *New York Times*, the letter could well have been drafted by any mainstream environmental advocacy group but for the Biblical citations that underscore each of its recommendations for a change in policy on the environmental issues it calls on the President to address. Specifically, it urges President Bush to "abandon his 'clean air' policy which seeks to dismantle the Clean Air Act of 1990, delays cleanup of harmful mercury pollution, adds to further global warming and allows polluters to avoid public health standards. In God's hands and entrusted to us is 'the life of every living thing and the breath of every human being' (Job:12:10)."[22]

What is most remarkable about this message is that it eschews generalities in favor of criticizing specific programs, namely the Administration's "Clear Skies" initiative on the legislative side and new rules that weaken the New Source Review provisions of the Clean Air Act of 1990, for failing to meet "fundamental moral responsibilities as set out in the Bible." The letter also laments the absence of mandatory standards of reduction of carbon emissions that harm the global climate, the protection of which "is an essential requirement for faithful human stewardship of God's creation on Earth." It notes as well our "paramount obligation to 'defend the poor and the orphans' . . . who have limited access to health care, senior citizens who may have compromised immune systems, and children who pound for pound breathe 50% more air pollution than adults, all disproportionately hurt by air pollution." Furthermore, these attacks are supported not only by Biblical passages, but by cited scientific authorities such as the National Academy of Sciences, the American Lung Association, and the U.S. Environmental Protection Agency. It even goes so far as to point to the "powerful corporate interests that have had disproportionate influence in shaping and reaping benefits from a clean air program which should serve the common good." It concludes by charging that "the Administration's energy, clean air and climate change programs prolong our dependence on fossil fuels, deplete Earth's resources, poison its climate, punish the poor, constrict sustainable economic growth, and jeopardize global security and peace." In reaffirming an organic relationship between environmental protection and fulfillment of obligations to do God's work on earth, a significant segment of the evangelical community brought their sacred mission directly into the political arena.

Just two months after its Open Letter to the President, evangelical Christians assembled at Sandy Cove, Maryland to reflect upon and nourish their "roles as stewards of God's creation." The *Sandy Cove Covenant and*

Invitation agreed upon at that event, while less explicitly political, nevertheless committed signatories "to make creation-care a permanent dimension of our Christian discipleship . . . to understand environmental challenges, and . . . to motivate the evangelical community to fully engage environmental issues in a biblically faithful and humble manner." It also committed attendees to developing a consensus statement on global warming within a year.[23]

Political participation was soon to become a central part of their mission. In October of that same year, the National Association of Evangelicals (NAE), comprising 51 church denominations, adopted *For the Health of the Nation: An Evangelical Call to Civic Responsibility*.[24] Its preamble soberly asserts:

> Never before has God given American evangelicals such an awesome opportunity to shape public policy in ways that could contribute to the well-being of the entire world. Disengagement is not an option. The basis for its civic engagement is that the responsibilities that emerge from that mandate [God's grant to our parents over the earth] are many, and in a modern society those responsibilities rightly flow to many different institutions, including governments, families, churches, schools, businesses, and labor unions. Just governance is part of our calling in creation.
>
> And it concludes with the commitment to "engage in political and social action in a manner consistent with biblical teachings."

That commitment was fulfilled, dramatically, in February of 2006, when a broad coalition of 86 evangelical Christian leaders of mega-churches and 39 presidents of evangelical colleges, all under the auspices of the National Association of Evangelicals, joined aid groups and environmentalists in announcing a plan to address global warming—*Climate Change: An Evangelical Call to Action*.[25] Remarkably, it regards the mitigation of human-induced climate change as a Biblical obligation as compelling as protecting the unborn, preserving the family and sanctity of marriage, defending religious freedom and human dignity, and taking the Gospel to a "hurting world."

It even goes so far as to call for federal legislation to reduce carbon dioxide emissions, specifically endorsing market-based mechanisms. The announcement was supported by a variety of media spots and public and private educational programs.

It must be pointed out that not all of the evangelical community supports the Initiative. In fact, its promotion has caused something of a schism in the ranks. An organization called Focus on the Family and two dozen other Christian leaders established the Interfaith Stewardship Alliance (ISA) for the sole purpose of challenging the *Call to Action*. They have assembled their arguments in a counterpart document called *A Call to Truth, Prudence, and Protection of the Poor: An Evangelical Response to Global Warming*, in which they argue that while global warming is real and potentially catastrophic, it is attributable principally to natural causes, not human activities. The ISA claims that a carbon reduction program will harm the poor by raising energy costs and advocates instead economic development programs in poor countries to enable them to adapt to the changing climate. The document is detailed and scientific, but, obviously, does not represent the consensus of the religious or scientific communities.[26] Nevertheless, the President of the National Association of Evangelicals and its Vice President of Governmental Affairs did not sign off on the Initiative in deference to the concerns of ISA.

In June, 2007, the Southern Baptist Convention, the country's largest Protestant denomination, passed a resolution not only questioning the science behind global warming, but, like the Interfaith Stewardship Alliance, expressed concern that governmental efforts to mitigate global climate change may well place undue hardships on the poor and the most vulnerable among the population.

Notwithstanding these divisions, the faith community's concerns with global warming continue almost unabated. The Evangelical Environmental Network and The Regeneration Project have each issued manifestos on their websites. In "An Open Letter to the President and Congress calling for immediate action on global warming," posted on its website in May, 2007, the Regeneration Project sets forth:

> *An Interfaith Declaration on the Moral Responsibility of the U.S. Government to Address Global Warming* . . . Each of our diverse traditions has a common concern for creation. The Hebrew Bible calls us to "till and to keep" the garden. The Koran declares that God created the Earth in balance, and that human beings are the trustees of creation. Christians, too, are challenged to be stewards of the garden . . . All of our traditions call us to serve and protect the poor and vulnerable. And it is the world's poor, who contribute the least to this problem, who will suffer the most from global warming.

Like the Letter to President Bush sent by the evangelicals, it endorses specific government policies: specifically, government imposed mandatory limits on greenhouse gases and public sector investments in renewable energy as means to reverse the warming trend. Like its predecessor, it invokes, as justification for aggressive government action, the plight of the potential human victims of our failure to act. Thus religion's responsibility for the health of the physical world is seen as inextricably linked to its responsibility to ensure and promote social justice.

Perhaps more importantly, these statements keep the issue alive both in the pulpit and in educational programs and videos around the country. Al Gore's documentary *An Inconvenient Truth* has obviously had a telling effect on national public opinion, but *The Great Warming*, a Canadian film, may in fact have more influence among the religious community. Gore is arguably too closely associated with the environmental movement to have credibility with evangelicals, and his documentary is, perhaps, too technical. *The Great Warming*, on the other hand, dramatizes the effects of climate change around the world, and is narrated in the voice of the new evangelical leadership. While Gore's film has captured a mainstream public audience, *The Great Warming* has been shown in hundreds of churches in countless cities around the country, and promoters have provided on the film's website Biblical study and discussion guides. A former supplementary website even suggested questions that the film's viewers can ask political candidates where they stand on the issue.

This new activism on the part of religious groups in the service of certain environmental causes has interesting but as yet uncertain political —and partisan—consequences. To a public whose religious leaders have historically been reticent to engage in partisan politics, preferring to stay above the fray so to speak, it has, at least on the surface, been surprising. In fact, federal law precludes religious organizations from supporting particular candidates and parties without jeopardizing special tax privileges, though they have routinely lobbied on behalf of social and moral issues like abortion, stem-cell research practices, and same-sex marriage rights that have no specific party identification. As long as they operate on a platform of "creation care," they will probably not compromise their legal status, though the previously discussed "Open Letter to George Bush" may be close to crossing the line.

What is at least as surprising is that the religious community's unwitting embrace of environmental causes represents if not a break, at least discontent, with the political right that they have been so identified with, and supportive of. It has been repeatedly documented that the Republican Party, in recent elections, has garnered as many as three out of every four Christian evangelicals' votes, and that those who attend church at least once a week have historically voted in substantially greater numbers for Republicans than Democrats. And it is the Republican Party, at least in the past six or seven years, that has opposed not only the environmental agenda in general, but action on the threat posed by global warming in particular. Whether or not the "creation care" campaigns occasion a shift toward the Democratic Party is unclear; less in question is that they will exert an influence on prominent lawmakers in particular and color the political discourse on a core portfolio of issues.

Global climate change has now been almost universally recognized as a genuine and pressing threat. It is impossible to discern, of course, just how much of the evolution in public opinion is attributable to recent religious activism. Surely there are a number of factors—social, economic, and scientific—at play. But environmentalists nevertheless welcome the support their agenda is receiving from an ally with substantial social capital and real moral authority and, unlike most interest groups, one with no financial stake in the policy outcome. Having their issues not only touted in the pulpit, but also supported and communicated directly to the Administration and Congress by a devout and trusted constituency, gives environmentalists a credibility they have rarely enjoyed.

Central Ideas

Both labor and the faith community have historically been involved in political activity. In its formative years, labor advocated for environmental causes not only for larger ecological concerns but also out of respect for the health of workers. But those concerns gave way during subsequent difficult economic times to an association with business that it felt would protect jobs. They now see their economic interests as better served by environmentalists, who advocate for a "green" reindustrialization of America. The faith community's involvement in a few environmental issues goes back several decades, but recently it has stepped out of the background and boldly into open advocacy under the banner of "creation care."

Chapter 8

Uncertain Science—
Uncertain Politics

Environment is one-tenth science and nine-tenths politics.
(Anonymous British Delegate
U.N. Conference on Human Environment)

The public has become used to conflicting opinion . . . Many have
come to feel that for every Ph.D., there is an equal and opposite Ph.D.
(Tim Hammonds)

Scientists, like journalists, see themselves as standing apart from the world
of politics. The scientific enterprise has historically been imbued with an
aura of objective authority, and the laboratory setting, where scientists
give free rein to their curiosity, is at the opposite end of the world from the
legislative chamber, where society's immediate problems and needs are the
focus of inquiry. The systematic pursuit of ultimate truths, the freedom
from coercion, the self-imposed isolation from the events, circumstances,
and pressures of the day—these represent the context in which scientists
ideally like to work.

But it is an ideal difficult, if not impossible, to realize, particularly at
this time in history, and especially in the areas of environment and ecology.
For a variety of reasons, science and its practitioners have, wittingly and
unwittingly, become deeply entrenched in the environmental politics of
the day. Though the research and experimentation that constitute the
substance of science inquiry continue at ever increasing levels of sophisti-
cation, the people, institutions, and processes that determine what is to be
researched, who will perform it, and to what purposes it will be put are
political matters, and it is over these issues that environmental scientists
are increasingly being drawn into the fray, both as subjects and as participants. It may, in fact, be argued that not since the Darrow-Bryan debates
over creationism in the mid-1920s has science been so publicly on trial. Its
very integrity, as well as its capacity to provide the necessary underpinnings to environmental policy, are being challenged almost daily. There

may be no more telling index to the status of environmental science in the latter years of the 20th century than the fact that the 1990s saw the publication of two books with the identical title *Science Under Siege*, but reflecting opposite sides of the ideological spectrum that their authors, Todd Wilkinson and Michael Fumento, represent.[1] Science was, in fact, under siege throughout the decade. We will discuss why and how this has happened, what battles were fought and to what effect, and just how environmental policy was affected by the struggle.

But the sparring over the implications of prevailing scientific thought on environmental policy at the turn of the last century have exploded into open warfare in this century. Not only politicians and their spokesmen, but also substantial segments of the scientific community have abandoned even the pretense of political neutrality and publicly aired their outrage at having their work distorted and misapplied. The reasons for this state of affairs will be detailed later in the chapter, but the unremitting ideological disposition of the George W. Bush administration is a principal factor.

At the core of the matter is the simple but significant fact that every environmental problem has, at its foundation, a scientific reality, and it therefore seems axiomatic that science must play a prominent, if not pivotal, role in formulating its solution. That is why every interest group, from the most ardent environmental activists to those who would have free market forces dictate environmental behavior, supports the notion that environmental policy should be guided by "sound science," though they differ radically on how they define that term. Whatever those differences, "sound science" is, and remains, a buzzword in almost all policy debates. Everyone agrees that, given the growing complexity and impact of potential problems and the social and economic resources that may be necessary to address them, the need to enlist science in making public policy decisions has never been greater. The unfortunate fact, however, is that science and public policymaking are fundamentally incompatible; there is a disjunction between the practice of scientists and the needs, demands, and expectations of the other major players in the political game such as lawmakers and regulators, the courts, the media, and the population at large. Science and scientists thus find themselves fighting a political war on several fronts simultaneously.

Science is Analogue; Public Policy, Digital

Let's look first at the different ways that scientists and lawmakers work, and the different missions they pursue. The scientific method is a measured, incremental, and systematic process of identifying a problem, collecting data, developing an hypothesis, establishing a tentative conclusion, testing it, and submitting the results and the methodology to others working in the same subject area, a practice called "peer review." Conclusions must not only be verifiable, but falsifiable, a process that takes time and depends upon self-imposed doubt.[2] Thus all scientific conclusions are tentative, the product of a collective meeting of minds with other scientists observing and studying the same or related matters. While definitive truth is, of course, an ultimate objective, it is rarely arrived at. Scientists generally require agreement among 95% of the relevant experts to establish cause and effect, a level seldom reached. More important, scientists are not only comfortable with uncertainty, but literally build it into their thinking.

It doesn't take much imagination to see how scientists and the scientific method frustrate the lawmaker and the policymaking process. They represent totally different cultures. Lawmakers are faced with problems for which the public demands prompt solutions and cannot wait for definitive data, whereas science is patient and tentative. Science develops gradually and changes, but once public policy is set, it is hard to modify. Whereas differences of opinion among scientists are simply part of their everyday world, lawmakers see such conflicts as not only complicating their decisions, but engendering public distrust, thus making anything they do suspect. Lawmakers understandably want a degree of certainty that scientists cannot provide. They find that scientists have a tendency to overqualify conclusions to the point of uselessness, or, more commonly, to avoid making recommendations entirely, preferring to remain separate from politically charged issues. On the other hand, if lawmakers are looking for science to sanction what is their disposition to do politically, they have no difficulty finding respectable scientists to support them, whatever that position may be. This dynamic is termed "forum shopping." Finally, politicians are put off by the inability of most scientists to simplify complex issues sufficiently to make them understandable.

Scientists, for their part, are generally reticent to participate in the political process. They feel that they are in fact most often brought into the policymaking process to sanction already decided upon policies rather than to help formulate them. They find lawmakers not only scientifically illiterate, but, more importantly, intolerant of uncertainty and unappreciative of the concept of probability. They see them as wanting black-and-white answers, often without apprising scientists of the context of the problem being addressed.

Beyond these, however, are fundamental differences between policy and science themselves. Public policymaking is priority setting, and involves considerably more than obedience to the bedrock scientific facts underlying problems. Science can, at its best, inform policy—tell us the relative probability of an environmental threat or estimate the likelihood of a particular consequence of that threat. But science cannot set political priorities; it cannot tell us how we should allocate our social and financial resources to meet these threats, or whether they are more or less deserving of attention than a host of problems in other areas. And it certainly cannot predict with any certitude the relative success of alternative courses of action to address them.

The uneasy relationship between scientists and lawmakers, then, and the disjunction between their respective missions and how they go about pursuing them, make science's role in policymaking tenuous at best. The obstacles are all the more difficult to overcome in the areas of the environment and the earth's ecology because of the interaction of a staggering number of forces, both natural and manmade, that synergistically impact the earth. The reasons are many, because to begin with, so many of the problems, potential and present, are global in scope; because many are nascent rather than manifest, and thus have delayed consequences; and because, in measuring their impact on human life, traditional trial and error experimentation is ethically unacceptable. Environmental scientists therefore have to develop their conclusions from computer models, statistical extrapolations, educated projections, and often just plain conjecture. For these reasons, their work in this area is inherently more technical and clouded with uncertainty—and therefore more vulnerable to second-guessing.

Congress' Love/Hate Relationship with Science

It is against this backdrop that the political conflagration in which science finds itself today can best be understood. Since Congress is the locus of policymaking, the recent history of its uneasy relationship with science is a useful place to begin. As noted earlier, the period prior to the administration of Ronald Reagan represented a burgeoning of environmental activism during which literally scores of environmental laws were enacted, each requiring a complex body of regulations. The demands they imposed on the scientific capacity of EPA and its sister agencies, academic institutions, and industry subcontractors were enormous. As the chapter on legislation suggests, Congress, in its zeal to "do the right thing" but not really knowing the regulatory implications thereof, directed EPA, under unreasonable deadlines, to implement its laws. There was simply no way that those regulations could enjoy the benefit of thorough and reliable scientific analysis and data. The result was an amalgam of different standards—technical feasibility, public health without consideration of cost, and best available technology, to name a few. In an era when environmentalism was so popular among the public, few were willing to challenge the tentative, shaky scientific foundations upon which so many of these regulations were based.[3]

But as the costs of compliance grew with increasingly stringent standards, that scientific foundation became the target of those whose practices are subject to environmental regulations. It was, not surprisingly, the

Reagan administration that made the first move. By advocating the primacy of risk assessment and cost-benefit analyses in environmental rulemaking, Reagan challenged EPA to justify the science upon which its regulations were based—and dragged science itself into a policymaking role. At the same time that he was publicly raising the stakes for what he regarded as good science, however, he reduced EPA's scientific resources by cutting its budget. While he met with only modest success, at best, Reagan clearly challenged the soundness of the science upon which environmental policies were developed and implemented. It should be noted, however, that his calls and those of his successors to document the scientific basis of regulations were largely clandestine efforts to defer, in some cases indefinitely, the adoption of those rules. Largely as a result of this, EPA scrambled to refine its agenda and sharpen its scientific focus, to establish defensible priorities, and to begin to measure success by empirical environmental indicators.

The partisan war on science was dramatically intensified by the 104th Congress under House Speaker Newt Gingrich. Picking up the mantle of Reagan, this Congress, in its "Contract With America" and in conformity with the Republican Party platform, again made risk assessment and cost–benefit analysis centerpieces of its regulatory reform effort. As discussed in Chapter 3, the platform directed regulatory agencies to "require peer reviewed risk assessments based on sound science." But even as it trumpeted the need for basing regulations on "sound science," Congress announced a series of initiatives to sharply reduce the scientific resources of the Executive Branch. The efforts were buoyed by a 1994 poll released by the Advancement of Sound Science Coalition, an industry-funded lobby group that found that almost two-thirds of scientists believed that public confidence in scientific research had decreased over the past 10 years, and that more than four out of five felt that policymakers used science only to achieve their pre-established objectives. It was the kind of support that the anti-regulatory Congress needed to justify proposals to abolish the U.S. Geological Survey, the National Biological Service, and the U.S. Bureau of Mines, as well as to substantially reduce the budgets of other federal agencies, most notably the National Oceanic and Atmospheric Administration. Interior Secretary Bruce Babbitt likened these proposals to "book burning."

While they never did come to fruition, on September 30, 1995, Congress did abolish the non-partisan Office of Technology Assessment (OTA), a 23-year-old executive branch agency whose mission was to assist Congress in dealing with the increasingly complex technical issues that affect society. While the public justification for doing so was that OTA guidance was not timely enough to inform pending legislation, and that the information they provided could be secured from other sources, the action seemed inconsistent with Congress' own stated principle. As Robert T. Watson,

Associate Director for the Environment at the White House Office of Science and Technology Policy, said in an interview: "The Hill is asking [the Houses of Congress] to look at comparative risk and cost–benefit analysis . . . good ideas basically . . . But comparative risk and cost–benefit analysis require good knowledge, good science, and good technology . . . In eliminating OTA, Congress cut the only independent, bipartisan scientific and technical group that provided effective advice for comparative risk."[4] By this action, Congress had, at least on the surface, raised questions about its own commitment to "sound science."

Those questions became even more pointed when, on the heels of the demise of OTA, the Subcommittee on Energy and Environment of the House of Representatives Committee on Science convened a series of three hearings on "Scientific Integrity and Public Trust: The Science Behind Federal Policies and Mandates."[5] Subcommittee Chairman Dana Rohrabacher and Committee Chairman John Doolittle, in their introductory remarks, said that the purpose of the hearings was to examine the question of whether the nation was "getting objective science from our regulatory agencies." It was transparent that the majority had as their agenda the undermining of the science that had, in fact, already gone into federal policy in the areas of stratospheric ozone, global climate change, and dioxin contamination, the subjects of the three hearings. These hearings not only broadened the scope of the attack on environmental science from the narrow regulatory issues associated with cost–benefit analyses to more global ones, but set forth the central line of attack that Congress and its anti-environmental constituencies would level at EPA for the remainder of the decade and beyond—that overzealous regulators were squandering public dollars on a politically driven agenda. As Representative George E. Brown, Jr., former Chair of the Science Committee and ranking Minority member on the Committee, described in his report in response to the hearings:

> They [the Subcommittee] implied that scientists themselves were part of a vast conspiracy with environmental regulators. The terms of the pact were that the scientists would exaggerate their certainty and consensus on environmental problems and the bureaucrats could use these statements, with help from their environmental activist allies, to push through ever more stringent regulations and ever greater funding for the researchers. Bureaucrats were funding science that justified their existence and scientists sold their integrity to the bureaucrats in exchange for steady funding.[6]

As one of the House's few science experts, Congressman Brown felt compelled to issue a sharp rebuttal to the Majority's claims. His report attacked the explicit mistrust of government science displayed in what were advertised as fact-finding hearings. It also exposed what to Congressman Brown was perhaps the report's most curious charge—that the views of scientists out of the mainstream of scientific thought were not allowed to influence policy decisions, implying "that scientific truth is more likely to be found at the fringes of science than at the center."[7] Brown saw this as a "disturbing repudiation of the scientific process and peer review . . . inimical to a constructive role of science in policymaking." Further, he saw the hearings themselves as advancing the dangerous notion that a Congressional committee could in fact serve as a science court capable of determining scientific truth through testimony and questions, thus promoting the very politicization of science that the committee was condemning.[8] Finally, Brown's report took exception to what he regarded as the overall message of the hearings—that "sound science is empirical science," implying that statistical analysis and models are "speculation," and that sound science resides exclusively in empirical fact or observational data.[9]

The hearings and the response they engendered have had little discernible effect on policymaking. But they do throw into bold relief the essential arguments of both sides in the debate over how science has been, and should be, used in the policymaking process. The Congressional majority, representing not only their own ideological disposition but the many business and commercial constituencies opposed to environmental activism have tried to exploit the inherent "weaknesses" of science as a policy tool. They principally exploit its inability to provide the certainty that lawmakers claim they need to impose financial and social burdens on the public. Absent this certainty, the underpinnings of those policies are, in their mind, reduced to mere hypothesis and speculation or, worse, hyperbolic claims of fear-mongers who would capture government and commit it to their "save the world agenda." Environmentalists, on the other hand, argue that, when it comes to phenomena like global climate change and stratospheric ozone depletion, or even the epidemiological consequences of exposure to air pollutants or pesticides, definitive conclusions are impossible, and to require certainty as a precondition to action is but a thinly veiled attempt to stifle regulatory activity altogether.

In what may well have been an attempt to save face, Speaker Gingrich commissioned the House Science Committee to review the country's science policy, specifically to write a sequel to the 1945 report, "The Endless Frontier," which had guided U.S. science policy for decades. In September of 1998, the Committee released its report, "Unlocking Our Future: Toward a New National Science Policy." While its main recommendation is for the U.S. to commit to stable and substantial funding for basic research, it does touch on the hot-button issue of peer review in specifically trying to fund "creative . . . speculative" studies that wouldn't be likely to be peer reviewed. Perhaps more significant, Congressman Vernon Ehlers, the principal author of the report, joined with 90 of his colleagues in co-sponsoring a bill to establish a National Institute for the Environment under the National Science Foundation, dedicated to improving the scientific basis of environmental decisionmaking. The Institute was not created legislatively, but it was brought under the umbrella of the National Science Foundation as the National Council on the Environment in February 2000, and later reconstituted as the National Council on Science and the Environment, where it is currently pursuing its core mission to "improve the scientific basis for environmental decision making."

For all the homage paid to science in the legislative process, it is at the regulatory level—principally at EPA—that science actually plays its most significant role. In fact, the credibility of rules and regulations depends upon the public confidence that our laws are being administered in observance of the best and most rigorous scientific principles. But, again, that expectation is not, and cannot, be fully realized.

First, EPA is not a scientific agency. Its principal charge is not to determine how best to attack environmental problems or even which problems to attack, but to implement and enforce Congress' mandates. Though it does maintain scientific offices and advisory boards and committees, its statutory obligations take precedence over the generation or evaluation of new information. Accordingly, EPA employs more attorneys than scientists, and its decisions are based as much on economic, political, or administrative considerations as purely scientific ones. Finally, because of the tight deadlines imposed by Congress to carry out the laws, its regulatory agenda cannot drive its research agenda, making it heavily dependent upon the science developed outside, rather than inside, the agency—some from consultants, some from previously developed research, and some from either the environmental community or the regulated community itself.[10] The inability of science to provide definitive and precise answers to many regulatory questions has led both Congress and EPA to seek political protection in increasingly prescriptive technology based standards, which identify both the ways those standards are to be achieved as well as the standards themselves. All of this makes EPA justifiably vulnerable to claims that its decisions rest on shaky scientific foundations.

The Courts' Struggle with Science

Though the political role played by courts is discussed more fully elsewhere in the text, it is appropriate to briefly mention the challenge that environmental science poses to the courts. In most ways, the courts are like legislatures, i.e. they are faced with specific cases that need prompt resolution; they cannot wait indefinitely for definitive information. Like legislatures, the judicial standard for decisions, except in criminal cases, is "preponderance of the evidence," closer to the 51% majority required to pass legislation than the 95% agreement among peers that scientists require to establish a scientific fact. Further, like legislators, judges and juries are faced inevitably with the prospect of sifting out the truth from a series of question-and-answer sessions with equally credentialed experts on opposite sides of the issue. Like their counterparts in the legislature, the judges are scientific laymen and thus largely incapable of arbitrating technical disputes.

Though courtrooms are no better suited than committee rooms to resolve scientific issues, the Republican Platform of 1996, in its section on "restoring justice to the courts," commits its party to "[e]liminate 'junk science' by opportunistic attorneys, by requiring courts to verify that the science of those called as expert witnesses is reasonably acceptable within the scientific community . . ." While the pledge addressed the political objective of minimizing or eliminating huge monetary awards like those enjoyed by plaintiffs in some recent high-profile cases, it is unrealistic to expect courts to be scientific referees. Proposals to establish specific courts to hear environmental cases, and to provide their presiding justices with specialized training in relevant subject areas, have not been adopted. The practical problems have seemed overwhelming, and the results far from assured. For both the legal system and the lawmaking process, an overriding concern is a social stability that derives from consistency of policy, which pure science cannot promise. As one critic put it, "science policy" is an oxymoron. And so the courts, though largely free of partisan pressures, also struggle to incorporate "sound science" into their decisions for most of the same reasons as their counterparts in the legislative and executive branches of government.

Science and the Media

The political role of science in public policymaking is by no means confined to the halls of government. The relationship between science and the media is as problematic as that between science and lawmakers. Scientists are commonly distrustful of journalists. Again, it's a question of incompatible missions. Because of the primacy of "newsworthiness" in the world of communications, what the media hope to get from scientists are breakthrough developments, pioneering findings, significant firsts, and bold predictions of significant consequences attendant upon environmental conditions or threats. But, of course, the cautious, plodding, tempered pace of science seldom provides journalists with what they want, and scientists are generally not given to public pronouncements.

Because the public gets virtually all their scientific information as well as their environmental guidance from the media, and because scientists who do want to affect public policy most often speak to lawmakers through the media rather than directly, the split between scientists and journalists has serious political consequences.[11] Despite the best intentions of people on all sides of the issues, science has not had an easy time constructively informing national policies. The incongruity of missions is only one relevant factor, however. Again, like lawmakers, journalists generally do not have the training and experience to understand the technical language of science, and scientists are often reluctant to provide them with explanations for fear that the nature and significance of their work will be oversimplified, and presented out of context. Further, editors and producers, if not journalists, see themselves not as educators but as chroniclers, and thus refuse to serve as publicists for research work. Therefore, an uneasy truce prevails between scientists and journalists and the public is left to sort out what is relevant and meaningful to them.

Of course, there is no shortage of offers to help the public reach its own conclusions on scientific matters related to policy issues. It is no doubt unfair and unproductive to speak of "the media" as if they constituted a monolith. While major city newspapers, general circulation magazines, and national networks must appeal to broad, general audiences, "the media" include, as well, a wide range of publications across the ideological spectrum that participate actively in environmental politics. And the broad media outlets welcome them, since they engage in just the kind of conflict that makes for lively disputes.

One of the most politically active of such publications has, surprisingly, been *Science*, the official organ of the American Association for the Advancement of Science. While its articles are invariably of high quality, peer reviewed and policy-neutral, it has not been hesitant in its editorials and in its letters column to give vent to a whole range of opinions on political issues. Its first agenda item, as might be expected, is to advance the role of science in public policymaking, and several of its columns in recent years suggested ways to do that.[12] But individual columnists, and any number of letters to the editor, have critiqued both ill-advised applications of science in public policy, and the "flight from reason" that critics of science display.

Clearly to the right of Science are the house organs, newsletters, and research papers of a number of think-tanks and foundations promoting free enterprise and unregulated markets—the Cato Institute, the Heritage Foundation, the Reason Foundation, and the American Enterprise Institute, to name but a few. They provide a platform for out-of-the mainstream scientists with estimable credentials and, usually, university affiliations, but whose work is nevertheless rarely peer reviewed. S. Fred Singer, President of the Science and Environmental Policy Project, is the most visible and influential of these since the death of Dixie Lee Ray, a former governor of Washington State, Chair of the Atomic Energy Commission, and a member of the zoology faculty of the University of Washington. Despite these credentials, in her subsequent work, she championed a counter-science movement that discredited generally acknowledged environmental concerns as "hysteria." A cadre of Singer's colleagues, e.g. Robert Balling, Hugh Elsaesser, Richard Lindzen, and Patrick Michaels, constitute a group of prolific scientists who consistently challenge the proponents of environmentalism and whose work is consistently picked up in the editorial pages of big newspapers and on talk shows like that of Rush Limbaugh.

The environmental community also has its own organizational support. Two of the more well known of these are the Union of Concerned Scientists and the Physicians for Social Responsibility. Each of these has attracted a strong scientific membership—some among the most prominent in their fields. Yet their activist policy disposition is transparent, and influences other professionals in the field as well as the general public.

It should be noted that each side has reinforced its policy positions— and rebutted those of its antagonists—in greater detail in a number of popular science books. Dixie Lee Ray's *Trashing the Planet* and *Environmental Overkill*, Ronald Bailey's anthology *The True State of the Planet*, Michael Fumento's *Science Under Siege*, John Baden's anthology *Environmental Gore*, and Ben Bolch and Harold Lyons' *Apocalypse Not*, have gained the most publicity as anti-environment science tracts. Counter-pointing them have been books such as Barry Commoner's *Making Peace with the Planet*, Paul Ehrlich's *Betrayal of Science and Reason*, and a spate of works published under the auspices of the Worldwatch Institute. Science has been the target of the right and a weapon of the left in a continuing media war for the public mind.

Given the respected reputation of science in general among the populace, it is not science itself but its exploitation that is the issue between the two camps. Each accuses the other of misusing, even abusing, science to serve its own agenda. It is therefore not surprising that a term for science appropriated for political purposes has gained currency in this climate— "junk science." Used as early as the mid-1980s by the U.S. Department of Justice in an unrelated context, it entered the public lexicon with respect to environmental issues in 1989 and in the early 1990s, and has continued to be an epithet routinely hurled by both pro- and anti-environmental interests across the ideological divide of environmental activism. The Washington Legal Foundation, one of the think-tanks whose mission is to promote free enterprise and less government, defines junk science as "phony science concocted to further activist regulatory agendas and profitable litigation."[13] The Union of Concerned Scientists, on the other hand, has defined it as "the 'data' and 'research' that some corporate interests and radio talk show hosts have been force-feeding America."[14] There is even a popular website, junkscience.com, whose motto is "All the junk that's fit to debunk," an obvious spoof of the *New York Times'* "All the news that fit to print." The site is a collection and exposé of what it regards as claims of phantom or exaggerated risks appearing in the popular media, and its creator and editor, Steven Milloy, an adjunct scholar with the Cato Institute, not only manages the site but writes editorials both for the site and for a variety of newspapers mocking the ungrounded fears environmentalists generate and their motivations. The website has already spawned a companion site, NoMoreScares.com, "dedicated to following the misanthropic adventures of Fenton Communications," the public relations firm retained to publicize such highly volatile issues as those surrounding Alar, silicon breast implants, bovine growth hormone, and endocrine disrupters. More significantly, Milloy now has an established link with a national network. He writes a regular Internet column for the Fox News website.[15] Junk science has apparently established a place on the media mainstream.

Obviously, the term "junk science" does not disparage science itself, but it does indicate how sensitive the competing sides in the environmental wars are to claims that science is on the side of their opponents. By disparaging the sponsors and motivations of the scientific findings ostensibly supporting their antagonists' proposed policy directions, the two sides hope to knock the props out from under each other's position, and pre-empt to the extent possible any public support for action based on their scientific assertions.

Underpinning the charge that science and scientists are policy driven is that science has no constituency of its own. Most scientists are reluctant to have their credibility compromised by political involvement and much of their work—and funding—have historically come from the necessarily secretive defense sector. But when defense as a national priority receded and environmental issues concomitantly rose to the fore, scientists looked to new sources of support. A substantial number, of course, work for the government as employees or by contract, for academic institutions with government grants, or by heavily regulated industries. In none of these capacities can their work be considered policy neutral. The fact that a large percentage of the funding for science in general, and for environmental science in particular, comes directly or indirectly either from government sources or from those regulated by government is sufficient to give credence to the competing claims of anti-environmental interests that science is being put to activist purposes, and of the environmental community that corporations and their hired scientists seek to roll back regulations.

It is because of these circumstances that scientists find themselves in a precarious position. On the one hand, they want to publicly establish themselves as experts in a relevant field of research and thus be considered for research grants and projects. On the other hand, prematurely going public with scientific conclusions may put them substantively at odds with institutional policies or industry positions that would disqualify them from those very same opportunities. Still, the paucity of sources of income from purely dispassionate research as well as public pressure to come down from their ivory towers to help solve problems increasingly pressure scientists to communicate more through public vehicles. Dorothy Nelkin may have put the resolution best: "Scientists ventriloquate through the media to those who control their funds." Whatever the perils, increasing numbers of scientists are recognizing the importance—personally as well as professionally—of talking to the media and making themselves available to policymakers. Their political isolation is grudgingly coming to an end.

Public "Uncertainty"

Science also faces challenges in enlisting the support of the general public at whom all these appeals are directed. The uncertainty at the source of its alienation from lawmakers and the media no doubt unnerves the public as well, who encounter it in their daily lives. The latter years of the 20th century witnessed a see-sawing of scientific opinion duly noted in the press on such matters as the threats posed by radon, by dioxin, and by MTBE (the gasoline additive required to meet Clean Air standards), each of which was downgraded and upgraded by turns as a genuine environmental threat. On an even more mundane level, there have been decades-long debates over the relative environmental impacts of brown paper and plastic grocery bags, of Styrofoam and paper beverage cups, and of cloth and disposable diapers. It is hardly surprising that a public that can't seem to get definitive answers to superficially simple scientific issues would question science's ability to understand global phenomena scores of years before their manifestation.

Of course, scientists are not that uncertain about radon, or dioxin, or MTBE, and can surely help us with our everyday environmental choices. But their answers, which are usually relative to the medium and duration of exposure, or the environmental problem to be alleviated, are not welcomed by a citizenry that is by and large scientifically illiterate, and not receptive to less than black-and-white responses. The one sphere that politics continues to prevail over substance is in the environmental wars. Another is technology's ability to detect pollutants in microscopic concentrations in air or water samples, which creates anxiety in the public because the presence of these pollutants often exceeds our capacity to remove them. Public perceptions of risk are thus skewed, leading to the situation whereby politically unacceptable risks get funding priority over real ones. Finally, simply as a matter of human psychology, the public is predisposed to overrate risks that are imposed upon them by external forces, and underrate those deriving from activities in which they voluntarily engage. In such cases, scientific information is pre-empted.

Further complicating the public's response to environmental science is their view of scientists themselves, a view colored by the almost invariable portrayal of scientists in movies and on television as strange, antisocial, "nerdy," if not outright sinister, types.[16] This characterization of scientists may well derive originally from *Frankenstein*, the immortal embodiment of science gone mad. The image of this monstrous creation still lives in the subliminal mind of the public and thereby serves as a constant reminder of the dangers of unfettered science and the need to enlist its services only with the utmost of caution.

The Precautionary Principle

Finally, it is appropriate to note that the previous century ended on an arguably optimistic note. A protocol for addressing the most thorny issue in environmental policymaking—whether and how to address problems that have not yet fully manifested themselves, or whose causes have not yet been definitively identified—was formulated. As has been discussed, those whose products and activities pose potential harm to public health and the environment have had some success in forestalling government action to address those threats by exploiting the scientific uncertainty we have been talking about. Specifically they have argued that in the absence of a convincing determination that those products or activities do in fact cause the alleged harm, public action to meet them would be, in many if not all cases, a ghost-chasing endeavor, squandering public and private funds, and diverting attention from known serious risks. To the environmental activists' warning that it is "better to be safe than sorry," the regulated community has retorted, "if it ain't broke, don't fix it."

This problem is a serious one, and there are solid grounds for both arguments. Surely there have been any number of alleged risks over the years that have failed to materialize—those from electromagnetic fields come immediately to mind—and public policy ought not to be held hostage to the claims of any single scientist, or any single study, that purports to identify an environmental situation that merits a public response. That would indeed carry caution to an unreasonable extreme, and have the effect of misallocating our finite fiscal and personnel resources. On the other hand, environmental interests have moved regulators to deal with some problems where they could credibly argue that waiting for scientific certainty to be established would preclude our ability to solve them at all because the potential harm was irremediable, as was the case with strip mining. As the scope and consequences of environmental problems grow, and as our detection systems become ever more sophisticated, this problem has become all the more intractable.

The protocol that promises to help resolve this dilemma is the Precautionary Principle. The Precautionary Principle, in concept born in Germany in the 1970s, was introduced in 1984 at The First International Conference on Protection of the North Sea and was given formal expression at the 1992 United Nations Conference on Environment and Development, to which the United States was a signatory. It progressively gained currency as the means to arbitrate the debate over when and if to act in the kinds of situations when waiting would be disastrous. While it has had only limited application in the United States, most notably in the 1990 Massachusetts Toxic Use Reduction Act, this principle constitutes an important component of over a dozen international treaties and laws, including the Montreal Protocol on Substances That Deplete the Ozone Layer (1987), The United Nations Framework Convention on Climate Change (1992), the Maastricht Treaty of the European Union (1994), and the Cartegena Protocol on Biosafety to the Convention on Biological Diversity (2000), which governs the international trade in genetically modified foods.

The prevailing definition of the Precautionary Principle is as follows: "When an activity raises threats to the environment or human health, precautionary measures should be taken, even if some cause-and-effect relationships are not fully established scientifically. In this context, the proponent of an activity, rather than the public, should bear the burden of proof [of the safety of the activity]." This definition was agreed upon by a group of activists, scientists, lawyers, legislators, scholars, and treaty negotiators convened at the Wingspread Conference Center in January, 1998 by the Science and Environmental Health Network, a consortium of more than four dozen environmental organizations dedicated to promoting the use of science to protect the environment and public health. The conference was organized in response to the several different practices and principles floating around under the "precautionary" umbrella.[17]

A few points about the principle ought to be noted at the outset. Its most salient feature is that it shifts the burden of proof from a prospective regulator to the party conducting the questionable activity or creating the potentially harmful product, a burden currently borne in the United States only by the pharmaceutical industry. But the "precautionary measures" it condones are not simple bans, or restrictions, or moratoria. Rather they are more anticipatory than remedial in nature. The kinds of questions that the precautionary principle would dictate are: "How much contamination can be avoided? What are the alternatives to this product or activity, and are they safer? Is this activity even necessary?" Ideally, questions regarding safety would be raised and answered at the earliest possible stages. In essence, the precautionary principle is almost indistinguishable from "pollution prevention," another protocol that has achieved wide acceptance following the enactment of the Pollution Prevention Act of 1990, whose guiding rationale is that products and processes be designed so as to minimize the pollution they produce in the first place rather than worry about minimizing their adverse effect on the environment after use.[18] The precautionary principle is, thus, a more nuanced strategy than those that have traditionally been adopted in response to alleged potential threats, where

the more conventional regulatory tools—particularly risk assessment—
have been employed. Here, the purpose is not to decide how much risk is
acceptable given the benefits, but whether the risks themselves can be
averted.

Because its most dramatic consequences are prospective and because its
causes are multiple even though its imminence is beyond serious question,
global climate change seems to be precisely the kind of problem that the
precautionary principle was designed to address. Yet the principle has
played almost no role in the policy deliberations over whether or how to
deal with it. Had the precautionary principle enjoyed wider support in the
United States these past several years, climate change would almost surely
not have become the lightning rod that it has. The spirit of the protocol
may well partly account for the fact that climate change is taken a good
deal more seriously abroad, and the world's other major industrial nations
are more receptive to taking actions to mitigate it. Political pressures from
the international community for the U.S. to join in the effort have continued to mount. What effect those pressures will have in this country,
however, will be the result of battles between competing interest groups,
not the consensus of a disinterested body of scientific experts.

Right Turn

The battle over global climate change is only the most prominent and
widely publicized of a whole host of issues that have brought scientists out
of the shade of their laboratories and classrooms and into open conflict
with the White House. In fact, a broad range of scientists, in a variety
of forums and media, have unsparingly damned the George W. Bush
Administration for at best ignoring, at worst distorting and misrepresent-
ing, science in order to advance personal ideological goals. Unprecedented
in scope and nature, their charges merit detailed exposure.

In February of 2004, the Union of Concerned Scientists (UCS) issued a
report signed by 60 leading scientists, 20 of whom are Nobel Laureates,
who charged the Bush administration with manipulating "the process
through which science enters into its decisions." More specifically, it
alleges that the administration has placed people professionally unqualified
or who have clear conflicts of interest in official posts or on scientific
advisory committees; disbanded existing advisory committees; censored
and suppressed reports by the government's own scientists; and failed to
seek independent advice.[19]

Two months later, in terms even more harsh, the editors of the pres-
tigious *Scientific American* compared Bush's policies to those spurning gen-
etics in favor of Lysenkoism in the 1930s, and further asserted that the
administration "disdains research that inconveniences it."[20] In October, an
extensive *New York Times* piece examined in detail the politicization of

science, explaining why 48 Nobel laureates justified endorsing John Kerry: "Unlike previous administrations . . . the Bush administration has ignored unbiased scientific advice in the policy making that is so important to our collective welfare."[21] And the American Civil Liberties Union (ACLU), in its own report on the corruption of science to serve political ends, reviewed government policies and practices that "have hampered academic freedom and scientific inquiry since September 11, 2001."[22]

If the Union of Concerned Scientists, the editors of *Scientific American*, the ACLU, and the *New York Times* could be written off as biased by reason of their having generally taken positions in opposition to White House policy, the same cannot be said of the American Association for the Advancement of Science, which is almost universally accepted as a nonpartisan forum for science. At its national meeting in February 2005, the Association decried FY 2005 budget cuts for basic research and investment in education to train future scientists, along with reciting many of the same complaints lodged by the UCS and the *Scientific American*.

The Union of Concerned Scientists followed up its initial report with another one two years later. Like its predecessor, it laments the misrepresentation of data for political reasons, and urges the restoration of scientific integrity in government policy. But this one was signed by 10,000 researchers, including 52 Nobel Laureates.[23]

Finally, another diverse group of scientists in various fields, science educators, and science writers launched a website—Defend Science!—in the summer of 2005. Its mission statement, like those of the previously cited critics, is to defend science from attacks of "powerful forces in and out of the Bush administration, who seem all too willing to deny scientific truths, disrupt scientific investigations, block scientific progress, undermine scientific education, and sacrifice the very integrity of the scientific process itself—all in the pursuit of implementing their particular agenda." Defend Science! sees the underlying agenda as that put forward by fundamentalist religious forces with influence in Washington.[24] Signatories of this mission statement include 2,000 science professionals and 100 members of the National Academy of Sciences.

The scientific community, then, has spoken out over the past half-dozen years with a single voice against its exploitation by ideologues and the misrepresentation and distortion of its findings by an administration with an agenda that is frustrated by free inquiry. The relationship between lawmakers and scientists has accordingly deteriorated into rancor, and the selfsame scientists who institutionally seek isolation from public affairs find themselves unwittingly immersed in politics.

But while their list of complaints is long and diverse, it is the administration's failure to take any significant action to address climate change that more than anything else has alienated scientists. The nascent and prospective consequences of global climate change have already achieved the 95% threshold of agreement among peers that science regards as the criterion for scientific fact. Only the threats of lead, asbestos, and tobacco have justified an unchallenged change in environmental policy. It has taken the George W. Bush administration's deliberate efforts to cloud the definitive results of climate research with propagandistic claims of uncertainty, and especially in light of the likely and soon irremediable catastrophic consequences of that indifference, to motivate the scientific community to participate in public policy formulation and put politics itself under siege.

Central Ideas

It is generally acknowledged that environmental policies ought to be guided by sound science, but the scientific process and public policymaking are fundamentally incompatible. This does not stop the combatants in the policy wars from exploiting science for their own ends. The principal obstacle to a decisive role for science in policymaking has been the tentativeness and uncertainty of its conclusions. But the scientific consensus that has been built to affirm the significance and potentially catastrophic consequences of climate change has brought scientists into a more vocal, prominent, and unaccustomed role.

Chapter 9

The Media Business

> For science, objectivity is tentativeness and adherence to evidence in the search for truth. For journalism . . . objectivity is balance. In the epistemology of journalism, there is no truth . . . there are only conflicting claims, to be covered as fairly as possible, thus tossing the hot potato of truth into the lap of the audience.
>
> (Peter Sandman)

> There is a tension between the scientific culture of caution and reticence and the media's penchant for drama, dread, and debate that keeps the show lively and the audience tuning in.
>
> (Stephen H. Schneider)

Journalists are almost invariably disturbed by any allegation that they are political. By and large, members of the mainstream news media see themselves as disinterested purveyors of information, and their professional code regards bias as heresy.[1] But in a complex way, the mainstream media have been, and continue to be, political. In no other area is this truer than in regard to the environment. They do not have an agenda to advance nor a particular set of environmental principles to promote. Yet by virtue of their intimate involvement in the debates among those who do, they play a significant, sometimes pivotal, role in forging public policies.

To call the mainstream news media political is not to suggest that print journalists, news anchors, and TV reporters—to say nothing of editors and producers—do not genuinely aspire to the estimable goal of dispassionate, objective communication. With few exceptions, they do. The reality is that the larger context of news in our society, the way it is produced, and the forces that shape it all pose formidable obstacles to the realization of their best intentions. And environmental issues, for a variety of reasons, make those obstacles almost insurmountable. This circumstance has far-reaching and profound implications for environmental policymaking, especially considering that the public that drives the environmental agenda is generally unaware of the limitations, discussed later, of the environmental reporting on which it depends, and which color its views of what is happening "out there."

Environmental journalism and the environmental movement virtually grew up together. We should not forget that Rachel Carson's *Silent Spring*, generally regarded as the clarion call to the modern environment movement, was first published in a magazine, the *New Yorker*, in 1961, and the shocked and dismayed reaction of its readers made the formal appearance of *Silent Spring* in book form a year later a literary event of major proportions. The story of *Silent Spring* was not only an important milestone in environmental journalism, but also, in many ways, a paradigm of the genre: the dramatic disclosure of the harmful, potentially lethal effects of a common practice imposed on an unsuspecting public by a powerful, indifferent industry. With only the details changed, this was the format for a story that would be told countless times in newspapers and magazines, and by the broadcast media, for decades.

At the core of the media's mission are two obligations—to inform their readers and viewers of events and circumstances that are important if not essential for them to know about; and to earn a profit, for press outlets and broadcast networks are, after all, businesses, and, as such, must maintain their economic viability. While these two mandates are by no means mutually exclusive, there is an inherent tension between them, and editors, publishers, and producers have had difficulty reconciling them.

The reconciliation was not difficult to achieve during the period from the late 1960s through much of the 1980s. The Love Canal and Times Beach chemical incidents, the Chernobyl and Three Mile Island nuclear malfunctions, the Santa Barbara and Valdez oil spills, and the toxic release at a Bhopal, India industrial plant—to name just a few—were all events of national, in one case international, significance that caused the death, illness, property damage, and/or relocation of thousands of people. They were blockbuster stories, and because most of America's population lives relatively near one or another factory, toxic or solid waste facility, nuclear power plant, potential oil drilling site, or other site that could pose the same or similar threats, they raised fears on the part of the public for their own safety and the security of their neighborhoods.

The media milked these events not only for their environmental implications, but also for their drama and dread, and, in so doing, drove the legislative agenda while increasing their own circulation and viewership. *Time* magazine rang in the 1980s with a cover story on the pervasive and growing threat of toxic chemical wastes,[2] and closed the decade by making "Endangered Earth" its "Planet of the Year."[3] *Time* was not alone in mining public anxiety over the environment. Even such stolid journals as the *National Geographic* asked on the cover of a special double issue, "Can Man Save This Fragile Earth?"[4] *Scientific American* published its own special issue on planetary ecological fragility,[5] followed a year later by a

New Republic issue on Earth's threatened condition, the cover of which pictured a greenish black funnel cloud bearing down on a lonely, helpless man.[6] And so the decade closed amid a barrage of apocalyptic soundings. It is not difficult to see why the principal catalyst for the halcyon days of environmental activism was the public's call for government action to protect them from the many ominous threats they were hearing so much about.

Fortunately, the disastrous events of 1970s and 1980s virtually disappeared in the 1990s, to be replaced by environmental issues that were more subtle, more technical, and more chronic than acute, though no less real and significant. Having raised public consciousness about environmental risks, the media were constrained to find—or, failing that, to generate—some of the same interest in such matters that the big events of the previous decades had commanded. These events "made news" by themselves. Subsequently, "making news" was left to writers, anchors, and production staffs.

Making Environmental News

These major disasters and foreboding circumstances earned the environment a place on the news agenda, alongside politics, finance, sports, entertainment, and health and consumer affairs. But absent such disastrous attention grabbers, the environment had to take its place in line, and fight for space and time against competing subjects. This meant that it had to become "news" in its own right. For the environment, this was, and remains, an especially challenging task, for almost every characteristic of most environmental issues goes against the grain of what has come to be regarded as "hot copy." The way environmental reporters have tried to meet this challenge has not only altered the nature of environmental coverage, but, in so doing, has drastically shaped the politics of the environment. Let us look now at how this has played out, and then examine some of its consequences.

Though the public's desire for a clean and safe environment has never wavered, as poll after poll has confirmed, its interest in media coverage of it waned at the turn of the century, if editors and producers are to be believed. In the minds of most of them, the environment went from nightmare to "snore," the word they use to characterize its newsworthiness.[7] Why are most environmental subjects so antithetical to engaging journalism? The reasons range from the limitations of the news genres themselves and the prevailing practices of news production, to the many demands they place on environmental reporters, to a professional ethic to which journalists are committed, to the pressures to craft stories coming from so many different sources.[8] Let's take up these factors one at a time.

First, it is almost axiomatic that, in an age of "infotainment" and short attention spans, any story has to engage the audience on more than an intellectual level. This was especially true as a steadily increasing percentage of the population gets their news from television and the Internet rather than newspapers. Television news has had to combine the traditional story line and relevance to the audience with strong visuals, which neither the Internet nor radio or newspapers could do to any substantial effect. Environmental events can satisfy these prerequisites—at least *certain ones* can—and that is where the media as political force have their origins.

Selecting News Stories

It might be best, then, to start with the criteria for what journalists call "newsworthiness," for if stories are not deemed newsworthy, they don't get into the press or on television in the first place, no matter how important they may ultimately prove to be. Journalism texts are pretty much agreed on the basic criteria.[9] A principal one is *conflict*. Where there is no conflict, there is no story line, and a narrative flow is an important element of contemporary journalism as it is a way to hold the diminishing attention spans of the viewing or reading public. The practice of conveying factual information through stories so as to engage the public and promote their understanding of otherwise "dry" material is called "narrative framing." It is often the "frame," not the incident or circumstance itself, that conditions the reader's or viewer's perceptions.[10] Indeed, the use of the word "story" to identify the genre is of relatively recent vintage. It was not so very long ago that what appeared under headlines in the newspaper were routinely called "articles," and their first paragraphs just as routinely answered the "five W's—who, what, where, when, and why." Today, they are almost always called "stories" and, accordingly, they begin, more often than not, anecdotally, with the introduction of particular people in a situation emblematic of the larger one that is the main subject of the piece. Such a change in treatment plugs into a number of the criteria of newsworthiness, but its principal achievement is to take what the readers may regard as academic, and make it into a mini-drama that they may someday find themselves involved in.

There is no shortage of conflicts in the environmental area, which is a principal reason that it can hold its own against sports, finance, and politics, provided, however, that the issues are chosen carefully and pitched the right way. The conflict between the rights of private property and government, for example, may be introduced by homeowners shocked to learn that they cannot build decks on their houses because they encroach on a wetland that has been identified and mapped since the house was built, while the battle between developers and environmental activists may well take the form of marchers protesting the siting of a major new subdivision in an area vulnerable to flooding. Conflicts between competing industries, between different segments of the same industry, and even between feuding scientists can be explored, but they are deemed more engaging to the reader if the history of how they developed, of who is in the middle of the fray, and of how it is likely to turn out is reported as well. But many big issues like the loss of biodiversity, overpopulation, and ozone depletion cannot be easily presented as conflicts and have no identifiable victims, nor are they readily cast as narratives, since their progression is, for all intents and purposes, imperceptible and their beginnings and endings highly speculative. That is why they do not get the copy that their significance merits. They are circumstances that must be revisited periodically as new information becomes available or as conditions change. There is simply no place in the newsroom milieu for tracking continuing developments.

Global climate change represents a unique case study of these factors. It was described by scientists more than three decades ago, and became a subject of intense concern in the late 1980s, as scientists generated pressure for government action and "focused the public's attention on potential remedies."[11] But like overpopulation, biodiversity, and ozone depletion, its progression until relatively recently seemed slow and undramatic, and its progenitors diverse and speculative. It failed to retain its currency as a media subject until the unexpected acceleration of its visible manifestations—some, like crumbling ice sheets, altered bird migration patterns, and stranded polar bears, starkly photogenic—have put it on the front burner of media outlets by the middle of the first decade of the 21st century. Cover stories on global warming in 2006 and 2007 in general circulation magazines were reminiscent of those on planetary peril in the 1980s. *Time* and *Newsweek* published issues with the same kind of apocalyptic soundings as their predecessors,[12] and *Newsweek* and the investigative journal *Mother Jones* devoted prominent coverage to dismissing climate change skeptics.[13]

Another criterion of newsworthiness is *novelty*. Again, the public is almost invariably attracted to the unusual and the bizarre, and less to conditions or circumstances to which they have become inured. This accounts, at least in part, for the great number of articles on genetically modified foods, for example, as opposed to the diminishing number on air or water pollution. *Timeliness* and *proximity* are other criteria. Whatever the substance of any particular concern, the public can be captured more easily by dangers or alleged risks that are present or impending, e.g. those posed by cell phones or microwave towers, than by those that are far off in distance or time. The public doesn't worry about threats too far into the future—witness their tentative acceptance of the reality of climate change in the face of a growing body of scientific evidence confirming predictions of impending cataclysm. Much the same can be said of threats posed to their own communities or lifestyles. Local news is clearly of more interest to them than threats far from home that have no immediate impact. This may well account in large part for the "domestication" of the policy agenda spoken of in the earlier chapter on legislative politics.

Public interest in media stories is also enhanced by *prominence*, by the involvement of celebrities. Actor Robert Redford's considerable allure has given credence to any number of environmental causes, and the Alar case from 1989 was much more widely publicized because of the active participation of Meryl Streep than it otherwise would have been. Actor Woody Harrelson's efforts on behalf of old-growth redwood forests and fellow actor Ted Danson's activities to raise public awareness about ocean water quality have brought public attention to otherwise silent causes. On the same theme, in the wake of the blockbuster movie *Titanic*, Leonardo DiCaprio, its star, made headlines as an ordinary citizen concerned about global warming, but his heavily advertised, eagerly anticipated interview with President Clinton was all but aborted because, in securing the interview, he upstaged the professional journalists who apparently could not generate comparable publicity for the issue.

More broadly, a whole cadre of entertainers have identified themselves with a wide range of environmental movements and causes, though whether their motives are public spirited or self-promotional is in some dispute. Formal organizational initiatives seek to capitalize on this phenomenon. The Environmental Media Association identifies itself as the premier organization of celebrities supporting the environment, whose mission was, in part, to get appropriate messages into films, television, and commercials.[14] Its awards program specifically recognized environmental messages in movies such as *Dances With Wolves, A River Runs Through It*, and *Free Willy*.

These criteria for "newsworthiness"—the dramatic, the new, the bizarre, the timely, the local, the glitzy—may or may not represent the ultimately most consequential threats or conditions, but they are, nevertheless, factors that determine what people read and hear about most frequently. Environmental issues suffer disproportionately by their application. The broad scope and reach of many significant environmental issues are often short-circuited, their issues oversimplified, and their effects trivialized by these criteria.

All this is not to suggest that social and environmental impacts are not themselves sufficient to "make news." Environmental happenings and circumstances that affect large numbers of people in serious ways do find their way onto the airwaves, but even such phenomena need to be carried by some element of immediate tangible consequence. For example, global warming began to secure increasing currency when it was arguably implicated in a drought or a flood, or when climatological statistics suggested that most of the hottest years in history were in the 1990s. Similarly, depletion of the ozone layer got fresh attention whenever an increasing incidence of skin cancer was reported. In short, the public seems to want their environmental stories to have some immediate relevance, or be of some practical consequence—"news you can use," so to speak.

Risk as Story

Quite beyond traditionally "newsworthy" events or situations are those that involve risk. They are especially difficult for the public to evaluate and for the media to communicate. Peter Sandman, a pre-eminent authority on risk communication, attempts to parse the nuances of this endeavor:

> The mass media are not especially interested in environmental risk. Reporters do care whether or not an environmental situation is risky: that's what makes it newsworthy. But once the possibility of hazard is established . . . the focus turns to other matters: how did the problem happen, who is responsible for cleaning it up, how much will it cost, etc. Assessing the extent of the risk strikes most journalists as an academic exercise. The reporter's job is news, not education; events, not issues or principles.[15]

The implications of this thesis are broad and significant. His studies concluded that "politics is more newsworthy than science." He finds proof of this position in the disclosures that risk coverage of hazardous events relied predominantly on government sources, substantially less on industry representatives, individual citizens and advocacy groups, and only minimally on experts. Put another way, the media prefer to get their risk information from people directly involved in the event, not uninvolved experts.[16]

Further, the media pursue their goal of "objectivity" in a balance of viewpoints, not in dispassionate expertise. It means giving both sides their chance to describe or evaluate the circumstance, and reporting accurately what they had to say. And the limited space or time allotments for their stories force them into either/or dichotomies—hazardous or safe, legal or illegal—not uncertain, complex judgments. This is one of the tendencies that alienate experts, whose views are more nuanced, and make them more reluctant to be cited as sources.[17]

Doris Graber, a prominent political scientist and mass communications expert, provides a somewhat different perspective on risk communication, but largely confirms Sandman's basic premise. The studies she cites find that, with respect to debates over global climate change and carcinogenic substances in the environment, expert opinion did not ultimately prevail. The scientific community's ambivalence about the efficacy of government actions to contain climate change led to a diminution of such efforts, and their testimony on toxic chemicals was deemed by the media to be too hedged to be convincing to the public. Environmental advocates, on the other hand, "make good storytellers." For these reasons, the disparity between the public's and experts' ranking of environmental threats varies significantly.[18]

Robert Cox finds an even more complex risk communication climate:

> while attempting to provide information about complex and serious hazards reporters and editors also must negotiate a thicket of journalistic norms: Is the story newsworthy? How shall it be framed? Will the story command the attention and interest of readers or viewers? Do sensational reports override substantive information?

The answers to these questions often skew priorities. Spectacular accidents garner disproportionate attention because of television's focus on visual images. Human interest displaces substantive health concern. The ambiguity and complexity of risk often overwhelm the reporter's, or the public's, understanding.[19] The media's reliance on government and industry allowed them to frame their respective stories to their advantage. "Government and industry were more likely to frame their accounts of risk in terms of official assessments and assurances of safety. On the other hand, members of the public spoke about environmental and health hazards . . ."[20]

The "Construction" of News Stories

What makes news is also conditioned by the form in which stories are cast, and the practices of newsroom production. Stories in the print media are presented in column inches, and on television in time slots—neatly delineated packages. While this factor constrains the presentation of any but the simplest subjects, it is especially fatal to most environmental problems, which are more often chronic than acute, and which commonly require scientific and/or economic background to be understood. Environmental stories are complicated, sometimes abstract and technical. The complex, inherently interdisciplinary nature of environmental issues does not easily accommodate itself to the space and time limitations of media presentation, nor are audiences prepared to give them the concentration they require, at least not when they are reading the newspaper or watching television.

Further, because of the necessary limitations on space or time in which they are presented, news stories are inevitably self-contained, discrete entities. This requires that they be "constructed" in the newsroom, that they be "framed," and, as they say in the business, given an "angle." Events that can be scheduled and pre-formulated have a leg up on those that can't. All these considerations obviously work to the disadvantage of environmental problems, since the most important are usually amorphous, have multiple rather than singular sources, and are rife with implications not only for the immediate situation at hand, but not infrequently for a host of large social issues, e.g. the proper role of technology, the relative demands of the economy and the environment, or the competing claims of social good and individual freedom.

Many of the same factors that make environmental subjects unattractive to media coverage impose enormous burdens on the environmental journalists themselves. First, environmental law is a huge and complicated labyrinth of statutes and regulations, beyond the grasp of the general public and all but the relatively few professionally involved in it. Explaining science to a lay public and making concepts like risk–benefit analysis accessible to the everyday reader or viewer are daunting tasks indeed.[21]

Second, the environment's interdisciplinary nature places unusual demands on reporters, so much so that there is a continuing debate over whether environmental journalists ought to be specialists, have their own beat, or at least have some training or special course work to prepare them for the myriad issues they will face. Such training would, presumably, enable them to understand and evaluate the information they get from the experts they interview in researching the stories. That element of their job is itself a challenge. There are, of course, the usual institutional sources to whom reporters can, and usually do, go to first—government officials with the relevant responsibilities and the appropriate politicians. But it is essential that they also seek out representatives of relevant private sector interests and of environmental organizations to fill out the story. Scientists also must be consulted when an issue warrants it. Each of these almost invariably brings his or her own interpretation of the problem or event, and it is the job of the journalist to tease out the hidden agendas from the facts. To ease the difficulty, journalists often build up a "rolodex" of trusted sources from whom they regularly seek out background and information. There rarely is enough time to examine a problem or event in detail and consult people with the relevant range of expertise, if they are so inclined.

The whole issue of sources introduces the factor most responsible for putting the media at the center of environmental politics, which is ironic because they have brought it upon themselves. As noted earlier, the journalism profession maintains, as an article of faith, the mandate of objectivity, or at least fairness, but pursuing that ideal has its consequences. In their effort to achieve balance, reporters are obliged to seek out, and publicize, the views of people on both sides of the issue at hand. (I use the word "both" advisedly, because the notion of a multiple number of sides in public disputes is atypical of Americans. As a society we tend to view things from a dual perspective—liberal or conservative, guilty or innocent, right or wrong, safe or dangerous.) In an effort to get "the whole story," journalists endeavor to be fair to all involved, which obliges them to report fully, and without editorial comment, what "both sides" say and think, however responsible or irresponsible—or isolated—a particular spokesperson may be. Thus, stories about environmental risk tend to represent opposing views rather than truths, leaving the determinations about the latter to the audience. Reporting the clash of views not only protects the journalist's claim to objectivity, but provides an element of conflict as well. Thus, even on issues where the weight of scientific opinion seems to be disproportionately on one side, conflicting versions of the truth are afforded virtually equal coverage. Again, global warming is a prime example. While the scientific community overwhelmingly regards the phenomenon as sufficiently real and serious to justify a comprehensive, systematic and deliberative public policy response, skeptics are routinely represented and quoted in virtually every story on it, thus giving the minority view equal coverage and weight.

The interest groups know all this, of course. Environmental organizations, whatever their honest appraisal of priorities, provide the media with a steady stream of scare stories about possible or prospective catastrophes, and thus keep the environmental pot boiling, as well as build their membership and contribution levels. The media, for all the reasons noted above, welcome them. Anti-environmental interests, even as they bewail the media's compulsive attraction to crisis, exploit the media for their own purposes. They know very well that reporters will present their opposing positions, however well founded, to *balance* the coverage. Thus, our newspapers and TV and computer screens serve as battlegrounds for dueling positions and ideologies on a wide range of environmental matters.

Superficially, there is nothing wrong with the media's serving as a forum for debates on environmental issues and happenings. Indeed, that is what they genuinely think they should be doing. But it should be obvious from the foregoing that the environmental subjects they choose to write about and, just as importantly, the terms in which they present them, engage their audiences in a profoundly emotional way. The public concern generated by such stories finds its way to their elected representatives, who take media stories quite seriously, however shaky their foundation. There is an historical correlation between environmental issues that have been regarded as high-profile and the body of environmental law enacted by Congress, though that correlation has been stronger when potentially cataclysmic events such as nuclear incidents, oil spills, and toxic releases generated the coverage. Absent of such events, the role of the media in setting the legislative agenda is less certain.

The relationship between legislators and the media is, in fact, somewhat complicated, and symbiotic. The media's constant surveillance of Congress is a fact of life that lawmakers have to be mindful of, and accommodate themselves to. Like private interest groups, they have to work within the media's characteristic communication envelope. Because the media are important to the Congressional agenda, legislators have increasingly sought more ways to publicize and promote their policy initiatives. The host of new technologies has been a boon to such efforts. Individual legislators have their own homepages, and local cable outlets are eager to host them at regular intervals. The political parties themselves have taken up the practice of preparing carefully structured issue memoranda for distribution to the media so that a consistent message is communicated. For their part, reporters depend on lawmakers and their staffs for information on prospective happenings. They need "sources" for their stories that are credible and timely. Thus, the media and the lawmaking community often work together in their mutual interest.[22] But beyond promotion of their specific legislative proposals, the two political parties try to exert influence by framing their cases in rhetorical terms as well.

The Battle Between Partisan Framers

At this point in environmental political history, it is appropriate—and revealing—to look at the great "framing war" that has been waged over the past half dozen years or so between linguists in the employ of the two political parties. Frank Luntz, Republican pollster and consultant for more than a decade, was enlisted to address what has been the principal electoral vulnerability of the Republican Party—environmental policy. It was Luntz that warned them that almost two-thirds of the nation's voters, and more than half of Republican voters, want Congress to more aggressively protect the environment instead of cutting regulations. To help the GOP cultivate a more environment-friendly image, he prepared a briefing book that set out a rhetorical strategy to be carried out in all their communications with the media.[23] As he sees it, the battle is as much over language as substance. Republican policies must be framed in non-threatening, simple, and positive language, not in the parlance of bureaucrats. The title of his memo, "The Environment: A Cleaner, Safer, Healthier America" itself embodies one of his core principles, that "safe, clean, and healthy" are "[T]he three words that Americans are looking for in an environmental policy." Much of his memo is a list of "dos and don'ts," but some general principles—"reinforce your sincerity and concern for the environment, set forth principles rather than policies, and emphasize shared rights and beliefs"—overarch the particulars, suggestions to make Republican positions more understandable and less threatening to the general public.[24]

To make matters interesting, the Democratic Party, and a number of environmental advocacy groups, have called upon their own wordsmith, George Lakoff, a teacher of Linguistics at the University of California at Berkeley, who himself has studied how political decisions are substantially the product of unconscious language frames to which we are subjected.

Unsurprisingly, many of his tenets are similar to Luntz's, though they derive from a wholly different metaphor. Like Luntz, he believes that language, not stronger positions, determines political winners. For example, the environment should not be spoken of as something "out there, separate from you." Rather it should be characterized as essential to our existence, vital to everything on earth. Environmental issues should be cast in terms of health and security, which people accept as desirable, not as abstractions.[25] "Thinking and talking about environmentalism in limited terms like preservation of wilderness is shooting yourself in the foot."[26] Both men, then, argue convincingly that how issues and policies are "framed" shapes how they are covered in the media, and, correspondingly, what policymakers perceive as priorities.

The forces shaping the selection and handling of environmental stories have other substantial political effects. It is a journalistic truism that "bad news drives out good news." For whatever psychological reason, people don't think that the communication of progress is "news." Thus, while new threats to the public health or environment quickly find their way into the public awareness, the real successes of programs designed to attack them do not. Thus the important but unspectacular improvements in air and water quality over the past several decades, reductions in solid and hazardous waste generation and improvements in their management, the achievement of significantly greater energy efficiencies across the board, and the *de facto* ban on nuclear power plant construction, to mention only a few examples, remain unacknowledged and unreported by the press and thus unknown to the citizenry. This not only distorts the public's perception of the state of the environment, but also implicitly undermines their perception of the effectiveness of government programs to solve environmental problems and manage risks.

Even more serious, media coverage that exaggerates minor risks in pursuit of the sensational and the bizarre diverts public attention and resources from real ones. Policymakers and regulators are continually frustrated by their having to allocate limited money and personnel in ways that they know are counter to good sense and good science in response to public perceptions and pressures, while more serious problems go underfunded. For example, the relatively minor health and safety risks posed by high-profile Superfund sites were systematically addressed at both the federal and state levels for more than a decade, and at great cost, whereas the more substantial, but clearly more low-key, threat of indoor air pollution was largely ignored. Time and time again over the past decade polls have graphically delineated the sharp disparities between what the public thinks is dangerous and what the experts think. This disconnect between perception and reality can be attributed only to the media stories that created these perceptions in the first place, and the consequences of these skewed priorities manifest in public policy are, of course, profound.

One more circumstance regarding media coverage of the environment merits mention, the consolidation of media companies and their acquisition by multinational corporations. This development has imposed additional commercial pressures on the media. Producers and editors now have to satisfy not only their historical audiences and sponsors, but stockholders as well. Again, this is a fact of life that most news areas have to deal with, but the threat to environmental reporting is perhaps more serious than to the reporting of other matters. As globalization takes hold, an increasing number of environmental issues take on international implications, and the transnational corporations have deep interests in how they are treated. The effects on U.S. environmental standards for international agreements like NAFTA and GATT, on its economy by treaties such as those signed at Rio de Janeiro and Kyoto, and on major biotech U.S. corporations like Monsanto, and of pacts such as that signed at Cartegena governing trade in genetically modified foods impose constraints. The corporate influence not only circumscribes the kinds of issues that may be taken up by the media, but it urges that they be framed in a less critical way. It is still another obstacle that environmental reporters have to steer around in covering the environment.

Everything in the culture of mainstream journalism, then, works against the responsible, comprehensive, and thoughtful presentation of environmental problems, circumstances, and developments. The prevailing criteria of "newsworthiness," the unique demands of newsroom practices, and increasing pressures from new interests like shareholders all contribute to an editorial policy framework that is inimical to the character of environmental issues. Few are inherently dramatic or newsworthy, and almost none comfortably fit into prescribed time slots or column inches. They are complicated, scientific or technical, and generally protracted. Their sources are multiple, their effects long-term, their underpinnings interdisciplinary. And their consequences frequently expose the financial interests of the very outlets that give them currency.

It is the synergistic effects of this set of circumstances and mandates that have inexorably drawn environmental journalists into the vortex of politics. Despite their best efforts to stay above the fray, environmental reporters have been understandably vulnerable to the persistent charge that they are "closet greenies." The factors described above predispose journalists to write about threatening events—some real, some exaggerated, some frankly non-existent—in an effort to attract audiences and satisfy commercial demands. In doing so, they have unwittingly served as the handmaidens of environmental interests. The media have thus constituted a conduit for environmental groups to Congress, for in publicizing these matters in the dramatic terms that they have, they have generated a level of public concern that policymakers have not been able to ignore. The media, then, have become a principal catalyst for an activist environmentalist agenda over more than five decades even as they have not recorded as faithfully as they could have the environmental gains achieved by that activism.

However strongly media coverage of the environment has influenced Congress, it has incurred the displeasure, if not the wrath, of two other interest groups. Scientists, who share some of the same obligations to the public as journalists but work in vastly different ways, often believe that the media misrepresent much of their work. According to a recent comprehensive survey, almost two-thirds of scientists think the media exaggerate the risks associated with various activities. Four out of five find the media more interested in "instant answers and short-term results"; and three out of four feel that "sensationalism" is more of a goal than scientific truth. These are no doubt the reasons that almost half prefer to avoid the news media altogether because they are suspicious of their motives. Again, one can see the hand of "newsworthiness" in shaping these attitudes, but the split with the scientific community it occasions has significant political implications, particularly when matters get to the policy stage. Not surprisingly, because of these attitudes, journalists are as unhappy with scientists.[27]

The Media and Anti-Environmentalism

Of equal political import, scientists' disaffection with the environmental media has been exploited persistently by the journalists' principal detractors —a loose consortium of anti-environmental interests comprising conservative economists and political scientists, "Wise Use" types, libertarian ideologues, conservative think-tank publicists, anti-government popular scientists, talk show hosts, and webmasters of environment-debunking websites. Despite their lack of authoritative credentials, these people and the larger philosophies or constituencies they represent are making careers out of opposing the government's historic and deep involvement in the environmental area. One even revived a journalism career by launching a glitzy and well-publicized attack on journalistic treatment of environmental issues in a national TV special. In it, ABC correspondent John Stossel characterized himself as a reformed sinner, a former consumer affairs reporter who earlier in his career exploited dramatic risk stories for their human interest, but since has come to see the error of his ways. His engaging production attributed the distorted priorities of our environmental polices to the triumph of fear over science and economics.[28] The anti-environmental forces enumerated above have sought to discredit prevailing environmental polices by discrediting the environmental media, painting them as "sky-is-falling" alarmists who seek out catastrophe for its marketability, and who generate needless and costly government action by foisting upon a fearful public, apocalyptic prophesies of doom.

That they can, and frequently do, enlist the testimony of a small cadre of sympathetic scientists in support of this indictment appears to make their case stronger.

Even as they chide the media for serving as shills for environmental groups, these anti-environmentalists are not above exploiting the power of the press themselves. For they also know that the media can be relied on to balance reports about dangers posed by new chemicals or technologies, or about the promise of proposed new laws, with their own opposing perspectives. After all, balance, not technical accuracy, is the overriding value, particularly for the regulated media such as radio and TV. And so, in the best traditions of both journalism and politics, these contrary voices are respectfully accorded "equal time."

So the mainstream environmental media have, inevitably, become deeply invested in politics themselves, Unlike the other interest groups taken up earlier in the book, they do not come to the table with any particular policy objectives. Rather, the communications climate in which they operate, the practices and mandates of their profession, and, perhaps most important of all, the commercial pressures to which they must always be responsive, clearly make them influential forces in the shaping of environmental policy, for better and for worse.

New Media Outlets

The mainstream media, over the past decade or so, have lost market share to Cable TV broadcasters and a host of independent stations and, with it, some influence over the public agenda, including the environmental agenda. Rapidly developing technology has been a major factor in this development. The proliferation of the Internet and the countless websites of the whole spectrum of political actors have displaced many of the network and newspaper and wire services as sources to which the public goes for their information. Of course, the environmental advocacy groups each have a homepage that presents carefully crafted arguments for their positions. Anti-environmental think-tanks and foundations, as well as business interests, challenge the advocacy groups for public support on their own sites. These are part and parcel of the clash of interests taken up in this book. But more general environmental education is the mission of other on-line services. Prominent among these are the "Environmental News Network" (www.enn.com), "Grist" (www.grist.org), the "Enviro-Link Network" (www.envirolink.org), and "Rachel's Environment and Health News" (www.rachel.org). "The Alternet" (www.alternet.org), while not devoted exclusively to environmental concerns, is only one of a spate of on-line services that take up public issues, but environmental issues are common subjects.

Also growing in popularity and influence are regional newspapers, such as *Appalachian Voices* and the [Chesapeake] *Bay Journal*, which publish extensive pieces on environmental matters relevant to their local audiences. Joining them are independent weekly newspapers in almost every major city. These newspapers, like the regional publications, target the issues relevant to their jurisdictions, but, again, environmental problems are frequently their subjects.[29]

Finally, most recently, we have seen the enormous popularity of documentaries. Al Gore's *Inconvenient Truth* and *The Great Warming* are both wake-up calls to the stark prospect of global climate change, and have been, by all accounts, influential in increasing public concern over this enormously significant phenomenon.

The gradual but inexorable drift from the mainstream media to a variety of new electronic and specialized print outlets is no doubt attributable to a number of social and economic factors. But, unlike the national networks and general circulation newspapers that have historically provided the public with their environmental news, the new outlets are not bound to the professional ethic of balance, objectivity, and fairness. Since they are not financially indebted to sponsors or corporate shareholders, they are free to advance unabashedly partisan positions. In fact, weeklies, and many regionals, are distributed free of charge. Nor are they constrained by space limitations; many weekly journal articles are very much longer than those most general newspapers can afford to run. And their audiences, especially in the case of websites, often choose them, so that readers come to the articles with more interest, substantive knowledge, and contextual understanding than the average person.

The new, balkanized public communications culture is now more open and accessible than ever before. Information and advocacy arguments flow in all directions, beyond the control of the relative few who "produced" the news in the last century. Whether or not this development will substantially alter the nature of the environmental debate or change environmental priorities remains to be seen. It is too early to tell if these new outlets will remain viable and grow in stature and support. What is true, however, is that they have complicated and enriched environmental policymaking.

Central Ideas

The ideal to which the media aspire is objective, non-advocacy reporting. Yet, by virtue of the criteria of newsworthiness, the practices of newsroom production, and the professional commitment to "balance," the media have become political actors. A complicated relationship with the science community, their obligations to their corporate owners and sponsors, and the technological complexities of communicating risk have made their jobs even more difficult. Yet they remain a force in agenda setting, so much so that the political parties have recruited professional linguists to help them with media presentation of their positions. During the past decade or so, new electronic and print outlets are challenging the mainstream for primacy as information centers and agenda setters.

Chapter 10

Federal Courts: A New Posture

> Cases presenting political questions are consigned to the political branches that are accountable to the people, not to the judiciary, and the judiciary is without power to resolve them.
>
> (Loretta Preska
> U.S. District Court Judge)

> EPA has offered no reasoned explanation for its refusal to decide whether greenhouse gases cause or contribute to climate change.
>
> (John Paul Stevens)

U.S. Supreme Court Justice

On April 2, 2007, the United States Supreme Court handed down its decision in *Massachusetts v. EPA*.[1] It is regarded by many observers as the most significant and far-reaching decision on an environmental issue in the Court's history. The decision came amid a flurry of lawsuits filed in federal courts around the country over the past several years addressing climate change in particular and, more generally, the myriad air pollution and energy issues related to that phenomenon. The lawsuits reflect impatience on the part of state governments, the plaintiffs in most of these cases, with the federal government's reluctance to address global warming in the face of the overwhelming consensus of scientists that it represents a potentially catastrophic threat. State plaintiffs have been further supported by the general public, who have become increasingly unsettled about global climate change by an uncommon number of severe weather events and a steady stream of media stories about its other potential consequences. The time for some definitive action was, as it is phrased in legal circles, "ripe."

But in this seminal case, the Supreme Court did more than some legal scholars thought was within its authority. The justices' ruling addressed not only the merits of the plaintiffs' request for relief, but, more relevant to this chapter, charted new political territory. The judiciary, like scientists and the media, regard policymaking as anathema to their sacred trust. Their formal responsibilities are principally to determine the constitutionality and scope of enacted statutes, evaluate the consistency of rules and regulations with their enabling statutory authority, and resolve jurisdictional disputes between branches of government. They enter the policy arena, if at all, at the back end of the policymaking process, upon the appeal of an aggrieved party—an administrative agency, an environmental group, a state or municipality—seeking relief from an allegedly unconstitutional statute or, more commonly, from a regulation that allegedly exceeds the scope of its enabling statute or abdicates the responsibility of an administrative agency to act.

Notwithstanding this superficially circumscribed responsibility, and the fact that they operate in accordance with strict procedural guidelines, courts do play a role in policymaking, and their decisions have policy implications. There is sufficient leeway in the language of most laws and rules to permit "interpretation," and a court's embedded ideological disposition affords it some latitude to rule as it will, as long as its decision is based on a legally actionable principle. Historically, courts have interpreted the laws and rulings in a variety of different ways. In a similar fashion, the EPA has, over the course of time, acted more or less strictly within the framework of its mission though it is required to follow any specific directive from its Administrator, who, unlike the line staff, is a partisan appointment. The results of court decisions vary; at times they have set or reshaped agency priorities, while in other cases, the court as acted so as to redefine the relationship between EPA and other agencies.[2] It is in another way, however, that the Supreme Court and, subsequently, lower courts have exerted their most pronounced policymaking influence in adjudicating the cases related to global warming in recent years, and that is through "defining the analytical basis for agency policies."[3] In agreeing to review *Massachusetts v. EPA*, in response to the formidable arguments brought forward by the defendants, and in crafting their ruling, the Supreme Court may well have charted an unprecedented, forceful policymaking role for itself and, ultimately, for the lower courts.

The Core Case

Massachusetts and a consortium of 11 other states, three cities, and a group of environmental advocacy organizations petitioned the Court to rule on two related issues: does the Clean Air Act of 1990 authorize the EPA to regulate CO_2 as a pollutant and, if so, did the EPA justifiably refuse to exercise that authority. Specifically, the plaintiffs pointed to EPA's failure in 2003 to order cuts in carbon emissions from new cars and trucks. Massachusetts and its co-plaintiffs prevailed on both counts. By a five to four majority, the Court ruled that the Clean Air Act of 1990 does, in fact, authorize EPA to regard CO_2 and other heat-trapping gases as pollutants and, further, that EPA must explain why it didn't, or couldn't, do so. Obviously the Court itself didn't mandate the regulation of the implicated substances; that would have clearly usurped the role of the administrative agency. But it did send EPA back to the drawing board to review and, if appropriate, alter its practices. The pressure the decision exerted on EPA has risen, not surprisingly, to the Congressional level. By the end of the year, Congress was already considering several bills addressing climate change.[4]

There is nothing unusual, or unorthodox, in this development. Court decisions have commonly proscribed regulatory practice and, in so doing, have prevailed upon Congress to clarify the obligations and practices of administrative agencies to resolve the contested issues. That is how the process often works. What is new and potentially precedent-setting is the Court's rationale for not only overcoming the legal obstacles to their reviewing the case in the first place but also how it worked its way through the novel and special challenges posed by this new environmental phenomenon.

Standing

Before the substantive issues of the case could be considered, the plaintiffs had to survive a procedural challenge: did they have standing? The requirement that parties seeking relief from a court have "standing" is one of the most difficult for environmental plaintiffs to satisfy. Under established doctrine, to demonstrate standing a litigant must claim a particular injury or injuries caused by an identifiable defendant's action or actions that can be redressed, or relieved, by the court. As one can readily see, these are difficult criteria for environmental plaintiffs to satisfy; environmental injuries are commonly broadly social and general, "caused" by a complex of factors from a variety of sources, only one of which may be implicated in the petition. In such cases, relief may require an impractical, or drastically uneconomic, remedy. One can also readily see that the planetary—and differential—impact of climate change on the world's population resulting from an untold number of sources emitting greenhouse gases and other heat-trapping emissions would make the procedural roadblock posed by standing seem almost insurmountable.

Fortunately for the environmental community, this hurdle was somewhat lowered by several cases over the recent decades, including the landmark Supreme Court case on standing, *Sierra Club v. Morton*.[5] In this case, the Sierra Club challenged a development near a national park. The court found that the Sierra Club, as a corporate entity, lacked standing, *but* that it may sue on behalf of any of its members who claimed that his or her interests were affected by the construction. Also pivotal was Judge William O. Douglas' prescient dissent in the case, which argued for standing for natural resources under threat. Douglas said:

> Contemporary public concern for protecting nature's ecological equilibrium should lead to a conferral of standing upon environmental objects to sue for their own preservation . . . The voice of the inanimate object . . . should not be stilled. That does not mean that the judiciary takes over the managerial functions from the federal agency. It merely means that before . . . priceless bits of Americana . . . are forever lost or so transformed as to be reduced to the eventual rubble of our urban environment, the voice of existing beneficiaries of . . . environmental wonders should be heard.

Douglas could have not written an opinion more pointedly supportive of the position of Massachusetts and the other petitioners. The qualification in the holding and Douglas' dissent in *Sierra Club v. Morton* no doubt provided grounding for the Court's decision to allow the case to go forward. In the face of fierce opposition from the Court's four conservative justices, who argued that the injuries claimed were too marginal and too speculative to "cause" that injury and make redress impossible, Justice John Paul Stevens, writing for the majority, held that the low-lying coastal areas of Massachusetts satisfied the injury requirement for standing, and that even modest reductions in emissions could ameliorate that damage.

Other Issues

Ironically, the substantive issues raised by the case were resolved with less dissension. EPA defended its decision to not regulate vehicle emissions on several grounds, which the Court dealt with individually. "The agency identified several factors that influenced its decision, including scientific uncertainty, unavailability of emission control technology, potential interference with foreign policy, and the belief that regulation . . . would address global warming in an inefficient, piecemeal fashion."[6] Of these, the thorniest was the scientific uncertainty surrounding claims about global climate change. As discussed in detail in Chapter 8, science's deliberate and time-consuming process, its standard of proof, and the invariable tentativeness of its conclusions, have always proven problematic to policymakers. So too have the sophisticated arguments and counter-arguments of scientists proven as challenging to scientifically illiterate judges as they are to most legislators. So problematic has this proven to be in an increasingly complex world that there have been proposals to create a judicial science court to resolve factual disputes, or to make special training in dealing with these issues available to judges.[7] In a light, but telling moment during oral arguments on the case, Justice Anthony Scalia, upon being advised that emitted CO_2 ultimately rises to the "troposphere," not, as he thought, the "stratosphere," said, "Troposphere, whatever, I told you before I'm not a scientist. That's why I don't want to deal with global warming, to tell you the truth." Justice Stevens no doubt fully appreciates the sophisticated challenges in utilizing science in formulating public policy. But he'd like proof in this instance: "If the scientific uncertainty is so profound that it precludes EPA from making a reasoned judgment as to whether greenhouse gases contribute to global warming, EPA must say so." In fact, EPA implicitly did the opposite when it acknowledged that a National Research Council report identifying a whole host of harms caused by climate change was an "objective and independent assessment of the relevant science . . ."[8] EPA had dug its own grave. Thus did the majority feel comfortable in remanding the matter back to EPA.

The majority summarily dismissed EPA's other rationales. It did not agree that automakers could not develop an economical and practical technology to minimize CO_2 emissions, affirmed that any foreign policy implications were matters for the State Department, and that any jurisdictional conflict with the Department of Transportation over the regulation of motor vehicles did not preclude their carrying out their environmental responsibilities. A less solidly founded aspect of their holding was related to the claim of EPA, supported by the Court's minority, that the promised relief of an automobile emissions reduction regulation would have a minimal, perhaps even negligible, effect on the advance of global climate change. Stevens dealt with that charge in an interesting way. Having granted standing to Massachusetts (the other plaintiffs carried along), he identified the "injury" as the damage wreaked by rising sea levels on its coast. He could thus conclude: "[A] reduction in domestic emissions would slow the pace of global emissions increases, no matter what happens elsewhere."

The Supreme Court's Aggressive Political Posture

In most ways, the Supreme Court's decision in the landmark global warming case, *Massachusetts*, et al *v. EPA*, et al (2007), represents something of a milestone in the Court's history. To be sure, in important ways, it performed its traditional responsibilities as a dispassionate arbiter of legal issues. It met, head on, the formidable procedural requirement of standing. It devoted much consideration to interpreting a federal statute—the Clean Air Act of 1990—and to examining why EPA, in failing to draft implementing regulations dealing with climate change, ignored the mandate of the Environmental Policy Act of 1969 to scrutinize and evaluate its consequences. It took up, successively, the claims not only of the EPA but also those of other respondents with substantive interests in the case's resolution. Finally, in returning the matter in dispute to EPA for further consideration, the court effectively disdained a policymaking role, and allowed the agency room to come to the same policy position if it could justify it on stronger grounds.

But in important ways, the Court participated in a policy debate. It clearly stretched one of the established criteria of standing to bring in a group of states and allowed Massachusetts to serve as an aggrieved party for them all, relying on a theory propounded 100 years ago.[9] It stretched other standing criteria as well, relying on a dissent in a 1972 case to allow "inanimate objects" a voice and to interpret an upset of the Earth's ecological equilibrium as a litigable injury. Finally, it found the broad, general environmental injury imposed by scores of sources and therefore not readily remediable globally, not sufficient to deny standing. It facilitated this ruling by narrowing the injury to a particular piece of vulnerable Massachusetts real estate.

And, finally, by accepting the prevailing scientific consensus as fact, or at least factual enough to hold EPA accountable, it surmounted a number of objections advanced by defendants. In so doing, it sought to fill a policy void created by federal inaction. As an indication that this decision was not an anomaly, but rather an influential and precedent-setting event, other global warming cases decided in its wake were obviously influenced by it. In September 2007, a U.S. District Court in Burlington, Vermont ruled that states can regulate greenhouse gas emissions from vehicles, rejecting automobile manufacturers' claims that states are precluded from doing so because they are pre-empted by federal law. Judge William Sessions affirmed that "[H]istory suggests that the ingenuity of the industry . . . responds admirably to most technological challenges . . . The court remains unconvinced automakers cannot meet the challenges of Vermont and California GHG regulations."[10] In November that year, a three-judge panel of the Ninth Circuit Court of Appeals in San Francisco, "voided new regulations for 2008–2011 model year vehicles and told the Transportation Department to produce new rules taking into account the value of reducing greenhouse gas emissions."[11] That directive, to "take into account the value of reducing greenhouse gas emissions," is not the kind of mandate any court would historically have made. And in December, a federal judge in Fresno, California dismissed a lawsuit filed by automakers that sought to overcome the State's law requiring a 30% reduction in greenhouse gas emissions by 2016. The Judge Anthony Ishii asserted that the goal of reducing greenhouse gas emissions must go forward. Clearly all these courts have implicitly prodded policymakers to take the effects of climate change into consideration as they address greenhouse gas emissions. The significance of this new direction was perhaps best expressed by Patrick A. Parenteau, an environmental law professor at Vermont Law School: "What this says to me is that the courts are catching up

with climate change and the law is catching up with climate change . . .
Climate change has ushered in a new era of judicial review."[12]

In this case, one can see, in microcosm, the new environmental policy
paradigm. The petition was brought by a consortium of 12 coastal states
and three municipal governments intent upon forcing the federal government to enact measures to forestall global warming, or at least to protect
their own efforts to do so from federal pre-emption. Heretofore, state and
local governments played a marginal role in policymaking. In the face of
the administration's intransigence, represented here by an EPA that
refused to regulate, state and local governments have adopted an aggressive political posture, and sought from the courts that which they could
not gain from the Congress. In this effort, they were joined by a consortium of environmental advocacy organizations. Both local governments
and environmentalists wanted to test the limits of federal statutes and
regulatory authority. It is interesting to note that among those who filed
Amicus ("friend of the court") briefs were the evangelical community
represented by the National Council of the Churches of Christ in the U.S.,
the U.S. Conference of Mayors, the scientific community represented by 18
climate scientists, and two major energy companies seeking regulatory
predictability. Automobile, truck, and engine manufacturers, utility air
regulators, and nine interior states expectedly joined EPA as respondents,
but most corporate interests stayed on the sidelines, not at all concerned
about any national protocols for ameliorating climate change. Indeed, they
have lobbied for such themselves.

And so the national, indeed global, need for a climate policy brought
together all these refocused and newly energized stakeholders, in a most
unlikely setting for major policymaking—the U.S. Supreme Court cham-
bers. What the Court did not do was forge a new policy. Instead, the court
reinforced the urgency for emission control measures and issued an
implicit directive to those directly responsible for policy to get on with it.
Climate change has made even the judiciary a more active player in
environmental policymaking.

But while *Massachusetts v. EPA* was, arguably, the most prominent and
far-reaching environmental case in recent years, courts at several levels
have handed down an impressive number of environment-related decisions, and face several others as their 2008 docket suggests. The busy court
calendars may be attributable to one of two factors. One is that this
judicial generation is especially sympathetic to environmental litigants. As
we have seen, this is a period of renewed public concern about environmental threats, and the leaning ideology of most courts may favor stricter
environmental regulation.

Another, more politically partisan, factor may be involved though. The
George W. Bush administration has been especially protective of business
concerns. Further, it has invoked, as a governing policy, the "unitary

executive philosophy," a doctrine that favors almost unlimited powers for the Chief Executive. The exercise of these powers, while evident across the policy spectrum, has routinely been invoked in environmental matters during the Administration, and the EPA, while an agency under executive branch jurisdiction, has generally been allowed the freedom to act in accordance with the dictates of science rather than politics. The intervention of the Office of the President in regulatory matters, implicit in most cases but explicit in some, has spurred environmental interests—local governments and advocacy groups—to challenge in court EPA actions, or inaction, that seem politically influenced. The following enumeration of selected court decisions betokens an active, and environmentally disposed, judiciary:

- on the same day that it handed down its ruling in *Massachusetts v. EPA*, the U.S. Supreme Court unanimously ruled that an EPA policy to circumvent the "new source review" requirements imposed on coal-generating facilities violated the intent of the Clean Air Act of 1990;[13]
- in September of 2006, California's Northern District Court restored the so-called Roadless Rule, enacted in 2001, granting the federal government authority to keep roads and development out of 50 million acres of wilderness, an authority granted by the present Administration to the states;[14]
- a three-judge panel of the DC District Court of Appeals charged the EPA with failing to observe the clear directives of the Clean Air Act of 1990 in setting emission standards for plants making bricks and ceramics, directing the agency to go to back to Congress if it finds the Act's standards improper;[15]
- in November of 2007, the Ninth Circuit Court of Appeals voided the U.S. Department of Transportation regulations for 2008–2011 model year light truck and sport utility vehicles on the grounds that they had failed to appropriately properly "assess the economic impact of tailpipe emissions that contribute to climate change";[16]
- a three-judge panel of the DC Circuit Court of Appeals struck down the EPA's rules establishing limits on mercury emissions from coal-fired power plants, arguing that the standards failed to require the strictest possible controls on toxic metals, or justify an alternative approach.[17]

On a somewhat different note, at the close of 2007 and early in 2008, two EPA actions clearly directly influenced by the President have rankled the environmental community, and, accordingly, both have been appealed. The first, an action taken in December of 2007, is the EPA's denial of a request by the State of California for a waiver of federal jurisdiction that would have allowed California, and more than a dozen other states, to impose more stringent greenhouse gas emission standards. The denial was issued in the face of the several cases decided by courts in favor of such stringency; waiver approval was considered perfunctory. What made the case litigable, however, is that the decision to deny the waiver was made unilaterally by the EPA Administrator Stephen Johnson against the advice of the staff and other EPA officials. Internal documents secured by Senate Environment and Public Works Committee Chair Barbara Boxer disclosed that "EPA officials had advised Johnson that California did have the 'compelling and extraordinary conditions' required under law," and that "EPA officials had concluded that the agency would likely lose in court if sued over denying the waiver." That suit has been filed and awaits legal resolution.[18]

In March of 2008, another EPA rulemaking decision will no doubt undergo court review. The EPA developed a rule reducing the allowable limits for ozone concentrations under the Clean Air Act of 1990, consistent with its best science advice. But those new limits were weakened just short of formal issuance by order of the President, according to documents released by the EPA itself. The last-minute change rendered the revised rules invalid under criteria the agency established, necessitating a corresponding last-minute revision of those criteria.[19]

It seems clear from the above that courts at all levels and in different regions have, over the past several years, taken on a substantially larger workload; the locus of environmental policymaking has shifted to the judicial branch. The reason, no doubt, is that the George W. Bush administration seems intent upon rolling back many of the laws and regulations in place when it took office and that the environmental community sees many of their past successes jeopardized. With an EPA that seems to have been "captured" by politics, and a business-friendly Congress in Washington, environmentalists and state and local governments clearly view the courts as a last refuge. The final year of the Bush administration promises to remain an environmentally active one, as interests adversely affected by strict regulation try to undo as much as possible of the legal framework in place. Struggles between and within branches of government will continue to dominate the court's agenda. But it will be interesting to see what changes a new administration will bring in 2009.

Central ideas

The federal courts, like the scientific community and the media, have no agenda, and thus do not participate actively in making policy. But in being called upon to arbitrate disputes over jurisdiction, the consistency of regulations with their enabling statutes, and the constitutionality of laws themselves, their decisions have had an effect on policy. But more recently, with the recognition of global climate change as a transforming phenomenon, and the presence of an Administration that seeks to control the regulatory process completely, the courts have taken a more aggressive stance in enforcing, in most cases, strict adherence to statutory and regulatory standards. They have even extended the reach of some policies to address climate change threats.

Chapter 11

Conclusion: A New Environmental Landscape

In conclusion, environmental policymaking has undergone a veritable metamorphosis in recent years. As documented in this book, the phenomenon of climate change has caused all the major participants in the policy arena to at least rebalance their agendas, if not recast their missions. State and local governments, frustrated by the failure of the federal policymakers to address the threat posed by climate change, have taken it upon themselves, individually and collectively, to develop scores of new policies and programs to mitigate its effects. The business community, long an opponent of environmental regulation, has recognized that climate change jeopardizes not only the environment, but also their bottom lines. Many have, accordingly, voluntarily undertaken efforts to reduce the sources of carbon emissions, promote the development of alternate energy technologies, and, most strikingly, vigorously lobby the federal government to enact nationwide climate control policies. Environmental advocacy organizations that just a few years ago pursued diverse goals and causes have coalesced around climate change as their common enemy. Groups with agendas across the spectrum from conservation to pollution control alike have subordinated their resources to this singular threat; their websites each accord prominent space to the science, effects, and remedial measures relevant to its mitigation. Organized labor, too, has been politically energized to respond to climate change; breaking from many of their alliances with certain business sectors, some key unions have joined with environmentalists to reconcile what were previously regarded as antithetical interests. For its part, the faith community sees in global warming a threat to God's creation, and has refocused many of its resources to "creation care" programs, even going so far as to take active part in the (for them) uncharted political territory. Not least affected have been scientists. The historically uneasy relationship between science and policymakers has been tested. While science's complexity and high standard of proof have previously limited their involvement in policymaking, the current overwhelming scientific consensus on the reality and effects of global climate change has been instrumental in moving climate initiatives forward. Global climate change apparently meets most stakeholders' threshold for actionable science. Finally, the U.S. Supreme Court case that is the principal subject of the previous chapter represents a legal capstone of this environmental policy evolution, engaging and embracing many of the forces of policymaking that have had to accommodate themselves to global climate change.

This evolution is thrown into bold relief by a speech delivered by two environmentalists in the Fall of 2004 titled, provocatively, "The Death of Environmentalism."[1] The speech, as one might expect from its title, incited a veritable civil war in the environmental community. Its thesis is that environmentalism as we have come to know it has lost its relevance and its salience as an effective movement, because the narrow policy prescriptions to cure individual environmental problems it has historically offered no longer command public allegiance. In short, they allege, environmentalism has become just another interest group, and not a politically popular one at that. Accordingly they argue that in order to remain viable, and a positive political force, the movement must expand its reach by incorporating a wider range of progressive activists and causes. Ironically, they point to environmentalism's failure to make any substantial progress in addressing global climate change as Exhibit A in their prosecution.

However justified the charge may have been in 2004, the national response, described in this book, from all sectors in the country that have joined environmentalism's campaign to deal with climate change call into serious question Shellenberger's and Nordhaus' claims. There is, of course, still much to do to adequately address the threat. Climate change, to say nothing of other environmentalist issues, remains far down on the public agenda, to judge from the attention given it during election campaigns. In recent years, though, environmentalists have, in fact, expanded their focus in much the manner prescribed by its critics. As we have seen, they have been joined by recruits from interests across the spectrum. Accordingly, the beginnings of success in controlling climate change have been prefigured. In short, Shellenberger's and Nordhaus' obituary may well have been premature.

Notes

Chapter I

1 http://www.cees.njit.edu/njtap/njtcpa.htm/ The Chemical Industrial Council's position, and the political context of its legislative consideration, are gleaned from personal experience.
2 Jim Carlton, "Business Coalition Protests U.S. Plan to Greatly Increase Logging in the West," *Wall Street Journal*, August 8, 1999.
3 Sam Verhovek, "A Land Use Struggle Over a Forest Bounty," *New York Times*, May 27, 2000.
4 Michael Janofsky, "Wyoming: A Plea to End Drilling," *New York Times*, August 30, 2000.
5 "Industry Doesn't Want EPA to Ease Lead Rules," (AP), *Orlando Sentinel*, February 18, 1999.
6 John Fialka, "Global Warming Treaty Is Sparking Differing Views From 2 Business Groups," *Wall Street Journal*, May 14, 1998.
7 "2 Textile Groups Face Off on CAFTA," *Raleigh News and Observer*, May 10, 2005.
8 Matthew Wald, "Tribe in Utah Fights for Nuclear Waste Dump," *New York Times*, April 18, 1999.
9 Michael Janofsky, "Methane Boom in Wyoming Proves To Be a Mixed Blessing," *New York Times*, April 8, 2000.
10 Martha Bryson Hodel, "Coal Firms and Union To Team Up," *Philadelphia Inquirer*, December 14, 1997.
11 Steven Greenhouse, "Longtime Foes Join to Promote Jobs and Earth," *New York Times*, October 4, 1999.
12 Jim Carlton, "Over a Mine, a Shootout of the Old West and the New," *Wall Street Journal*, August 17, 1999.
13 James Brooke, "Rare Alliance in the Rockies Strives To Save Open Spaces *New York Times*, August 14, 1998.
14 Michael Janofsky, "U.S.—Utah Land Accord Incites Unlikely Critics," *New York Times*, May 23, 2003.
15 Elizabeth Becker, "Unlikely Allies Press to Add Conservation to Farm Bill," *New York Times*, June 18, 2001.
16 Jim Robbins, "Rail Plan Splits Scenic Montana Area," *New York Times*, December 13, 1998

17 Jim Robbins, "In the West, a Water Fight Over Quality, Not Quantity," *New York Times*, September 10, 2006.
18 Timothy Egan, "Drilling in West Pits Republican Policy Against Republican Base," *New York Times*, June 22, 2005. See also Susan Moran, "Fight Against Coal Plants Draws Diverse Partners," *New York Times*, October 20, 2007.
19 There are, of course, countless discussions of this issue, but perhaps the most comprehensive and incisive can be found in Holway R. Jones, *John Muir and the Sierra Club: The Battle for Yosemite* (Sierra Club, San Francisco, 1965), 82–169.
20 Rachel Carson, *Silent Spring* (Houghton Mifflin, New York, 1962).
21 Ralph Erenzo, "Wilderness Selectively Defined," *New York Times*, August 7, 1998.
22 It is interesting to observe that both the contemporaneous drought in the Southeastern states and the wildfires in California in 2007 have been attributed to the "drying" effect of global climate change.

Chapter 2

1 A useful discussion of this stage in environmental lawmaking history can be found in Martin H. Belsky, "Environmental Policy Law in the 1980s: Shifting Back the Burden of Proof," *Ecology Law Quarterly*, Vol. 12, No. 1 (1984), 5–12.
2 The Federal Water Pollution Control Act can be found at 33 U.S.C. s/s 1251 et seq. (1970); the Clean Air Act of 1990 (a reauthorized version of the Air Pollution Control Act) can be found at 42 U.S.C. s/s 2401 et seq (1977).
3 Walter J. Oleszek, in "Congressional Procedures and the Policy Process," (CQ Press, Washington, D.C., 1996), 92, notes that "of the thousands of pieces of legislation . . . introduced in every Congress, a relatively small number become law . . . of the roughly ten thousand measures introduced during the 102nd Congress . . . 1,405 (13.8 percent) were reported from committee and only 590 (5.8 percent) became public law." Walter Oleszek's book is a definitive work on the subject. My discussion of the legislative process is indebted to it generally, as well as on those points specifically cited in footnotes.
4 For a fuller description of the process, see for example Betsy Palmer, "CRS Report for Congress: Conference Committee and Related Procedures," December 8, 2006, 96–708.
5 Glen S. Krutz, *Hitching a Ride: Omnibus Legislating in the U.S. Congress* (Ohio State University Press, Columbus, 2001) 3–7. See also Barbara Sinclair, "Unorthodox Lawmaking: New Legislative Processes in the U.S. Congress", 2nd edn. (CQ Press, Washington D.C., 2000), 3–7.
6 P.L. 104–170 (August 3, 1996).
7 Stephen Engelberg, "Wood Products Company Helps Write a Law to Derail an E.P.A. Inquiry," *New York Times*, April 26, 1995, National A18.
8 George Lardner Jr. and Joby Warrick, "Pesticide Coalition Tries to Blunt Regulation," *Washington Post*, May 13, 2000, A01.
9 Oleszek (see note 25), 94.
10 Oleszek (see note 25).

11 Krutz (see note 27), 4.

12 Ibid. 6

13 Oleszek (see note 25), 119.

14 John W. Kingdon, "Agendas, Alternatives, and Public Policies," (Harper Collins, New York, 1995), 197–208.

15 This background was provided in the "Insider," a newsletter of the League of Conservation Voters, Spring, 1999.

16 A package of measures the Republican candidates for office in the 1994 pledged to enact if elected. Environment measures included a requirement for a strict cost/benefit analysis in regulatory adoption; a federal mandate/federal pay requirement; and a requirement that government pay lawndowners for loss of value attributable to regulations.

17 "National Environmental Scorecard," League of Conservation Voters, October 1996, 104th Congress, 3–4, 17–18.

18 "National Environmental Scorecard," League of Conservation Voters, October 1998, 105th Congress, 4.

19 Evan Osnos, "Federal Court Ruling May Reduce Coal Mining in West Virginia," *Chicago Tribune*, June 6, 2002,

20 The League of Conservation Voters continues to track, scorecard, and discuss anti-environmental riders in its biannual Scorecards. The Natural Resources Defense Council continues to track riders at "www.nrdc.org/legislation/legwatch.asp." Defenders of Wildlife also tracks and discusses anti-environmental riders at the "search riders" link on its website, "www.defenders.org."

21 The Antiquities Act of 1906, 16 U.S.C., 431–433.

22 Presidential Proclamation 6920, September 18, 1996.

23 P.L. 109–058, (August 8, 2005).

Chapter 3

1 U.S. Code, Title 5, Chapter 5, sections 500 et seq.

2 Executive Order 12291 (February 17, 1981); Executive Order 12498 (January 14, 1985).

3 The Toxic Catastrophe Prevention Act, N.J.S.A. 13:1K-19 et seq. (1993).

4 A full discussion of this history can be found in Jack Doyle, "DuPont's Disgraceful Deeds: The Environmental Record of E.I. DuPont de Nemours." *Multinational Monitor*, October 1991, Vol. 12, No. 10.

5 P.L. 104–121, (March 29, 1996).

6 The entire document can be accessed at http://govinfo.library.unt.edu/npr/library/rsreport/251a.html#principles.

7 Transferred to the newly created Environmental Protection Agency were water pollution and certain pesticide functions from the Department of Interior; air pollution, solid waste, and certain pesticide functions from Health, Education, and Welfare; radiation responsibilities from the Atomic Energy Commission, and other pesticide control duties from the Department of Agriculture.

8 Fuller discussion of this, and succeeding, history can be accessed at http://www.whitehouse.gov/omb/inforeg/chap1.html.

9 Ibid.
10 Ibid.
11 An interesting discussion of the difficult relationship between the EPA and the Council on Competitiveness, albeit from a not disinterested party, EPA Administrator William Reilly, can be found at http://www.epa.gov/history/publications/reilly/26.htm.
12 See, for example, "No Greens Need Apply," *New York Times*, Editorial, August 19, 2001, 12. For a detailed list, albeit from a partisan source, see "A Sweetheart Deal: How Republicans Have Turned the Government Over to Special Interests," The Democratic Policy Committee, issued April 14, 2003. Additional examples can be found in "The Bush Administration: Corporate Connections," http://www.opensecrets.org/bushn/cabinet.asp.
13 Executive Order: Further Amendment to Executive Order 12866 on Regulatory Planning, issued January 18, 2007. It can be accessed at http://www.whitehouse.gov/news/releases/2007/01/print/20070118.html.
14 See http://news.bostonherald.com/editorial/view.bg?articleid=181067&format=text.
15 Executive Order: Further Amendment to Executive Order 12866, see note 58.
16 Ibid.
17 Ibid.

Chapter 4

1 Reproduced in *American Journalism Review*, July/August 1998.
2 Martin H. Belsky, "Environmental Policy Law in the 1980s: Shifting Back the Burden of Proof," *Ecology Law Quarterly*, Vol. 12, No. 1, 1984, 1–65 (passim).
3 Ibid., 61–65.
4 Proposal number 8 of the *Contract With America*, http://www.nationalcenter.org/ContractwithAmerica.html.
5 www.sso.org/ecos/GeneralInfo.htm.
6 Ibid.
7 30 U.S.C. §§ 22–24, 26–28, 29–30, 33–35, 37, 39–42 and 47, May 10, 1872.
8 Brief but incisive discussions can be found in Helvarg, *The War Against the Greens* (Sierra Club Books, San Francisco, 1994), 64–65, 67–68; and at http://www.vcdh.virginia.edu/PVCC/mbase/docs/sagebrush.html.
9 http://www.knowthecandidates.org/ktc/BushGang/gailnortonexpose.htm.
10 *Solid Waste Agency of Northern Cook County v. U.S. Army Corps of Engrs.* [SWANCC]. 532 U.S. 159 (2001).
11 www.rggi.org.
12 www.westernclimateinitiative.org.
13 www.ef.org/westcoastclimate/WCGGWI_Nov_04%20Report.pdf.
14 http://www.midwesterngovernors.org/govenergynov.htm.
15 http://www.usmayors.org/climateprotection/agreement.htm.
16 http://coolcities.us/.
17 www.iclei.org.
18 www.iclei.org.

Chapter 5

1 A good discussion of this can be found in Joseph M. Petulla, *American Environmentalism: Values, Tactics, Priorities* (Texas A&M University Press, College Station), 43–56.

2 An account of the changing ideology of the Sierra Club between the 1940s and the 1960s can be found in S.R. Schrepfer, "Perspectives on Conservation: Sierra Club Strategies in Mineral King," *Journal of Forest History*, October, 1976, 177–190.

3 Philip Shabecoff, *A Fierce Green Fire: The American Environmental Movement* (Hill and Wang, New York, 1993), 101–102.

4 The settlement, and preliminary discussions and negotiations were widely reported in the media. Two such reports were Andrew Ross Sorkin, "A Buyout Deal That Has Many Shades of Green," *New York Times*, February 26, 2007; and Jasmina Kelemen, "United States: TXU's emissions U-Turn shocks power industry," http://www.ecoearth.info.

It should be noted that a number of less prominent environmental organizations were not supportive. One concern was the less publicized allegation that TXU never intended to build all eleven of the plants and that, in any case, in light of the air quality implications, none of the plants should have been agreed to. There were also rumors that, following the published reports of the settlement, TXU had outlined new loopholes. For an explanation, see Rebecca Smith and Jim Carlton, "Environmentalist Groups Feud Over Terms of the TXU Buyout," *Wall Street Journal*, March 3, 2007, A-1.

5 "Rainforest Action Network: the inspiring group bringing corporate America to its senses," *The Ecologist*, February 16, 2006.

6 A useful discussion of this period can be found in David Helvarg, *The War Against the Greens* (Sierra Club Books, San Francisco, 1994), 63–89.

7 A critical look at the "unholy" support of environmental organizations by corporate interests can be found in Wallace Kaufman, *No Turning Back* (Harper Collins, 1994), 81–83.

8 See Mark Dowie, *Losing Ground* (MIT Press, Cambridge, 1995), 105–124.

9 Executive Order 12898, issued February 11, 1994.

10 David Warner and James Worsham, "The EPA's New Reach," *Nation's Business*, October 1998, 18.

11 The definitive work on environmental justice is, arguably, Robert D. Bullard's *Unequal Protection: Environmental Justice and Communities of Color* (Sierra Club Press, San Francisco, 1994).

12 See, for example, "Environmentalists Are On the Run," *Fortune*, September 19, 1994; and Timothy Aeppel, "Green Groups Enter a Dry Season as Movement Matures," *The Wall Street Journal*, October 21, 1994.

13 Christopher J. Bosso, "Seizing Back the Day: The Challenge to Environmental Activism in the 1990s," *Environmental Policy in the 1990s*, Norman J. Vig and Michael Kraft, eds. (CQ Press, Washington, D.C., 1997), 63–4.

14 "Global Warming Urgent Say Unions for 10,000 EPA Workers," *Environment News Service*, November 29, 2006. PEER is a non-profit alliance of local, state, and federal scientists, law enforcement officers, land managers, and other professionals committed to the responsible management of public resources and the strict enforcement of laws and regulations.

Chapter 6

1 The 1980 Republican Party Platform, *Congressional Quarterly Weekly Report*, July 19, 1980, 2,030–2,056.

2 *Policy Analysis: Concepts and Practice (4th Edition)* by David Weimer and Aidan R. Vining, Chapter 12.

3 Executive Order 12291, February 17, 1981, 46 FR 13193, 3 CFR, 1981 comp., p. 127

4 A description of the Sagebrush Rebellion can be found at http://www.library.unr.edu/specoll/mss/85-04.html. A more critical discussion is in David Helvarg, *The War Against the Greens* (Sierra Club Books, San Francisco, 1994), 64–68.

5 See David Helvarg, *The War Against the Greens*, Chapter 3 (Sierra Club: San Francisco, 1994).

6 http://pubs.acs.org/hotartcl/cenear/980112/responsible.html; http://www.chemicalguide.com/.

7 http://ceres.org/ceres.

8 http://www.gemi.org; http://www.bsr.org/Meta/About/index.cfm.

9 http://www.equator-principles.com.

10 "Wall St. Develops the Tools to Invest in Climate Change," *New York Times*, May 24, 2006; "Power Companies and Wall Street Firms Begin to Assess Climate Risks," at http://www.ceres.org//news/pf.php?nid=242.

11 "New combatant against global warming: insurance industry," at http://www.csmonitor.com/2006/1013/p01-usec.htm; see also "The Insurance Climate Change," *Newsweek*, January 29, 2007, 44–46.

12 http://www.lloyds.com/News_Centre/features_from_Lloyds/climate-_change_adapt_or_bust.htm; see also http://www.planetizen.com/node/22117.

13 "Ski resorts combat global warming with clean power," at http://www.eenews.net/Greenwire/2006/08/02/archive/8/>Greenwire.

14 http://www.us-cap.org.

15 Felicity Barringer, "A Coalition For Firm Limits On Emissions," *New York Times*, January 19, 2007.

16 Claudia H. Deutsch, "Companies Pressed to Define Green Policies," *New York Times*, February 13, 2007; http://select.nytimes.com/search/restricted/article?res=F30814F6345B0C708DDDAB0894; see also Katharine Q. Selye, "Environmental Groups Gain As Companies Vote on Issues," *New York Times*, May 29, 2003.

17 Steve Hargreaves, "10 global warming dinosaurs," *CNN*, February 13, 2007. See also Ron Scherer, "Investors turn up heat over carbon emissions," *Christian Science Monitor*, February 14, 2007.

18 U.S. Environmental Protection Green Power Partnership, http://epa.gov/greenpower/aboutus.htm; also http://www.epa.gov/greenpower/partners/top10retail.htm.

19 "Is Wal-Mart Going Green? CEO vows to be 'good steward' for the environment in announcing goals," at http://www.msnbc.msn.com/id/9815727/; see also "Wal-Mart To Seek Savings in Energy," *New York Times*, October 25, 2005.

20 Martin LaMonica, "Wal-Mart readies large-scale move into solar power," http://news.com.com/2100-11395_3-6146851.html?part=rss&tag=2547-1_3-0-5&subj=news.

21 Elizabeth Souder, "Will Wal-Mart sell electricity one day?" *Dallas Morning News*, January 29, 2007.

22 "Wal-Mart Announces Goal to Sell Sustainable Electronics; Retailer to Score Electronics", http://www.prnewswire.com/cgi-bin/stories.pl?ACCT=109&STORY=www/story/03-12-2.

23 Mari Margil, "Companies' support goes against the environment," *Seattle Post-Intelligencer*, February 13, 2007.

24 William Kevin Burke "The Wise Use Movement: Right-Wing Anti-Environmentalism," http://www.publiceye.og/magazine/v07n2/wiseuse.html.

25 David Helvarg, " 'Wise Use' in the White House: Yesterday's 'fringe,' today's Cabinet official," http://www.sierraclub.org/sierra/200409/wiseuse.asp.

26 A full list of such anti-environmental think-tanks, and their corporate sponsors, is in Carl Deal, ed., *The Greenpeace Guide to Anti-environmental Organizations* (Odonian Press, Berkeley, California, 1993). A good discussion of right-wing think-tanks can be found in Bob Burton, "Battle Tanks: How Think Tanks Shape the Public Agenda," Center for Media And Democracy, at http://www.prwatch.org/prwissues/2005Q4/battletanks.

27 Chris Mooney, "As the World Burns: Think tanks and journalists funded by ExxonMobil are out to convince you global warming is a hoax," *Mother Jones*, May/June 2005, 36–49.

28 http://www.house.gov/house/Contract/cre8jobsd.txt.

29 February 12, 1990.

30 June 25, 2003.

31 Jed Greer and Kenny Bruno, an updated version of the 1992 "The Greenpeace Book of Greenwash," Third World Network and CorpWatch, 1996, see http://www.corpwatch.org/article.php?id=244. For a more recent critique, see Bill McKibben, "Hype vs. Hope: Is Corporate Do-Goodery for Real?" *Mother Jones*, November/December 2006, 53–56.

32 A new website, "GreenBiz.com," tracks the developing record of business with respect to their efforts to foster a greener environment. It introduces the "GreenBiz Index, a set of 20 indicators of progress, tracking the resource use, emissions, and business practices of U.S. companies."

Chapter 7

1 A comprehensive and nuanced treatment of this subject can be found in Brian K. Orbach, *Labor and the Environmental Movement* (MIT Press, Cambridge, Massachusetts), pp. 27–46.

2 *The American Federationist*, June 1970, Vol. 77, No. 6.

3 David Moberg, "Brothers and Sisters," *Sierra*, January/February, 1999, 50.

4 Ibid., 48.

5 http://www.apolloalliance.org/about_the_allliance.

6 http://www.usw.org/usw/program/content/4104.php.

7 A précis of "Securing Our Children's World" and a link to the full

document can be found at http://www.minesandcommunities.org/Action/
press1407.htm.

8 http://grist.org/news/maindish/2005/01/13/doe-reprint/. The Grist website
also served as a forum for debate on various perspectives and evaluations of the
paper.

9 As cited in "Sierra Club, United Steelworkers Announce 'Blue-Green' Alliance:
Good Jobs, Clean Environment, Safer World Cited as Uniting Principles"
available at http://www.uswa.org/uswa/program/content/3035.php.

10 Lynn White, "The Historical Roots of Our Environmental Crisis," *Science*, Vol.
155, March 10, 1967, 1,203–1,207.

11 Speech to the Royal Society of London, as cited in *Evangelical Environmental
Network & Creation Care Magazine*, accessible at http://www.creationcare.org/
resources/climate/Houghton.php.

12 To reinforce the Vatican's commitment to this concern, Pope Benedict XVI,
in his first address to the United Nations on September 2, 2007, said, "Before
it is too late, it is necessary to make courageous decisions that reflect knowing
how to recreate a strong alliance between man and the earth." Later that week,
he noted a "pressing need for science and religion to work together to
safeguard the gifts of nature and to promote responsible stewardship."
James Macintyre, "Pope to Make Climate Action a Moral Obligation," *The
Independent UK*, September 22, 2007.

13 http://earthrenewal.org/Open_letter_to_the_religious_.htm.

14 http://www.webofcreation.org/DenominationalStatements/joint.htm.

15 http://www.nrpe.org.

16 http://www.coejl.org.

17 http://www.creationcare.org.

18 http://www.creationcare.org/resources/declaration.php.

19 http://www.noahalliance.org/.

20 http://www.theregenerationproject.org.

21 http://www.christiansforthemountains.org/Flyout%20Topics/Links/Chris-
tian%20Groups/S.

22 Accessible at http://www.ncccusa.org/news/04bushonair.html. Reprinted in
New York Times, April 28, 2004.

23 http://www.google.com/search?hl=en&ie=ISO-
88591&q=The+Sandy+Cove+Covenant&btnG=Google+Search.

24 http://www.google.com/search?hl=en&ie=ISO-8859-
1&q=For+the+Health+of+the+Nation&btnG=Google+Search.

25 http://www.christiansandclimate.org/statement.

26 http://www.google.com/search?hl=en&ie=ISO-8859-
1&q=A+call+to+truth%2C+prudence&btnG=Google+Search.

Chapter 8

1 Todd Wilkinson, *Science Under Siege: The Politicians' War on Nature* (Big Earth
Publications, Boulder Colorado, 1998). Michael Fumento: *Science Under Siege:
How the Environmental Misinformation Campaign Is Affecting Our Lives* (William
Morrow, New York, 1996).

2 "Falsifiability" is a key concept in scientific methodology. "It means that every

scientific idea must be framed in such a way that experiments can be designed which have the possibility of demonstrating that the idea is incorrect. For an idea to be falsifiable, someone must be able to create an experiment which, if carried out correctly, could yield data that contradict predictions previously made." Michael Zimmerman, *Science, Nonscience, and Nonsense: Approaching Environmental Literacy* (Johns Hopkins University Press, Baltimore, 1995).

3   A comprehensive and incisive analysis of the problems in reconciling good science with responsible regulatory policy can be found in Mark R. Powell, *Science at EPA: Information in the Regulatory Process* (Resources for the Future, Washington, D.C., 1999).

4   *Chemical and Engineering News*, June 9, 1995.

5   Hearing[s] Before the Subcommittee on Energy and Environment of the Committee on Science U.S. House of Representatives, 104th Congress, First Session, September 20, 1995 [No. 31]. First Session, March 6, 1995, [No. 39], and Second Session, March 6, 1996 [No. 49].

6   *Environmental Science Under Siege: Fringe Science and the 104th Congress*, A Report by Rep. George E. Brown Jr., Ranking Democratic Member of the Democratic Caucus of the Committee on Science, U.S. House of Representatives, October 23, 1996, p. iii.

7   Ibid. 10.

8   Ibid. 14.

9   Ibid. 15.

10   Powell (see note 169), passim.

11   Jim Hartz and Rick Chappell, eds., *World's Apart: How the Distance Between Science and Journalism Threatens America's Future*, First Amendment Center, Nashville, Tennessee, 1997. This study is a comprehensive and useful analysis of the relationship between journalists and scientists.

12   See, for example, William J. Madia, "A Call for More Science in EPA Regulations," *Science*, Vol. 282, October 2, 1998; Nathan Myhrvold, "Supporting Science," *Science*, Vol. 282, October 23, 1998; Sydney Brenner, "The Impact of Society on Science," *Science*, Vol. 282, November 20, 1998; and Angela Merkel, "The Role of Science in Sustainable Development," *Science*, Vol. 281, July 17, 1998.

13   Daniel J. Popeo, "Junk Science Strikes Back," *New York Times*, February 8, 1999.

14   "Is Junk Science Trashing Our Planet," *Nucleus: The Magazine of the Union of Concerned Scientists*, Vol. 18, No. 4, Winter 1996–1997. See also the USCs Sound Science Initiative, established in 1995, a national network of scientists committed to debunking junk science.

15   http://www.foxnews.com/science/junkscience/index.sml. See also Steven Milloy, "The EPA's Secret Science," http://www.foxnews.com/science/junk-science/index.sml.

16   An interesting discussion of this is at George Gerbner, "Science on Television: How It Affects Public Conceptions," *Issues in Science and Technology*, Spring 1987.

17   A comprehensive and authoritative discussion of the precautionary principle can be found at Joel Tickner, Carolyn Raffensberger, and Nancy Myers, "The Precautionary Principle in Action: A Handbook," Science and Environmental

Health Network. Another useful discussion can be found in Nancy Myers, "The Rise of the Precautionary Principle/A Social Movement Gathers Strength," *The Multinational Monitor*, Vol. 25, No. 9, September 2004.

18 U.S. Code Title 42, Chapter 133, ss. 131101 et seq.

19 See complete 38 page report at http://www.ucsusa.org/scientific_integrity/interference/scientists-signon-statement.html. The most public example of the last of the cited charges was the extensively edited report on global climate change prepared by the National Research Council (NRC) commissioned by the White House in 2001. The report concluded that man-made emissions are warming the earth. But the chief of staff for the Council on Environmental Quality made hundreds of substantive changes to the text before it was made public, changes that emphasized the uncertainty of the phenomenon. A selection from the texts, together with the handwritten edits, can be found in "See No Evil: How the White House edits out global warming," *Sierra*, January/February 2006.

20 "Bush-League Lysenkoism: The White House bends science to its will," http://ad.doubleclick.net/adi/N33271.Scientific_American/B2473889.5sz=160×600;ord=[[ti.

21 "Bush vs. the Laureates: How Science Became a Partisan Issue," Andrew C. Revkin, *New York Times*, October 19, 2004.

22 "Science Under Siege" can be accessed at www.aclu,org/scientificfreedom.

23 "US scientists reject interference," *BBC News*, December 14, 2006, http://news.bbc.uk/2/hi/science/nature/6178213.st.

24 http://www.defendscience.org/about.html.

Chapter 9

1 For all but the last part of this chapter, "media" include the news networks, newspapers, and general circulation magazines, but do not include publications of organizations or interests across the partisan spectrum or newly emerging alternate media that unabashedly advance positions on carefully selected issues, and pick and choose the subjects for their investigative journalism. Alternate media are addressed in the last part of the chapter. With respect to their anti-bias protocol, the mainstream media observing a professional ethic of *American* journalism. British citizens, for example, expect to get their views from two or more sources with competing perspectives rather than from one "balanced" one.

2 "The Poisoning of America," *Time*, September 22, 1980.

3 "Planet of the Year," *Time*, January 2, 1989.

4 "Can Man Save This Fragile Earth," *National Geographic*, December, 1988.

5 "Managing Planet Earth," *Scientific American*, September, 1989.

6 "The State of the Earth," *New Republic*, April 30, 1990.

7 Everette E. Dennis, "In Context: Environmentalism in the System of News," in Craig L. LaMay and Everette Dennis, eds. *Media and the Environment* (Island Press, Washington, D.C., 1991), 55.

8 Ibid., 57–64.

9 The widely accepted criteria of news value are described in any number of journalism studies. See, for example, Brian S. Brooks, George Kennedy, Daryl

Moen, and Don Ranly, *News Reporting and Writing* (St. Martin's Press, New York, 1988), 4–16; or Anthony Sadar and Mark Shull, *Environmental Risk Communication: Principles and Practices for Industry* (CRC Press, Boca Raton, 2000), 46–47.

10 A good discussion of this practice can be found in Robert Cox, *Environmental Communication in the Public Sphere* (Sage Publications, Thousand Oaks, California, 2006), 186–189.

11 Doris Graber, *Mass Media and American Politics* (CQ Press, Washington, D.C., 2006), 166.

12 "Be Worried. Be VERY Worried," *Time*, April 3, 2006; "Save the Planet—OR ELSE," *Newsweek*, April 16, 2007.

13 "Global Warming is a Hoax," *Newsweek*, August 13, 2007; "As the World Burns," *Mother Jones*, May/June 2005.

14 http://www.ema-online.org/.

15 Peter Sandman, *Explaining Environmental Risk: Some Notes on Environmental Risk Communication* (United States Environmental Protection Agency, Washington, D.C., November, 1986), 4.

16 Ibid., 5–6.

17 Ibid., 8–9.

18 Graber (see note 201), 166–169.

19 Cox (see note 200), 227–230.

20 Ibid., 230.

21 Lack of understanding of the nature of science and technology is the most common of twelve media limitations cited by scientists in translating their work to the general public. Interestingly, more than 75% of journalists agree. Jim Hartz and Rick Chappell, *World's Apart* (First Amendment Center, Nashville, Tennessee, 1997), 31, 33.

22 See Walter J. Oleszek, *Congressional Procedures and the Policy Process*, 4th edn (CQ Press, Washington, D.C., 1996), 39–42 for an elaboration of this point, and an illustrated example of a political party's "Conference Notes."

23 "Straight Talk," www.ewg.org/briefings/luntzmemo/pdf, 131–146.

24 Ibid., 131–134.

25 Interview by Kathy Butler, *Sierra*, July/August, 2004, 55.

26 Ibid., 56.

27 op cit., Hartz and Chappell, 27–36.

28 John Stossel, "Are We Scaring Ourselves to Death"? ABC News Special, 1994.

29 A more detailed discussion of alternate media can be found in Cox (note 200) 191–197.

Chapter 10

1 549 U.S. 1438 (2007).

2 Fiorino, Daniel, *Making Environmental Policy* (University of California Press, Berkeley, California), 82–83.

3 Ibid., 83.

4 The bill favored by most interests and, consequently, most advanced in the legislative process at the close of 2007, is the Climate Security Act, S–2191,

sponsored by Senators Leiberman and Warner. This bill would create a national cap-and-trade system for greenhouse gas emissions that would give polluters credits for the amount they could emit and allow them to trade with others who cannot meet the limitations imposed.

5 405 U.S. 727, (1972).

6 Justin R. Pidot, "Global Warming in the Courts: An Overview of Current Litigation and Common Legal Issues," Georgetown Environmental Law and Policy Institute, 2006. Though issued prior to the disposition of *Massachusetts v. EPA*, it is a comprehensive and authoritative study of the context of that decision, discussing in detail all the legal issues raised by global climate change regulation, the scientific background, actions by other states on the matter, and a compilation of other deciding and pending court cases.

7 Two excellent book-length studies on this issue are: Sheila Jasanoff, *Science at the Bar* (Harvard University Press, Cambridge, Massachusetts, 1997); and David L. Faigman, *Laboratory of Justice* (Times Books, New York, NY, 2004).

8 68 Fed. Reg. 52930.

9 *Georgia v. Tennessee Copper Co.*, 206 U.S. 230, 237 (1907).

10 www.vtd.uscourts.gov/Supporting%20Files/Cases/05cv302.pdf.

11 Felicity Barringer and Micheline Maynard, "Court Rejects Fuel Standards on Trucks," *New York Times*, November 16, 2007.

12 Ibid.

13 Pete Yost, "US Supreme Court Gives Boost to Environmental Groups on Power Plant Cleanup," Associated Press, April 3, 2007.

14 Deborah Zabarenko, "U.S. Judge Rejects Bush Rule on Logging Roads," Reuters, September 21, 2006.

15 Felicity Barringer, "Judges Say E.P.A. Ignored Order in Setting Emission Standards," *New York Times*, March 14, 2007.

16 Felicity Barringer, and Micheline Mayard, "Court Rejects Fuel Standards on Trucks," *New York Times*, September 16, 2007.

17 Felicity Barringer, "Appellate Panel Rejects E.P.A. Emission Limits," *New York Times*, February 9, 2008.

18 See   http.//ap.google.com/article/ALeqM5jJh569kQSBI-FfOe4F9IiGjADk 3gDj8UCGG8H00; "Memos Show Pressure on EPA Chief," Associated Press, February 26, 2008; and "Confessions on Climate," *New York Times*, Editorial, March 4,2008 for perspectives on the decision.

19 Juliet Eilperin, "Ozone Rules Weakened at Bush's Behest," *Washington Post*, March 14, 2008, A01.

Chapter 11

1 Michael Shellenberger, and Ted Nordhaus, "The Death of Environmentalism," delivered at the meeting of the Grantmakers Association, October 2004. It was printed in essay form, and is accessible at www.grist.org/news/ maindish/2005/01/13/doe-reprint. The essay is preceded by a foreword by Peter Teague, Environmental Program Director, Nathan Cummings Foundation.

Annotated Bibliography

Sources and Resources

Following is a selected list of books and articles that helped me formulate and organize many of the issues, ideas, and principles presented in this text. Some were cited in the book, while others provided important perspectives and background. I have also included works that offer thoughtful counter-arguments to the ones I have advanced. Individually and collectively these works may profitably serve as springboards for discussion, further study, or writing.

Chapter I

A number of fine books trace and analyze the development of environmentalism and environmental policy. Two that I found especially enlightening and insightful, while offering sharply different critiques of the environmental movement, are Dowie, Mark, *Losing Ground: American Environmentalism at the Close of the Twentieth Century*, MIT Press, Cambridge, 1995; and Kauffman, Wallace, *No Turning Back: Dismantling the Fantasies of Environmental Thinking*, Basic Books, New York, 1994. Other useful studies are Hays, Samuel, *Beauty, Health, and Permanence: Environmental Politics in the United States, 1955–1985*, Cambridge, 1987; and Dunlop, Riley E., and Mertig, Angela G., *American Environmentalism: The U.S. Environmental Movement, 1970–1990*, Taylor and Francis, Washington, D.C., 1992. A recent comprehensive history of environmentalism is Shabekoff, *A Fierce Green Fire: The American Environmental Movement*, Hill and Wang, New York, 1993.

Two "histories" that look ahead are the somewhat controversial Easterbrook, Gregg, *A Moment on the Earth: The Coming Age of Environmental Optimism*, Viking, New York, 1995, and the estimable addition to the environmental history literature that looks back but anticipates new directions is Gottlieb, Robert, *Environmentalism Unbound: Exploring New Pathways for Change*, MIT Press, Cambridge, 2001.

Chapter 2

General descriptions of the legislative process can be secured from, among other sources, The Congressional Research Service. The elements of lawmaking—legislatives, regulatory, and judicial—are discussed in Fiorino, Daniel, *Making Environmental Policy*, University of California Press, Berkeley, 1995, Chapters 2 and 3; Rosenbaum, Walter A, *Environmental Politics and Policy*, 6th edn. CQ Press, Washington, D.C., 2005, Chapter 3; Switzer, Jacqueline Vaughn, *Environmental Politics: Domestic and Global Dimensions*, St. Martin's Press, New York, 1994, Chapter 3; and Buck, Susan, *Understanding Environmental Administration and Law*, Island Press, Washington, D.C., 1991, Chapter 3.

A comprehensive and detailed study of the legislative process is Oleszek, Walter J., *Congressional Procedures and the Policy Process*, Washington, D.C., CQ Press, 1996. A full discussion of the mechanics and effect of conference committee actions can be found in Palmer, Betsy, *CRS Report for Congress: Conference Committee and Related Procedures*, December 8, 2006, 96–708.

Extensive studies of new legislative strategies, including omnibus legislation, are: Krutz, Glen S., *Hitching a Ride: Omnibus Legislating in the U.S. Congress*, Columbus, Ohio State Press, 2001; and Sinclair, Barbara, *Unorthodox Lawmaking: New Legislative Processes in the U.S. Congress*, 2nd. edn, CQ Press, Washington, D.C., 2000. A full-length study of the legislative process in general and agenda setting in particular is Kingdon, John, *Agenda, Alternatives and Public Policies*, Harper Collins, New York, 1995.

The website of the League for Conservation Voters (www.lcv.org) is a detailed and up-to-date source of congressional proceedings, and its annual Scorecard is the best summary of the year's significant legislative activity, as well as the voting records of each Senator and Representative on major issues.

Chapter 3

A study of the policy implications of regulation might well start with two classics in the field that represent opposing points of view: Wilson, James Q., *The Politics of Regulation*, Basic Books, New York, 1980, especially Chapters 8 and 10; and Tolchin, Susan J. and Martin, *Dismantling America: The Rush to Deregulate*, Oxford University Press, New York, 1983, especially Chapters 1, 4, and 6. Other challenging works include: Yandle, Bruce, *The Political Limits of Environmental Regulation: Tracking the Unicorn*, Quorum Books, New York, 1989; and Hoberg, George, *Pluralism by Design: Environmental Policy and the American Regulatory State*, Praeger, New York, 1992.

Two critiques of the EPA that are indispensable to an understanding of its functioning and the political pressures under which it has operated are

Landy, Marc K., Roberts, Marc J., and Thomas, Stephen R., *The Environmental Protection Agency: Asking the Wrong Questions*, Oxford University Press, New York, 1990; and *Setting Priorities, Getting Results: A New Direction for the Environmental Protection Agency*, National Academy of Public Administration Report to Congress, April 1995.

Shorter pieces that provide valuable perspectives on the EPA's regulatory responsibilities and history are Portnoy, Paul, "EPA and the Evolution of Federal Regulation," in Portnoy, Paul (ed.), *Public Policies for Environmental Protection*, Resources for the Future, Washington, D.C., 1990; and Rosenbaum, Walter A., "The EPA at Risk: Conflicts Over Institutional Reform," in Vig, Noman J. and Kraft, Michael E. (eds.), *Environmental Policy in the 1990s*, 3ʳᵈ edn, CQ Press, Washington, D.C., 1997.

Clinton, President Bill and Gore, Vice-President Al, *Reinventing Environmental Regulation*, a National Performance Review report issued on March 16, 1995. This document not only sets forth the 10 principles for reinventing environmental regulation discussed in the text, but also reviews the past 25 years of regulation, provides the administration's vision for the next 25 years, and enumerates 25 high-priority actions. It was the most succinct and authoritative statement of the administration's anticipated direction for the EPA and the rationale therefore.

Some of the excesses of regulation that the Clinton administration presumably sought to address are given delightfully mock treatment in Reich, Robert, "The Origins of Red Tape," *Harvard Business Review*, May/June, 1987, reprinted in Reich, Robert, *The Resurgent Liberal*, Vintage Books, New York, 1991, pp. 34–47, esp. 44–47.

Chapter 4

The literature on state and local governments as political interests is scant. The standard volume on the subject is Harrigan, John. J., *Politics and Policy in States and Communities*, 4ᵗʰ edn, Harper Collins Publishers, New York, 1991, especially Chapters 1 and 16. Other, briefer, treatments are in Switzer, Jacqueline Vaughn, *Environmental Politics*, St. Martin's Press, New York, 1994, pp. 67–69; Daly, Herman, Goodland, Robert, and Cumberland, John H., "An Introduction to Ecological Economics," Costanza, Robert (ed.), St. Lucie Press, New York, 1997; and Davis, Sandra, "Fighting Over Public Lands: Interest Groups, States, and the Federal Government," in Davis, Charles (ed.), *Western Public Lands and Environmental Politics*, Westview Press, Boulder, Colorado, 1997.

The environmental positions and activities of states and localities can be tracked by consulting their respective publications and websites: *State Legislatures* by the National Council of State Legislatures; *Government News* and *Eros* by the Council of State Governments; the American Legislative

Exchange Council (ALEC.org), and *Governing*, an Online Magazine publishing news and information on state and local governments.

The newly energized and expanded political activities of state and local governments discussed in this text to address climate change are available at www.coolcities.us and at the site of the Mayors Climate Protection Agreement. The National Caucus of Environmental Legislators (NCEL) tracks state climate change legislation.

Chapter 5

The environmental advocacy groups—their role and development—are treated in the environmental histories identified under Chapter 1.

Much quality work has been done on the environmental justice movement. Its ideological roots can be found in Smith, James Noel, *Environmental Quality and Social Justice in Urban America*, Conservation Foundation, Washington, D.C., 1974. Prominent studies of the movement are Bullard, Robert D., *Unequal Protection: Environmental Justice and Communities of Color*, Sierra Club Books, San Francisco, 1994; Foreman, Chrisopher H. Jr., *The Promise and Peril of Environmental Justice*, Brookings Institution Press, Washington, D.C., 1998; and Bryant, Bunyan (ed.), *Environmental Justice: Issues, Policies, and Solutions*, Island Press, Washington, D.C., 1995.

Two governmental issue briefs are Durrett, Dan, *Environmental Justice: Breaking New Ground*, 2nd edn, National Institute for the Environment, 1994 and Cooper, Mary H., "Environmental Justice," *CQ Researcher*, Washington, D.C., June 19, 1998. A brilliant academic treatment is Tesh, Sylvia N., and Williams, Bruce A., "Identity Politics, Disinterested Politics, and Environmental Justice," *Polity*, Spring, 1996.

Eco-terrorism has understandably been accorded less attention, but see: Sullivan, Robert, "The Face of Eco-Terrorism" *New York Times* (magazine), December 20, 1998; Markels, Alex, *Backfire*, Mother Jones, March/April 1999, and Russell, Dick, "The Monkeywrenchers," *Amicus*, Fall, 1987.

Chapter 6

For the best study on the change in thinking going on in the business community with respect to environment, see Hawken, Paul, *The Ecology of Commerce: A Declaration of Sustainability*, Harper Collins, New York, 1993.

Other useful works on business and the new environmentalism are: Smith, Denis (ed.), *Business and the Environment: Implications of the New Environmentalism*, St. Martin's Press, New York, 1993; and Makower, Joel, *The E Factor: the Bottom-Line Approach to Environmentally Responsible Business*, Random House, New York, 1993.

The bible of the Wise Use movement is Gottlieb, Alan M., ed., *The Wise Use Agenda*, Free Enterprise Press, Bellevue, WA, 1989. See also

Arnold, Ron, *Ecology Wars: Environmentalism As If People Mattered*, Free Enterprise Press, Bellevue, WA, 1993; and Arnold, Ron and Gottlieb, Alan, *Trashing the Economy: How Runaway Environmentalism Is Wrecking America*, Free Enterprise Press, WA, 1994.

Three book-length studies of the anti-environmental movement are: Switzer, Jacqueline Vaughn, *Green Backlash: The History and Politics of Environmental Opposition in the U.S.*, Lynne Rienner Publishers, Boulder, CO, 1997; Rowell, Andrew, *Green Backlash: Global Subversion of the Environmental Movement*, Routledge, London, 1996; and Helvarg, David, *The War Against the Greens*, Sierra Club Books, San Francisco, 1994.

Brief but informative articles on corporate codes of conduct are: Nash, Jennifer and Ehrenfeld, John, "Code Green," *Environment*, January/February 1996; Bavaria, Joan, "An Environmental Code for Corporations," *Issues In Science and Technology*, Winter 1989/90; and Rayport, Jeffrey and Lodge, George C., "Responsible Care," *Harvard Business School*, March 18, 1991.

"Greenwashing" is discussed extensively in Athanasiou, Tom, *Divided Planet: The Ecology of Rich and Poor*, University of Georgia Press, Athens, 1998 and in the format of an expose in Bruno, Kenny, *The Greenpeace Book of Greenwash*, Greenpeace International, Washington, D.C., undated.

Chapter 7

Two books provide useful but different perspectives on the recent political evolution of the labor/environmentalist relationship. Obach, Brian K., *Labor and the Environmental Movement: The Quest for Common Ground*, MIT Press, Cambridge, 2004, is a comprehensive study of the history and development of the relationship between organized labor and environmentalists. Schwab, Jim, *Deeper Shades of Green: The Rise of Blue-Collar and Minority Environmentalism in America*, Sierra Club Books, San Francisco, 1994, documents the convergence of two movements—conservation and social justice.

The new political activism of the faith community is too recent to have gotten scholarly study. The best way to track the activities of the faith community is through the Evangelical Environmental Network, www.creationcare.org and its magazine.

Chapter 8

To gain an historic perspective on the relationship between politics and science, I recommend the old standby, Greenberg, Daniel S., *The Politics of Pure Science*, New American Library, New York, 1967. Another historical perspective on science that illuminates policy issues is LaFollette, Marcel C., *Making Science Our Own: Public Images of Science 1910–1955*, University of Chicago Press, Chicago, 1990.

The alternately symbiotic and adversarial roles of scientists and journalists in contemporary policymaking is treated extensively in Hartz, Jim and Chappell, Rick, *Worlds Apart: How the Distance Between Science and Journalism Threatens America's Future*, First Amendment Center, Nashville, 1997.

A formal attack on government regulation, albeit in the form of exploratory hearings, was conducted by Congress in 1995. Testimony at these hearings was compiled in two volumes as *Scientific Integrity and Public Trust: The Science Behind Federal Policies and Mandates: Hearings Before the Subcommittee on Energy and Environment of the Committee on Science*, U.S. House of Representatives, 104th Congress, 1st Session, September 20, 1995 (No. 31) and December 13, 1995 (No. 39), on stratospheric ozone and dioxin respectively.

A dissenting report on the hearings was issued by George E. Brown, Jr.: *Environmental Science under Siege: Fringe Science and the 104th Congress*, U.S. House of Representatives, October 23, 1996. See also *Environment*, March 1997 and May 1997 for exchange of letters on the debate. See also Brown, George, "Science's Real Role in Policy-making," *Chemical and Engineering News*, May 31, 1993, pp. 9–11. The resulting new proposal on how science should be incorporated into policymaking was issued as *Unlocking Our Future: Toward A New Science Policy*, a report to Congress by the House Committee on Science, September.

A study of how science has been developed and applied over the years at EPA is Powell, Mark, R., *Science at EPA: Information in the Regulatory Process*, Resources for the Future, Washington, D.C., 1999.

An indispensable discussion of the problems, and some suggested solutions, regarding how to apply science to policymaking is Ruckelshaus, William D., Science and Democracy, Issues in Science and Technology, Spring 1985, pp. 19–38. See also Wilson, James D., and Anderson, J.W., *What the Science Says: How We Use It and Abuse It to Make Health and Environmental Policy*, Resources for the Future, Summer 1997, pp. 5–8. The scientific community's call for more science in policymaking was represented by Madia, William J., "A Call for More Science in EPA Regulations," *Science*, October 2, 1998, p. 45.

Attacks on government's alleged misuse of science are represented by two book-length studies: Bolch, Ben and Lyons, Harold, *Apocalypse Not*, Cato, Washington, D.C., 1993, and Fumento, Michael, *Science Under Siege: Balancing Technology and the Environment*, William Morrow & Company, New York, 1993.

For a healthy dose of anti-environmental rhetoric aimed at the general public, see Bailey, Ronald, *Eco-Scam: The False Prophets of Ecological Apocalypse*, St. Martin's Press, 1993; Ray, Dixy Lee and Lou Guzzo, *Trashing the Planet*, Regnery Gateway, 1990 and *Environmental Overkill: Whatever Happened to Common Sense, 1993*; Baden, John A. ed., *Environmental Gore: A Constructive Response to Earth in the Balance*, Pacific Research Institute for

Public Policy, San Francisco, 1994; and Bailey, Ronald, ed., *The True State of the Planet*, Free Press, New York, 1995.

The assertions and arguments in the above cited tracts have been compellingly challenged by Ehrlich, Paul R., *Betrayal of Science and Reason: How Anti-Environmental Rhetoric Threatens Our Future*, Island Press, Washington, D.C., 1996.

Works lamenting the scientific illiteracy of the public that complicates public policymaking include: Miller, Eliana Beth, "Public Alienation from Science and Science Illiteracy: Post-Sputnik Education and the Media as Causative Agents," unpublished senior thesis, Swarthmore College, 1993; Zimmerman, Michael, *Science, Nonscience, and Nonsense: Approaching Environmental Literacy*, Johns Hopkins University, Baltimore, 1995; and Howell, Dorothy, *Scientific Literacy and Environmental Policy: The Missing Prerequisite for Sound Decision Making*, Quorum Books, New York, 1992.

The problems that the courts have with incorporating science in policymaking are treated in two long journal articles: Abraham, Kenneth S. and Merrill, Richard A., "Scientific Uncertainty in the Courts," *Issues in Science and Technology*, Winter, 1986, pp. 93–107; and Burack, Thomas S., "Of Reliable Science: Scientific Peer Review, Federal Regulatory Agencies, and the Courts," *Virginia Journal of Natural Resources Law*, 7:27. 1987, pp. 27–110.

Finally, for an unabashedly partisan, but well documented, study of the misuse of science by the George W. Bush administration, see Chris Mooney, *The Republican War on Science*, Basic Books, New York, 2005.

Chapter 9

Study of media coverage of science and the environment should begin with the classic, Nelkin, Dorothy, *How the Press Covers Science and Technology*, W.H. Freeman & Company, New York, 1995.

A collection of essays by journalists on the issues, problems, and challenges of environmental journalism is LaMay, Craig L. and Dennis, Everett, *Media and the Environment*, Island Press, Washington, D.C., 1991. Other perspectives on environmental journalism by insiders are Prato, Lou, *Covering the Environmental Beat: An Overview for Radio and TV Journalists*, The Media Institute, Washington, D.C., 1991, and Frome, Michael, *Green Ink: An Introduction to Environmental Journalism*, University of Utah, Salt Lake City, 1998. Finally, Gregory, Jane and Miller, Steve, *Science in Public: Communication, Culture, and Credibility*, Plenum Press, New York, 1998, especially Chapters 5–7, well documents the history of communicating scientific issues to the public.

The best short work on the interrelationships between science and the media with respect to risk communication is Sandman, Peter, *Explaining Environmental Risk*, U.S. EPA, Washington, D.C., 1986.

Insightful discussions of the practices and procedures involved in producing environmental stories are: Hannigan, John A., *Environmental Sociology*, Routledge, London, 1995, especially Chapters 2 and 3; and Hansen, Anders (ed.), *The Mass Media and Environmental Issues*, Leicester University Press, Leicester, 1993, especially Chapters 2–4.

Useful pieces on media coverage from periodical literature are: Edwards, David, "Can We Learn the Truth about the Environment from the Media?" *The Ecologist*, January/February 1988; Gerbner, George, "Science on Television: How It Affects Public Conceptions, *Issues in Science and Technology*, Spring, 1987; and Stocking, Holly and Leonard, Jennifer, "The Greening of the Press," *Columbia Journalism Review*, November/December, 1990.

The following are a representative sample of the crusade against the media's allegedly sensationalist and irresponsible coverage of the environment: Bailey, Ronald, *Eco-Scam*, St. Martin's Press, New York, 1993; Ray, Dixie Lee, *Environmental Overkill: Whatever Happened to Common Sense?*, Regnery Gateway, Washington, D.C., 1992; and Wildavsky, Aaron, B., *But Is It True?*, Harvard University Press, 1995.

The most authoritative counter-attack is that of Ehrlich, Paul R., *Betrayal of Science and Reason: How Anti-environmental Rhetoric Threatens Our Future*, Island Press, Washington, D.C., 1996.

Chapter 10

A comprehensive and authoritative study of the American judicial system, though it does not treat, to any significant extent, how that system handles environmental matters: Carp, David, *Judicial Process in America*, 7th edn, CQ Press, 2004. Hoban, Thomas More and Brooks Richard Oliver, *Green Justice: The Environment and the Courts*, Westview Press, Boulder, CO, 1996, is an excellent discussion of the principles and process of environmental law.

Briefer discussions of environmentalism and the judiciary can be found in: McSpadden, Lettie, "Environmental Policy in the Courts," in Vig, Norman J. and Kraft, Michael E. (eds) *Environmental Policy in the 1990s*, 3rd edn, CQ Press, Washington, D.C., 1997; Fiorino, Daniel, *Making Environmental Policy*, University of California, Berkeley, 1995; and Buck, Susan, *Understanding Environmental Administration and Law*, Island Press, Washington, D.C., 1991.

Index